Soverei Goddess

Table of Contents;

Introduction

Chapter 1; Ritual of Her

Chapter 2; The Island of Lusciousness

Chapter 3; Not all things Planted are Prosperous

Chapter 4; Meeting the King

Chapter5; When you Squeeze an Orange

Chapter 6; Ala Wai Mansion

Chapter7; Blending with Different Cultures

Chapter 8; The Dragon Under the Moon

Chapter 9; Freshwater Pearls

Chapter 10; The Docks of Honolulu

Chapter 11; Tiki and Ali'i

Chapter 12; In Mailie's Arms

Chapter 13; Moori Comes to the Island

Chapter 14; The Christian Family from the Farm

Chapter 15; Turning Purple

Chapter 16; Repaying the Debts Owed

Chapter 17; Full Moon Party to the Goddess

Chapter 18; Big Waves

Chapter 19; Auntie Angeline's

Chapter 20; Heading Home

Chapter 21; Truth is, we are All Different

Chapter 22; The Blue Fairy

Chapter 23; Pipi

Chapter 24; Andara's

Chapter 25; Twenty Month's

Chapter 26; We Lost the House

Chapter 27; My Desert Oasis

Chapter 28; Underlying Issues

Chapter 29; What's up Kauai

Chapter 30; My Dreamwork

Sovereignty and the Goddess

Introduction:

It is the 21st Century, I mean, come on. Nearly everyone is fighting for their Sovereignty in one way or another. The days of the tribe have been over for some time. Well of course, sure, we all have our tribe. Our family, our friends, the people we work with, our neighborhoods. Maybe we have our Facebook friends and Instagram follower's. Or perhaps a neighborhood co-op, or community center. A favorite Yoga studio? Those MMA Fighting Groups are popular these days.... sheesh pretty brutal though and can be quite bloody. And then there's always your favorite bar, coffee shop or poker squad.

The tribes are indeed happening, and yes, they are out there, but often, I sense this underlying and gnawing craving to be free from the relentless grips of conditioning and from the culture. Our forefathers paved the way, but with their strides, they left behind large black footprints in pavement that is now worn like snakeskin on the layers of the human being.

Even in trying to gather like a tribe. Let's say a yoga event. You must schedule time off work, drive to the event, get gas in your car, get through traffic, find parking. All of this, to simply gather and do a little stretching with a tribe you resonate with. Or perhaps a

Jennifer Lin Phillips

football game. Beer in hand, arms in the air, you and your tribe.........Goooooo Bears!!! It's just that, the amount of effort it takes to get to your tribe, as an individual in your own flow anymore, stress-free, can be a challenge.

It sure is interesting the modern culture we all now live in. More of us, if we are smart, are working from home, shopping nearby, walking, simplifying and engaging in events in our own neighborhoods. I think that's where I really vibe and tribe, in the subtle. In my neighborhood and the people there, the parks and markets, and events nearby. Tribing in the simple. Although I do reach out often on social media or with friends to connect with like-minded and high vibe tribes. Hehe. And I take off often on journey's, travelling high above it all. Simply to just breathe and experience freedom, expansion in my being and of course, newness.

So, I kind of determined that this need to belong, yet to be free from the pressures we all now deal with, is simply the character of our instinct. If you examine a young child, once off mama's boob for nourishment, those independent characteristics, seem to arise from within.

Last week I was hanging out with a girlfriend of mine. We did a healing session together and I practiced my sound healing and singing bowl therapy on her towards the end of the session. It was beautiful. Her three-year-old daughter, Sasha, managed to get through the session with us. Thankfully, she stayed engaged nearby doing her little three-year-old thing, and if it wasn't for the stash of fuchsia flood lipstick and mineral fusion gloss, that she had discovered in my purse, we would've been chasing her around in her independent flails and fits.

I looked at Sasha as she reached into my purse for more gloss. "Baby girl, I think you have enough lip gloss on already," I said to her. I have two sisters with three daughters, and I call all my nieces by the nickname baby girl, and the oldest of them, Amelia, is six years old.

"I am not a baby girl! I am a big girl!" She gave back to me with attitude.

"And I want to look pretty too!" She whined.

Her mama and I just laughed together at her demand for respect and acknowledgement of her maturity. I later thought to myself about the symbolism in her behavior that day. It could be a basic human need, I thought. To be the one in charge of one's own life and destiny. I know for certain, that I want to be the leader, co-creator and master of my life and existence. And I think most people think this way. Like somehow that is our wholeness. To be wholly, or holy, who we are.

Jennifer Lin Phillips

In reflection, those desires have pushed me into the unknown so many times, balancing on an invisible beam that only I can see and sense safely. Many times, it looked like I was going to fall while balancing there and striving for this independence and sovereignty. But somehow, I maintained my own weight and equilibrium. I am not saying that things turned out for me exactly as I had envisioned or had planned for them too. But the unexpected gaps in my plans or expectations, were filled somehow by the flow of and pull of existence, of connecting with the tribe, yet standing in my own flow or integrity. And in harnessing the power in the inescapable pull of both life and death.

It wouldn't be possible for me to have accomplished what I have in my short life, if it wasn't for the assistance from spirit through my intentions. I've learned over the years, through observing and reflecting on my own instinctual traits, that we are all fighting in one way or another, to be free from the pressures we place on each other. The interrogation from the culture and from society. In this fight, at least, we are all together in sync somehow, acknowledging one another's plights, yet moving strangely in our own unique rhythm's.

Chapter 1: Ritual of Her

Have you ever just paused, stopped to observe a divine rush of ecstatic energy and Aaahhh? You find yourself witnessing a moment so stunning and illuminating that it could only be the dust from Goddess' wand. And you watch in wonderment as the golden dust sprinkles delight, color and passion all around before your eyes. You know when you've been caught in such a moment when you keep replaying it in your mind's eye over and over again, sniffing in the air of its memory like it could be the very last one like that. That moment happened to me last week and as I rest in its vibrant grips, I release it back to wherever it came from, thankful for its play before me.

The yellow of my heart opened as fall leaves played for me like a musician plays its violin. The aroma of such a song and dance whispered to me and I breathed in deeper the hush of yellow fall leaves all around me. The smell of fresh dirt swooped up into the strands of my strawberry blonde hair. The roots of the trees moved deeper into the Earth beneath my feet. A movement so subtle, the air seeping up from its plumage softened beneath my nostrils sending scents fulfilling my desire, the deeper I breathed in.

I was in my familiar neighborhood again. One lined with cutesy shops, a new bed and breakfast, two

Jennifer Lin Phillips

health food stores, a beer and cider house, and elegant flowers aligning the streets in up hinged baskets.

I spent four of the past five years here. An exciting road trip led me to the desert and country, including Idaho, Utah, New Mexico, Oklahoma, Kansas and the snowy mountains and hot springs of Colorado. I had fallen back into the beauty of the Pacific NW. And in my return, I was finally feeling grounded as the golden fall leaves played for me like sunshine streams play for spiders spun in webs, in the corners of dusty rooms. Shedding their mystery and truth on me in an enchantment that nearly hypnotized me. I am a part of this, I thought.

And I exhaled, feeling welcome back at home.

Providence Hospital is directly through the walking trail and park where I play basketball with old friends from High School times. Last year a client of mine, I practice bodywork and healing therapies, did a photo shoot of me in a long white dress on that trail beneath the tall fir trees. I run through those woods often in the chilly, cool mornings to awaken my body and mind. The woods are right behind the basketball court and one of my favorite purple flowering spring trees.

Woody and I shot hoops there the other day when he came down from the town of Seattle. Just north of here up in Washington State.

Sovereignty and the Goddess

I lived up in that area once, in this adorable town called Sumner. I spent the whole summer hiking Mt. Rainier and swimming in cold lakes, framed by wildflower's, that one could discover halfway up the mountain trails. The town was known for its daffodils that were grown for the entire state and local markets. And all around the area coffee was served by young girls in bikini's working from tiny coffee trucks.

I don't think I had walked close to a hospital in some time. Probably not since my mother's sickness. Or yes there was that one time I visited my older sister after she had a benign cyst removed from her cervix.

I was looking for red leaves that day, that had fallen from the trees. And after practicing sound healing with my new prayer singing bowl made from quartz earlier that morning, I thought that I would like to play it in hospitals for patients healing from one thing or another.

Why Not?

I had a dream last week about being shot in the head. I know yes, that sounds awful, but in the dream the prayer bowl was being played and the sound and vibration was in fact healing the trauma in my brain and cellular structure. Yeah, super creepy, but sort of amazing.

Jennifer Lin Phillips

And if we were speaking metaphorically. The bullet wound in the psyche of my brain from being used by others, abused by a few, dealing with the guilt and alcoholism in my family, the anger, the cancer and disease, the loss and death of my own mother at the young age of fifteen, and the betrayal from a few Ex's was easing. It seemed that playing the bowl and allowing its sound to penetrate my being was calling me to align with truth and heal.

Much of my trauma had been around since I was a very young girl. And it really felt like it was being lifted. Psychically and energetically removed from my being, by simply listening and opening to the sound and frequency that was entering me.

My bullet wound of thirty-eight years on the planet. Of trial and error, voyage and vonkage, was somehow being soothed by the sound coming from this bowl at 432 hz. frequency. I've done my research. And that is the same frequency that green grass grows from and which entices flowers to bloom. Could be a revelation, I thought.

The wind that day was light, it moved through me in purpose. It didn't feel awesome to walk up to the hospital flooded with images of my mother's bald head and the look of hope mixed with hopelessness streaming through each of her eye's. As I approached the hospital there was a statue of deer and fawn. Mother and child. The strong doe cradled her soft chest, and the writing in steel below the images read;

"Mischief Underfoot."

I walked through the outdoor hallways observing female doctors, visitors rushing to see patients. I could smell the health and sanitation, the correct posturing, the stale food. Sensing the sick, the injured and recovering, the dying, and the hope for all the children inside. I could hear the paper towels being pulled from bathroom walls drying clean hands, and needles and syringes being carefully wrapped and tossed into waste baskets.

As I walked around the corner and back to the busy street of Cornell and the lines of trees along the sidewalk, I noticed many of the red leaves had already fallen. I scooped some of them up and put them in my bag, along with some pine cones. I walked through the wooded running trail to find small purple flowers and some cute green sprouts, resembling parsley shapes.

The rosebuds on the edge of the woods had turned to seed and I gathered a few orange buds known as rosehips, extremely healthy and high in vitamin C.

This should be enough for my prayer offering to She, I thought, as I continued back to my apartment.

Still connecting each breath with her breath, the wind

Jennifer Lin Phillips

and breath of the Mother. Mother Earth or Gaia as many refer to this blue and green planet we occupy. I breathe with her now as often as I can, since no hospital could save my own mother, and no western doctor could cure her illness. I then took a nice deep breath and exhaled the emotion and memory from that experience out from within me.

When I returned to my apartment, I created a grid with flowers, seeds, rocks, leaves, crystals, feather's and pine cones. The entire experience of gathering the tools for the offering was infused in my being and the warmth in my heart and mind was seeping out from my fingertips as I placed each ornament in its proper place. Remembering the wind upon my back and shoulders, shuttering around me like wings.

I lit a candle and texted the man I had been loving for the past year.

He was halfway across the country and I was praying for his safety and prosperity. I then began my prayer, singing and chanting aloud to Goddess Lakshmi. The beautiful Goddess of prosperity, beauty and abundance.

The mantra echoed throughout my apartment as my fingers touched and arranged my collection from nature. I picked a few white mums from my patio to brighten the grid and add life. The holographic offering displayed beautifully upon my tablecloth was like a crop circle to the heavens and stars. Etched perfectly in my mind's eye, expanding in form out to the universe and beyond, to the God's and Goddess'. I was igniting my prayer with the forces of the planet and knew that my sincere message and request would be heard.

I sang as I played my bowl, and I knew that spirit would decide what to enhance in love's request and what to burn into love's dusty ashes. But after dancing, I stopped to kneel down. I bent my head down with hands in prayer by my forehead and I gave thanks to She, the One who provides all things bountiful.

Thankyou Goddess for all your blessings.

Jennifer Lin Phillips

Chapter 2: The Island of Lusciousness

It had been almost five years since I had returned to the magical and wet island of Kauai. Mama Kauai is what people refer to the island as, being the oldest of the eight main islands on the Pacific Island Chain.

After returning to Oregon this past year from my yearlong western, desert road trip. I decided to spend some time on the islands again. My body was aching for the ocean. I needed to swim, relax, collect shells, walk the shores, visit some old friends and splash around in waves like a mermaid again. I spent a week on Oahu, then flew to Kauai where I spent three weeks.

I couldn't believe he was still living in that house on one of the most gorgeous and secluded beaches on the island. The sands on that beach collected the tiniest and most precious shells. They were red in color and different shades of pink, purple and white spiraling their delicate bodies.

The locals pick the shells using small bamboo chopsticks made specifically for the trade. The incredibly crafted jewelry is weaved like leis are and worn in stunning cultural flare. They speak the story of the history and heritage there. Of the islanders travelling from island to island in pursuit of each islands unique offering. The shells are called Kahelelani's, also known as "The Many Pathways to Heaven." And they end up on Kauai after travelling many miles across the ocean taken by waves from the very small island of Niihau.

When I lived on Kauai at 23 years old, and worked on an organic farm in Moloa'a, I would collect the shells. I collected hundreds of them. So many some days, that at night when I slept in my tent by the ocean and closed my eyes, they were all I would see, spiraling in my mind.

I made my own style of the jewelry and gave many of my craft away to friends, also selling a few handmade pieces. Many kinds of people landed on the beaches and islands from all over the world, just like the shells had, seeking their own pathway to this mystical paradise and heaven.

When we drove by the house, I panicked inside. What a liar! He deserves a Grammy, I thought. But really what was I to expect from a person with his deceiving characteristics. His charm and intelligence sucked me into him when we had first met on the

Jennifer Lin Phillips

island of Oahu, at the health food store I was working at in Honolulu.

In reflection of our meeting and everything that transpired, and just what it took for us to get to Kauai five years before, I was in shock and subtle terror. I was now fully feeling the trauma from my experience at that house finally surfacing. Giant ocean island waves of un-trust and damage stormed through me and began to bellow up from inside of me.

The waves splashed on rocks outside the truck door. We drove to the end of the road, where I used to clean my crystals and hike up the hills to the local bank in town.

I spent a full year on this long incredible beach, which trailed up and down a windy road past horses and beach houses. The road ended at the canal. Many mornings at sunrise, I would run up and down the sand, splashing in the water in my swimsuit. I would connect inside with the movement happening there and flip my wet salty hair from side to side, releasing tension and pressure. The subtle energy in my pelvis and hips began to rise and move about too. I would spin, turn, breathe, bow, raise and extend my arms and hands in motions like as they do in hula to honor the sun.

This was all instinctual.

I would allow the negative ions coming from the salt

and ocean water to pour into me, and with that exchange I would dance, release, stretch and uplift the soft air around me.

It was so surreal being here on the same road in Jesse's truck again. One of the last times I saw Jesse on island, was right here, where we had just parked his truck at the end of the road. I was out on a run that day and he happened to be on a job site.

That was five years ago, and it was perfect timing to connect then like we had. That accidental meeting connected Jesse and I and bonded us along our individual life path's. And the amazing friendship and experiences we have shared since then are because of that spot at the end of the road, where the canal meets the ocean.

I heard that spot is a sacred portal. I had done ceremony there before and ran to the canal in my adidas many times when I lived on island. We turned his truck around and began heading back down the road, back towards the house.

"I am here for you Jennifer! That guy is such a douche bag. I'm glad he is not in our lives." Jesse said to me as we approached the house again, coming back from the other direction.

I just smirked at him, in disbelief and sarcasm showing

on my face.

"His intentions are so twisted, and he has lied and hurt you so many times. He's bad energy, you know it. Let's just keep moving forward and let the bounty and the fruits of this island continue to heal us. This is the best thing for us right now, and I will take care of you." Jesse said as we drove past the house.

He was right. Jesse and I had remained friends over the past few years, since we met at that house. And here I was back on the island. I had finally returned to Mama Kauai.

With Jesse as my friend and guide, I did feel safe and welcome back to the island. It was nauseating to feel what I felt as we passed by the house again. I knew that I was safe in Jesse's company, but I was feeling the darkness and sickness inside me starting to weep out.

Like a poisonous mold.

The memories wanted to devour me right there, from that year on island that I was still suppressing and avoiding really remembering. My feelings wanted to turn me into dirt. Icky, moldy, nutrient deficient, island dirt.

Chapter 3: Not all Things Planted are Prosperous

I had decided to make tomato soup that day. I marched on out to the gardens down the backdoor of the kitchen.

We had planted two big gardens, and I had grown everything from seed. There was an array of tomatoes; pink speckled, roma, cherry tomato and an orange heirloom variety. The gardens were producing well, and there was even a melon corner where we were growing watermelon and cantaloupe.

I learned to put the melons on pieces of cardboard, to keep them from rotting in the island rain. I did notice that some of the tomatoes were rotting but most appeared to be ripening beautifully.

The soup came out very flavorful and it was exciting to be making food from the crops we harvested from our own gardens.

I got sick that night.

The temperature in my body was rising and something nasty was gurgling up from inside my tummy. After a few, let's say, icky deposits in the toilet, I was returning

Jennifer Lin Phillips

to equilibrium.

Gosh, something in that soil was off. The molds on the property had been harassing my wellbeing for months. It was safe to assume that the mold was in the soil too. After all that effort growing everything, this was going to be the outcome? Food we can't eat? Nathan handled assimilating the soup well that day. But his immune system was different than mine. He wasn't allergic to mold and wasn't responding as poorly to living on site with the mold as I was.

I admired the papaya trees that I had also grown from seed and was hoping that they would bare healthy fruit for us. It was amazing watching them grow along the backside of Nathan's office. But only time would tell if they would grow to bare healthy fruit or not.

Things were running smoothly overall, at the house now. After being on the property for nearly eight months, there seemed to be somewhat of a consistency finally. Nathan and I had worked hard on creating a business together. Our business was rentals. We had successfully rented out the open rooms and the cottage. Everything was in motion and now in full effect.

Initially, we just had only the cottage occupied. But for the past month or so, everything was rented out. All our current tenants were young. Including Nathan and

I, there were three couples all in our 30's. Which honestly made for an interesting mixture of things.

The attached one-bedroom studio housed a cute young couple from Vermont, and they had a little two-year-old baby boy. The energy at the house was pretty good now.

Me and my partner, Nathan, were in the middle room. I had painted the hot salmon, pink bathroom, with the skylight, to a cool liquid blue, with dazzling golden butterflies and flowers. The room had the best view of the Ocean, and the sounds at night, after the noise of the day had died down, sent waves of warmth and seawater air through the tall wide screen doors.

We rented the master bedroom to a fun young couple from Northern California. I loved that area of the country and had lived there for a few years, just before returning to the islands in 2011. The area was so pristine, giant redwood trees would parade all the way out to the Golden Coast that displayed pampas grass along windy roads.

The couple was grateful for and indulging in the bathtub I loved so much and that I had soaked in nearly every evening since we began living at the house. The tub had colorful blinking lights all along the rim, the lights would change color in synthesis with the jets bubbling up through the water.

Oh, and that water!

Jennifer Lin Phillips

It came down from a small hole in the ceiling and streamed perfectly into the bathtub like a contained waterfall.

The front room we rented to a middle-aged man who was working at the Princeville Hotel. He worked in marketing and events for the Hotel and was gone nearly all day and would cruise up after sundown in his van. He would park on the opposite side of the street, oceanside, just down from the front of the house.

I absolutely loved the hotel he was working at.

He had come to the island from New York, and with his experience, he found an excellent spot to work. I went for happy hour, mostly sushi and a fun frufru martini, and sat on the outdoor patio there at the Princeville Hotel once. I think that was when I was working at the organic farm in Moloo'a back in my early twenties.

The views were breathtaking of the Coastline, the Kalalau Valley Mountain Range that was curved, peaked and trailed up along the North Shore. There was often live music there too. The notes from the piano playing that night, moved through me elegantly, and could be heard throughout the hotel many nights during happy hour. The music echoed from the large main room inside that night I was there, and I sat outside at sundown, witnessing warm waves splashing sips of water on the legs of the building below the deck. And I sipped too on my martini in awe at the mystical and sensual beauty of this island, Kauai.

Oh, my Goddess...... Seriously?!!! I am in a cafe right now, down from my apartment in Oregon, typing and recalling this story of mine and one of my favorite Hawaiian Vocalists is streaming from the speakers right now! This is lovely!! Wow, lol......"Somewhere over the rainbow bluebirds fly, and the dreams that you dream they really do come true, ooooooooohhh....wake up where the clouds are far behind me.....that's where you will find meeeee.......Oh somewhere over the rainbow...."

I remember crying at my best friend Damon's mothers house when I heard this song maybe ten years ago.

I was missing the ocean and the energy of the Hawaiian people and culture. "Ooooooooooooo ah ah ah ah ah ah ah"......What an amazing vocalist. Brother Iz, or Israel Kamakawiwo'ole. I know for certain, Bradda Iz, made many people cry with his soothing gentle voice and loving spirit. What a giant, gentle, Hawaiian angel he was and anyone who knows of him and his story was saddened by his death at the age of only 38.

He was just beginning to see the huge success of "Over the Rainbow." His obesity was too much for him to handle and he lost his dear life due to respiratory

Jennifer Lin Phillips

failure.

My story of the islands continues...... Everything was going really pretty smooth at the house on Kauai. Maybe a little tension between couples and housemates, with the division of male and female energy, three couples in close quarters. It was so cool and mystifying how we all had been brought to the house, led by spirit, to live and grow, and learn at this incredible house along one of the most seductive and private beaches on the entire island.

Claire was living in the closely attached one-bedroom studio, the bubbly and charming young blonde and recently new mother, had one of the most amazing singing voices I had ever heard from a friend and peer.

I remember her walking in through the back door one warm, island day, humming and seducing the air before her with her fresh tones. She would come over often to do laundry. It was perfect, we all shared the washer in the main house, and we had set up three cords outside for hanging the clothes to dry.

It was kind of magical, watching the laundry air drying in the yard some days. Color and comfort dangling outside. Cotton resting and shaking out the nights and days, and the special or challenging moments of the one who hung them, or perhaps their loved ones.

Rachel and Travis in the master bedroom were a vibrant and very energetic couple. Rachel would blink uncontrollably while talking, she had Hashimoto's disorder and I learned a little about that and how she took care of herself to stay healthy. Travis was into fungi and medicine. We definitely resonated on that level and would have talks about how to make homemade kombucha or jun. Jun, he told me, is a healthier version of kombucha, which was made from live cultures or positive bacteria without all the extra added sugar.

Rachel belonged to a girl group that danced, and she even danced with fire. That mesmerized me. I always thought I would pick up the practice, but even as much as I carry and work with the element of fire, being that close to it kinda frightens me. With my extremely sensitive, pink freckled skin, I am almost always in a state of doing things to cool my skin, not flare up its warm expression.

I remember how Rachel and I would share our meditations and talk spiritual.

I would show her how to use the ocean water to cool and clean crystals that I had used for ritual or ceremony. I told her how much I loved the Hindu culture, the gods and goddess. The colors and spices

Jennifer Lin Phillips

they created their clothes and foods with. I loved the mantras they spoke, and how they worshipped the Beloved. Whispering sincerely to Lord Shiva, Lakshmi, Hanuman, Ganesha. There were old men in sarongs and robes, and candles dripping wax aligning pictures of their Gurus around them. The men and women sitting peacefully for meditation.

I really felt that the culture was in surrender to God's heart in earnest request to quiet and soothe ones very soul.

Rachel talked often of her connection to the Buddhist culture.

She took me one day to the temple on island where she led meditation for a group mostly of women. The temple was set up out in the open air. We sat outside in the garden along those metal and wooden wheels one island day.

Traditionally the mantra "Om Mani Padme Hum" is written in Sanskrit on the outside of the wheel. At the core of the cylinder is a "Life Tree" often made of wood or metal with certain mantras written or wrapped around it.

I drug my fingers and hands along the wooden ornaments, also known as a prayer wheel. I spun them as I walked behind the row of girls there. I spun them elegantly, head relaxed and swaying, hair dangling over shoulders, mouth whispering prayers to She. I remember how safe I felt with the ladies there. I also felt electrified by each of their unique presence and energies.

And as we kneeled on the blankets in the grass below them, my heartbeat calmed and rested with each of theirs. All of us, sisters, mothers, daughters, and each a divine link to the Goddess.

Ever since we got the gym equipment downstairs beneath the house in the open garage at ground level below the house, Nathan would only leave the house to swim at the beach across from the home or skip out to the health food store for some desirables.

I did get him out to dinner and lunch a handful of times in our year together on the island of Kauai. Or on a shopping trip to buy something for the house, or some clothes for him. But it was nearly impossible to get him to take me on a hike or to another beach and spend the day with me.

He had to be one of the most disciplined boyfriends I had ever dated. I was usually the one inspiring my lover to be more health conscious, or aware overall. But not in this relationship. I was the one now learning a lot from him.

We would always start the day out with tea that had steeped naturally overnight, out on the long patio being blessed by fresh evening air and the ocean waves at dawn.

It was the first thing we tasted in the mornings.

A swim and workout in the morning was routine, a smoothie afterwards, some breakfast of oatmeal, peanut butter, banana, hemp seeds and eggs and then off to work for both of us.

He would sit in his office doing research. All kinds of research on laws. How to acquire a loan so we could do more work on the house and then possibly sell it. And then he would also do his work for the Kingdom, where he was given the position as the Minister of Finance. The Kingdom was in the process of creating their own currency. And Nathan used his own money to help them and to create gold and silver coins with the face of the King etched into them.

Many of the local Hawaiians loved the coins and he gave many of them away to the them, to show his appreciation for their culture and their struggles. The Kingdom was also working on developing an offshore bank. Perhaps in Tahiti, or one of the other islands of French Polynesia.

Nathan's work was fascinating to me. The challenges and the vision they were creating made my heartrate increase and palm's sweaty. Quite honestly, so did being in the company of the King, the Queen, his wife, and some of the other Hawaiian people seeking sovereignty from the predominantly white government of the USA.

They had an anger, a purpose so ocean deep. You could feel its intense persistence and urgency expressed in their gestures, from their eyes. And the excitement of sovereignty, of reclaiming the island. They were determined to return the land to the people whose families really, truthfully owned it. And regain their peace and sovereignty. Their dignity.

I remember Nathan telling me how the land was taken by missionaries and other white men who had landed there. Much of the land was ruthlessly taken by white men with fancy paperwork. The innocent and uneducated Hawaiians had their land taken by the new lawmakers who carried guns, quick speech and ink in their writing pens. And many of the white men taught Christianity.

It was both sad and interesting to see how the Hawaiian people were camped out in long stretches of highway on the island of Oahu. And living in extremely small lots in old and worn houses on acreage that was now being occupied by million-dollar homes on many of the other islands.

I saw all this first hand.

A Polynesian lady across from the house where Nathan

Jennifer Lin Phillips

and I were, was living in nearly a shack that housed bulldogs behind a small fence. The dogs would bark fiercely as one walked by.

She came to the house one or two times. Explaining to us how the entire block all the way down to the campground was in fact her families land. And that our house, which sat along a tiny canal with interesting red geese, was built on an old creek and pond that had been diverted into two small canals and ponds on each side of our house. Her grandfather used to canoe just below our house along the pond and fish when she was a girl.

Now at night in one of the ponds, a toad would croak alone under island stars that remembered the history of its people.

When Nathan told me about the house, we were living in Waikiki together. He had been working on creating a document, that would put a lean on the house. He had found the house on a trip over to the island with a member of the Kingdom. The member had shown him the house and shared with him his dream of taking it over for him and his family one day.

I remember when I first met Nathan. I was working at the vegetarian market and health food store in Honolulu. We chatted once or twice and then one day he walked in with a few freshly picked island wildflowers and a grin on his face. I decided that day I would hang out with him and see just what he was all about.

He seemed nice, unusual character, I thought. But I knew I felt intrigued by him. He came in singing and humming that day to me down the isle of vitamins and royal ginseng that I was standing in. I decided I would meet him later for a talk.

At that time, I was going through a breakup with a longtime friend, sort of boyfriend of mine. We had decided to give dating another try. He was a painter and an incredible artist. He painted island scenes and was usually in between three or four paintings at a time. We just weren't working out being together romantically, although there was a lot of love and history there between us.

Our differences were too much. I didn't drink much alcohol. And I just couldn't binge on tv every other night either.

Unfortunately, there was a lot between us, and I was found most nights hiding away in the bedroom meditating and stretching. I knew I was ready to move on, but I wasn't quite sure how to.

I ended up moving in with Nathan almost immediately, faster than I wanted to. My ex, Josh, had found out that I had hung out with him a few times and was pissed.

I knew it was time to make the leap into another direction.

Nathan was living in a small, dirty apartment in Waikiki with bus soot on the windowsills. It was a lot to clean when I moved in, but wow, what an exciting turn in my life. I was very attracted to Nathan's passion, his healthy and strong body and his interest in me.

Come nightfall, we would walk along the strip that lined the beaches of Waikiki. He picked white and pink plumeria's from trees along the Ala Wai Canal and would sing to me. He would pull me close into him and carefully place the plumeria flowers he had just picked in my hair behind my ears. He told me he understood me, my flow and my energy. And that he could see the strength of my spirit. He referred to me as GG, or Graceful Goddess and often called me a pure bred. Like a horse who was strong and built to run. I felt like he could really see me, my struggles, and my striving, where I came from and my journey.

"I'm falling in love with you Jennifer." He whispered to me, while we were standing in line at the health food store I was working at.

I was off that day and spending the day with him.   As

I approached the cashier with my groceries, my heart turned rosy pinks inside myself. Cheeks blushing different shades of red on my face. I could hear the beep from the organic food crossing under the register in front of me and then placed into paper bags. It felt like the ceiling was spinning above me dark purple kale leaves and sprouted alfalfa clovers all around. I knew right then I was falling for him too.

"You should work at my friend's spa in Honolulu. You would be great there! You've been talking about getting into massage and possibly going to massage school. Why not go to work for my friend and see if you like it?" Nathan said to me one day in his apartment in Waikiki over lunch.

It wasn't a bad idea. We could make some quick money too and then head over to Kauai and get to that house he had been telling me about for a few months. We could build a life there together. It's so remote on Kauai. Really, we could have a much more peaceful and secluded way of living. It certainly seemed like our next step forward. We were just making one step after the other. And plus, I could tell the pressure from the city was really getting to him.

He burst out in road rage several times while travelling in his car throughout the city some days. And would speed fast and foolishly around other cars putting both of our lives in danger.

It's true that Waikiki can get to you while living there after a while. Tourists and loud buses. A party scene every night. Hookers casually aligning their next prey.

I loved Kapiolani Park, named after the once Queen Kapiolani.

People were so active there. Volleyball by the beach in the sand, joggers, people practicing Chi-Gong on the lawn. Across from the park was my favorite beach, Queen's Beach. The name was given due to the amount of gay men that frequented that corner of the strip. At least that's what I was told.

I felt good there, usually a cute local lifeguard on site. I almost always ended up there after grabbing an ahi poke bowl with avocado from a fresh fish market. I loved to watch people and tourists swim. I swam daily, most likely every single day and the ocean water was always the release that I needed.

Across from the sands of people, the surfers, and sailboats and loads of cheap sunscreen was the famous Pink Hotel in the center of the city. Every Friday night fireworks went off above the thousands of people in condo's and hotels. High above the statue of the famous surfer Duke, which is always adorned with fresh flowered leis from tourists.

The blowing of the conch shell or pu, at sunset in

Waikiki is sounded to inform everyone that the fireworks would be set off soon. The blowing of the pu was tradition of the people and was often used before ceremony to mark the official beginning.

Jennifer Lin Phillips

Chapter 4: Meeting the King

I had lived on the islands on and off for fifteen years, most likely six years total and almost three years on Oahu. Waikiki and Honolulu were special to me. Down the street from where I lived you could get cheap, authentic and very good acupuncture and oriental herbs. I loved the weird smells that came from Chinatown from something being fried or some strange meat I hadn't heard of being roasted.

The stores in Chinatown had incense, little trinkets from Asia, silk slippers and bra's wrapped in plastic that were literally only a few dollars. I enjoyed observing the odd island fruit, dragon fruit was particularly interesting with its pink and green horns coming off its rounded back.

I had my picture taken in Chinatown once standing next to the beautiful statue of the Bodhisattva Kuan Yin, the Goddess of Compassion. I was holding an Asian fan I had just purchased, smiling like the daughter of my mother. Her smile and grace beaming through me as I held the open fan perched beneath my wild eyes, and soft sun kissed cheeks.

Friday night art walk with exuberant young college kids showcasing their artwork was a total kick. I remember tasting sake or elderberry martini's in between dancing on the dance floor and relaxing under the evening air beneath the warm Hawaiian moon.

I rode my bike home with the cute bell and basket attached on front a few times, feeling a bit tipsy with Josh. He on his cute Schwinn bicycle too. We would ding our bells to one another, swerving and gliding along the dark, humid streets at night. Of course, riding along the sidewalk when at all possible to avoid any possible danger from cars driving by.

We usually continued the dance party at home with his amazing choice of music and fun grooves. Everything But the Girl was one of his favorite bands. How did he always know how to choose the music?

Dancing was our forte. We also got out a lot to hike to really see the islands and also attended a few of the art festivals up North Shore.

Josh was my dear friend who captured on film my years exploring the islands with him and I was very thankful to him for that and our friendship that had endured for fifteen years. Josh could also almost always make me laugh with his quick wit and humor. He made everyone laugh, but I realized quickly again, our second time around that anytime there is too much drinking by one party in the relationship, trouble soon follows.

Jennifer Lin Phillips

When I met Nathan, he was so refreshing to me. He drank maybe a beer in a week, if even that. Although he did enjoy his weed. He smoked daily, and it was his medicine that calmed his nerves and put him at ease. He smoked and wore hempseed oil all over his body. I remember walking up to the apartment we shared, and the nutty scent would enter me. That nutty warm smell of pressed hempseeds into oil.

Nathan was so green and so different. He told me stories of being tied in with the Kingdom of Atooi. A group of Pacific Islanders and Hawaiians longing for and rebuilding their sovereignty. Atooi was defined as "The Light of God," and that really felt sincere and impressed me.

I couldn't help but giggle sometimes when Nathan would sing to himself in the mirror...."I'm a millionaire"......He would look at himself confidently and smile. He explained to me how he was actually once a millionaire due to his weed business but got sold out by his ex-girlfriend.

Apparently, she turned out to be into women, screwed him over good too and you could tell that he still had feelings for her when he spoke of her.

She went ahead and went behind his back and ruined his business somehow. He told me also how he had pursued a career in singing in the LA area. Hadn't had any big record deals granted thus far. Frankly, he didn't have any real talent in singing. But it was awfully sweet when he did burst out into song. Or when he would serenade me or just sing casually aloud.

One day, he explained to me just what that term really meant to him, "I'm a millionaire!" Although I know he chose to say it and bring the term into his awareness as a means of creating its actuality in his life. He also explained that it was a way for him to shine from the inside out. Like he was a true winner, a Champion......which happened to be the title of one of his songs on the record he created.

He told me about the time he had been robbed and beaten up in Honolulu in his condo while distributing and selling weed. He then, after yet again losing everything he was working on, decided to try another avenue of work and began working for some hotels and he even started his own water business. With his water biz, he would make routes for his clients and drop off gallons and jugs of pure alkaline water that he would fill up from his $3000 Kangen water machine.

I remember when I met the King from the Kingdom. He dropped over to the tiny apartment downtown for some herb, and Nathan had phoned me a few minutes before to tell me that he would be by shortly. Yea, Nathan had put me to work in his small business selling

Jennifer Lin Phillips

weed right away.

"Hi! Wow nice to meet you." the King said to me as I opened the door. It was like he had never actually talked with a haole girl before with red hair.

Haole; a derogatory word used for white people, but which I was told means "shallow breather".

"Nice to meet you too!" I said back to the King as he walked in.

He definitely had a presence. Tribal tattoos on his face and cheekbones. An incredible smile that captivated me in its warmth. He had love in his eyes and a fierce determination that one could easily pick up on.

I walked to the backroom where the weed was, and he followed me. The weed and scale were in the bedroom. While weighing it, I had my back to the King. While I was pulling fresh buds out of a bag, he leaned over to me and said, "Oh my gosh, you look so good! Can I touch it?"

My face paled over in expression and I thought what? What is he asking of me? My boyfriend's friend and the King of the Kingdom? I glanced towards him as he looked me up then down. I felt his hand reach out and touch my bare skin and booty. Just a quick grab and that was it. I could sense his embarrassment mixed in with his satisfaction. "Thank you, sorry, oh sorry."   He said to me.

"Okay, okay." I said back to him and handed him his bag of weed. And then he left.

Jennifer Lin Phillips

Chapter 5: When you Squeeze an Orange

I was more than ready for the move across island. Nathan showed me the house he had discovered and pictures of the outside and the inside online.

The house had been abandoned for nearly five years and no one had occupied it since then. The previous owners were a family. But the man of the house had committed suicide by driving a car off the coast up in Washington State. He had been charged many times over for fraud and had worked in real estate or financing.

I cannot remember the exact story of that family but apparently, he had been taking people's money, investing it and not returning it forthright. He was convicted of numerous crimes, his wife and children were sideswiped and shocked. He was going to lose the house and everything he had invested and would be sentenced to years in prison. I believe it was after his sentence that his body was found along the coastline up in Washington State outside of Seattle somewhere. I did read some of his story but was learning so much about the Kingdom, the house and how to acquire it, that I could barely keep up on everything.

I do remember Nathan explaining to me how one of his best friend's was in his seventies, Jamaican, and a lawyer living in the LA area.

"We can secure the house with his help, clean it up and live there. Eventually we can sell it and make a lot of money. My friend in LA knows the laws and the correct ways to do the appropriate paperwork. He is also an ordained minister and can marry us on the beach. Let's keep going forward babe with our move and get off Oahu."

He called his friend who was the owner of the spa, and I began working nights right away. It was a means to save some quick money for the exotic adventure across the islands.

We were walking on the bustling streets of the city of Waikiki that day and Nathan had decided to help me sell my handcrafted jewelry. The Niihau Shell jewelry I had been working on for months. He was in a fast pace and frustrated and I was kind of looking forward to who we would meet and who would like to buy my craft.

Before we even got set up, we broke down. I made a remark about his hostility and he left me there on the strip with my things. I felt pretty humiliated at the people around watching and I just packed up and went back to the apartment trailing behind him. I didn't

Jennifer Lin Phillips

really feel like it was the right energy to run trying to sell my craft, when I had previously spent hours and hours on my jewelry, poking holes in each tiny shell, stringing them intently with love.

When I returned behind him to the apartment we began to argue.

He told me how much I needed him and how I would be down in the streets without him. I found it ironic since I had just bought him hundreds of dollars' worth of clothes and I was the one with the active credit card that we had talked about using to get to the house and furnish it.

He was peeling an orange and squeezed it so hard that its juice and seeds splattered out across the room and down from his fingertips. I just looked at him, in disbelief, recalling how he, maybe a month prior, was sharing the knowledge of one of his favorite life coaches with me. Dr. Wayne Dyer used to say in his talks about being in control of one's emotions. And taking responsibility for how we respond to situations. Dr. Wayne Dyer would say literally "When you squeeze an orange what comes out?"

In other words when you are squeezed, when life squeezes you, what comes out from you? This is what we are all working on. Those knee jerk responses and reflexes. With each new challenge of the day, we are being squeezed like oranges.

Hey, I've been squeezed before, and out came sauerkraut. And yes, I know, it sure is a lot to walk ones talk, but after the episode of him leaving me on the street and then ironically squeezing that orange like he did right there. I knew I needed to get some space for myself.

I am in control of my life, I thought. And I wanted to feel like I was going to determine my next choice, not him. Not Nathan. I was going to need the mind room and clarity to see things right.

There had also been a few intense arguments before this one.

I remember one evening on the Fourth of July when we went out for sushi. I had offered to take Nathan out. He had been generous and bought groceries so many times. This was my treat. I had been working late hours now at the spa, and I had some extra cash to treat us with a bit.

He was so stoned that night, he said maybe two words to me at dinner. When I asked him why he was so aloof, he replied that I was taking HIM out to dinner, not the other way around. So why would he need to put the extra effort into engaging my company?

Jennifer Lin Phillips

I've been crazy stoned before. I know what it's like when you get spacey, unavailable and anti-social. But I wanted him there with me. Present and engaging me. I also thought it was an odd way to look at things, like I was the masculine energy now trying to win his affections because I had the funds to pay for the meal? It was a weird way of thinking. All righty then, fine, ignore me then, I thought.

He was frustrated at my response to his mood and as we left the restaurant, he sped up leaving me walking alone behind him. We had been living now together in Waikiki for a few months and things and emotions were starting to surface.

At first, I tried to keep up with him while walking outside, but instead I let him walk quickly ahead of me and I decided to get lost in the crowds of tourists beneath the Waikiki lights.

With the exuberant energy of the city, the people in groups all around, families, couples, shops open late, I just let myself get lost in the night's energy. I ended up on the beach across from some of the shops, and watched the fireworks being shot into the air. I felt sad about our argument and was trying to get a grip on my feelings and what had just happened. It felt odd to me that he would even think like that. And I felt taken advantage of.

I was sitting with arms around my knees pulled in on

the sand when a young man approached me. He asked me how my night was and why I looked a little sad. We talked for a few minutes, ocean waves splashing around us, between the words being exchanged.

He complimented me on my dress and told me I looked very pretty. His gestures were sweet, and he was sincere. It was what I wanted to hear from Nathan that night and didn't. That's all I wanted to hear and feel. Like I mattered and was beautiful.

But sitting on the sand that Fourth of July evening, I at least felt the comfort from this stranger and knew he was there somehow to ease inches off my hurt. We talked a bit more, laughed aloud about the night, about the island and the crazy happenings of the city, and said goodnight. I went home to Nathan and I crawled hesitantly into bed.

Jennifer Lin Phillips

Chapter 6: Ala Wai Mansion

After the orange incident, I was really feeling the pull to branch out on my own. The words, "I would be out on the streets without him" played over again in my mind and I was not going to feel like I would be lost in Waikiki or my life without him. I knew his words were not the truth. I had always been in charge of me, and spirit had also always had my back. Always.

I was sitting on the front porch the next morning, skimming through craigslist ads and rooms for rent. **$900 room along the Ala Wai, fully furnished, private bath**. Hhhmmm……I thought to myself, this could be a good fit.

I called the owner of the condo and room for rent, it was a fifteen-minute walk from me along the Ala Wai Canal. The building was called the Ala Wai Mansion, and we made plans to meet that afternoon.

After a quick shower, I skipped on down the Ala Wai to meet him.

You needed a key to access the elevator, so we met downstairs outside in the parking lot. When I approached the garage, the Owner of the condo Richard walked over to greet me warmly. He seemed very kind, and a rather generous being I felt right away.

Sovereignty and the Goddess

We took the elevator up to the 10th floor and got out. His condo occupied half of the floor and we went inside through the doors to the right of the hallway.

When we walked through the front doors inside, I was immediately ignited by the aroma of love and enchantment coming through the artwork on the walls. The older man, early 60's, was a Hare Krishna and had vibrant paintings all over his home. A bright mustard yellow mural in the kitchen depicting a love scene of Radha and Krishna, the lovers, in a canoe with lily pads and colorful flowers springing from the water and grass. The artwork of the lovers, them gesturing sweetly to one another, gazing into each other's eyes with love, devotion and admiration was all over the three-bedroom condo. I knew that I had just entered a portal to another world.

The front room was very spacious with couches, wide oriental rugs, chairs, and an elegant alter with statues of Bodhisattvas, candles set out, incense dust and flowered offerings.

The lanai wrapped around 180 degrees of the condo with views of the Ala Wai Canal and he led me to the room for rent down its own private hallway. We passed the elegant bathroom with tub to the room. Upon entering the room, golden satin bedding and pillows poked at my senses. There was a nice size closet, a desk with chair, some more of the artwork above the bed of the lovers and a sliding door to the

Jennifer Lin Phillips

lanai.

I smiled to him showing my delight at such a sensually intoxicating place and opened the sliding doors to step outside. There was a tall palm like plant in vase, a lounging chair and an Asian screen door separating the lanai into two parts. Around from the screen was an open, long, glass sliding door that lead into his room, and I peeked around to see. The view was oceanside and really nice, some hotels and buildings and then the ocean's blue waters along the horizon in the distance. Only about a five-blocks walk to the hotels that lined the beautiful blue water of the sea.

He told me that you could see the Friday night fireworks from the lanai too. We then talked about deposits and expectations. His compassionate nature just oozed from him and allowed me to feel very welcome right away.

And I felt so stimulated by the images of lovers, the colors around, the view of the canal and also the ocean. It was nice being up so high too, elevated and up off the pavement of the crowded city.

I gave him cash right there and secured the room for myself. I knew it was my best decision and probably just what I needed. To feel elevated from some of the distress I had been experiencing and get a clearer perspective on where to put my energies and how I was going to make my next move.

I moved in the following day and said a quick goodbye to Nathan while gathering up the rest of my things. Explaining to him calmly how we both needed some space for ourselves. I didn't have much. I came to the island less than a year before, and this was my second time back living on Oahu. Nathan was friendly and cooperative. Reassuring me that he was sad to see me move out, but that the room for clarity was most appropriate for our current situation. Of course, we would stay in touch, and continue to move forward, wherever our paths would lead us was still very uncertain.

The room was perfect for me. It was so sensually gratifying, and I began doing mantra and sound vibration on my lanai with my new wooden prayer beads that Richard had given me. He even gave me a specific mantra to work with. I remember reaching a really tranquil space one day, chanting Hare Krishna along the mala beads outside on the lanai one gorgeous Hawaii day. It was refreshing being in my own space and energy finally. I was now able to relax deeper into myself and my chakras and senses were naturally opening without all the added stresses around me.

There were two other people living in that condo also. A Thai woman and her son. Well, Richard's son also. And the Thai woman, was also Richard's wife. They had

Jennifer Lin Phillips

married when she was very young. Richard had found her on a trip to Thailand and brought her back to the islands. They were married, and she gave birth to their child. At some point, she began working at a night club, and Richard said things got weird and they became very distant from one another. I think they even separated. But she came back to him one day, needing a place to live. They shared custody of their son. He was 18, I believe when I met him. And him and his mother slept on a mat on the floor in a middle room next to the kitchen and Richard's room.

The woman's name was Tia, and we got along well, building a friendship almost immediately. She was very sweet and had a beautiful smile.

We began going to Chinatown together, and I would drive her and I both down in the car I had bought from Richard. A 1978 blue Mercedes, stick shift with a sunroof. She was easy company for me to be around. We would shop together at the market and if she needed to run another errand, maybe to the bank or somewhere, I would take her. She cooked for me in exchange sometimes and made some really pretty good Thai dishes. Even my favorite, green papaya salad. She even gave me my own pounding gourd, or bowl to make my own salad with.

I was surprised at the amount of clothes and all the expensive purses she had. It was odd seeing her and her son on the floor together like that, with only a few blankets and pillows.

Her son was practically a man now, considered to be an adult. And he had a job working at a fast food establishment. It could've been McDonald's where he was working, but I can't remember now. I do remember when her son started to act like a real teenager, a troubled and confused teenager. And it reminded me of how I acted at that age.

He came home drunk one night, it was really a pretty late night for him. I was sitting on the couch in the front room unwinding from my night from working at the spa and I was reading.

The mood was so good in that room by the alter and above the Ala Wai Canal. The silence just permeated everything come dark. The blackness that had taken over the sky and the winking and blinking of stars that extended past sky-scraper's. The water shimmering on the canal from street lights down below that were built into the cement of the sidewalk.

His demeanor startled me when he came in to sit by me there in the silence of the front room. His behavior was odd, and he was kind of flirting with me. He was so young, and I had to laugh a little at how he was acting about. I pretty much told him that drinking and getting drunk like that is pointless and will only get one into trouble. But one had to learn on his own, right? I think we all have had to learn by experience. He let me talk and I think he listened a little, and then I went down the long side hallway to sleep.

The following week, Tia told me that he had chipped his front tooth out on the pavement. He was walking home drunk again and fell flat on his face. I know it was confusing for him having different girl's rent out the Golden room down the hall.

I know he didn't quite understand why his dad barely spoke to his mom, but instead hid out in his room binging on images of Radha or Krishna or fantasizing about another time in his life when he was really living and happy. Richard and Tia seemed to only converse over food. Which was just fine, because at least there they could come together. He would pay for the food, and Tia would do the serving and cook some very healthy and pretty amazing meals for them.

Honestly, they had worked out a pretty good balance at the condo. And it was a peaceful place to live. He was really acting out like most teenagers do anyways. What's normal right? Kids grow up in some interesting arrangements these days. He was well fed, and safe.

But I have a feeling, that it was probably odd for him to see his mom on the computer all day, skyping a man from another state, in hope's he would finally come and rescue her. He had, she told me one day, promised to come for her, and he had lots and lots of money. She had known him for a few years, and he had a great reputation, she said. I really was hoping he would come to her soon and take her away with him somewhere nice and take good care of her. Her and her son could go too.

Jennifer Lin Phillips

Chapter 7: Blending with Different Cultures

I had been working at the spa maybe a month and was making really pretty good money some nights. The hours were rough, 5pm-2 or 3am most nights. My schedule was consistent. I was working maybe four days every week.

To get to the building I would walk along the canal about 25 minutes from where I was living now in the condo in the opposite direction from where I had lived with Nathan.

I was working mostly with Thai women and younger girls, ages anywhere from 21-40s. I did feel welcome at the spa right away but there were obviously some cultural differences that I was being challenged with. I couldn't speak Thai, which was fine because many of the girls spoke English quite well. The owner of the spa, Karla, was from Thailand and was running the business while her husband watched their 5-year old daughter, Ella.

There were four main rooms for massage that had dynamite views of the canal, the city and ocean, and the misty mountain and Manoa Valley behind. One of the rooms was for us to dress, put on makeup, rest, read, listen to music, play on our phones, eat and gather. There were blankets, a massage table, that was often used for naps, and an amazing alter to the Buddha and other deities.

The mists from the mountain beside the building, sent soothing breezes outside the spa with all glass windows surrounding in each room.

The theme was Thai with statues and flower offerings in the hallway and in each massage room. The girls would cook together most nights and I tried their food often, spicy as it was. I really enjoyed the fresh herbs, sprouts and all the flavors that complimented one another. I think it was humoring the other girls some days, watching me try some of the hotter dishes they had prepared. With water nearby to sip on, extinguishing the flames upon my pink tongue.

I loved it when Ella would march in to see us and bring with her the joy she naturally exuded with her presence.

One day in the girls lounging room, Ella and I were playing together. I was lying on my stomach face down in front of the alter and she playfully mounted my back to touch my hair with her tiny fingers. I told her to lie down and put her arms out like wings. She decided to follow my instructions. It was special to me how we had a little bond between us. Even though she really loved all the ladies there.

With her little chest resting on my back, both of our

arms spread out sideways, her arms above mine, we both flew in that room. Our wings spread out ready to swoop and soar.

With the air under our wings from the valley's gape, we flew high above the statues of the Buddha and the candles in the room. Above the sheets of paper with Thai mantras and prayers. We kept flying over and above the wet mists seeping out from the depths of the valley outside. It felt like we soared down the long narrow Ala Wai Canal together and up to the peak of Diamond Head Crater to perch up and look out over the water.

And then to sit under the midnight black of the night sky, like a couple of curious island birds. We laughed and giggled and one of the young Thai girls who used the nickname Twinkle, had been watching us. She looked at me in amazement, her eyes now appearing open, like a tunnel, a long silky hallway that had carried her into another way of seeing. I could sense her yearning and amazement at the magic little Ella and I were creating right there together.

The owner of the spa had decided to take full advantage of the new redhaired girl working for her, Me. She used pictures of me on her ads to bring people in that were seeking a different look than the mostly Thai women working there. She befriended me right away and liked that I was reliable and showed up on time. Even if I was tired from the late night before. I averaged on 5-6 massages in a night, and even though I was just learning, I had always possessed an intuitive touch naturally. I was able to do the work with the strong hands that I had developed from a lifetime of playing team sports.

One day a few of us were standing around talking and making up the massage table with clean sheets, when the owner, Karla, pointed up to the ceiling and said, "Look, a spark, I saw a flash right there in the corner of the room, Jennifer's going to bring me good luck here!" I was a bit surprised at her exclamation. And watched her closely.

I think she could sense that I had an energy of abundance, perhaps charm, and a willingness to work. It was true, many of her clients began requesting me and would also come back weekly, or bi-weekly as repeat clients.

Karla was showing signs of curiosity about my touch, so we planned a massage exchange on one of the slower evenings. I think we were both needing a soothing exchange of feminine touch. As I rubbed both of her temples with my fingers, then pulling them through the long dark strands of her thick, black hair, we agreed that we both had strong, nurturing hands. It was then, that the authenticity of our friendship began to bloom.

Jennifer Lin Phillips

She exhaled a deep breath after her session with me had ended. Allowing some of the stress from running a business of that caliber go a little.

I was having lunch one day at a vegetarian cafe in my neighborhood downtown when a younger man sat at the table beside me. He began eating and then casually looked up at me to smile in between chewing his food. I smiled back.

Our tables were very close to one another and he began to casually talk with me. He complimented me on my hair and how I looked. I got the usual, "You know I just really have this thing for redheads." I get that a lot from men. Not all the time or anything, but I do hear it quite often. Along with the, "Well you know, I hear redheads are amazing in bed!" Or...."You redheads really are a lot to handle I've heard, quite the temper."

Okay....like telling someone you just met and don't even know, that you heard they have a temper, isn't slightly irritating? Hear that one a few fifty times and see if it sparks a little fiery response. I would just smirk a little, blow the remark off and think to myself.... "Yes, I hear you are a real annoying jerk, who believes everything you hear. Ddddrrrrrrrr"

Some of the assumptions I would hear are pretty ridiculous, and although some flattering, could really be used on anyone of any ethnicity or hair color.

I usually tell them, yes, I am a real honest to Goddess Redhead, and yes some of us are a lot to handle. We get assumptions made about us all the time, unnecessary judgements, rude and interrogating nicknames, and asked constantly from women as well as men...."Hey, is that your real hair color?" Seriously?!! If I was given a hundred bucks for every time, I was asked that I would be the richest redhead on the planet.

Yes, it's my real color, and no I will not show you pubes to prove it. And please, stop going around asking every redhead you see if that is their real hair color. Do you not realize that you are turning their hair grey? Sheesh!

I just mostly tell people when they ask about my character now, "Yes, a redheaded woman is a lot like a Spanish woman. She's spicy, sexy, full of passion and flavor, sensual, perhaps wild or exotic, and could be prone to an outburst here and there."

But seriously, I'm just a girl in the world.

We continued our conversation and laughed about a few things while we talked. I was happy to have his

Jennifer Lin Phillips

company really. I was also wondering what part of the country he was from. I figured he was a tourist, being that we were in Waikiki, and mostly tourists frequent the area. He was visiting from Middle America and only in town for a week.

He asked me what I was doing in town and what I was up to later as for dinner plans. I had to work that night and mentioned to him that he could come see me for a session if he wanted. I gave him the address to the spa and he said he would set an appointment at the spa later that day. We said our farewell's, and I left feeling a bit curious if I really would see him later.

Karla phoned me to tell me that I had a 5pm session, and that the gentleman had requested me. I thought perhaps it was the man that I had met at lunch. I finished getting ready and walked the canal for work.

The spa was busy that night.

When my appointment arrived, I was forced to use the meditation and the ladies hang out room for the session, because all the other massage rooms were occupied.

When I got the knock at the door of the room, I reached for the handle, and opened the door to see him, the guy from the cafe standing there. He had shown up right on time and my very first client. We closed the door behind us, and I mentioned to him there was a bathroom for use and shower if he needed it. Although he appeared to be well groomed and looking quite nice.

He dressed down and got under the sheet on the table. He seemed confident with himself and relaxed. We talked about travelling mostly, and halfway through the session, it was time for him to flip over.

While on his back, I could see the features on his face, he had brown hair and was attractive. He happened to be a bit younger than me and admitted he was in his mid-twenties. I was almost always attracted to men closer to my age, if not older, but he was charming. He was incredibly fit and spoke with ease and experience. And he appeared to be well travelled, which I like.

I had just had my Golden birthday as they call it, my 33rd. The number is considered a master number of universal service. It is supposed to be a special and sacred number and year. The year for me had proven to be a challenging one, with so much change happening, and although I had struggled a lot, I felt like I was going somewhere colorful and positive.

After putting some oil mixed with lotion on his chest, he opened his eyes and looked at me. I grinned back at him and felt awkward with him watching me massage him now.

After massaging both his arms and stomach, he asked if he could have a little more time with me. I walked the hall to let Karla know and she confirmed it was fine. I had no other clients for at least another hour.

When I returned to the room, I felt the shift in the air. He was watching me now move about the room. I was searching for the oil to begin again. When I approached him at the table with the oil in my hands, he grabbed my hand and sat up. He pulled me into him and began kissing me. He smelled really good to me, his breath was sweet and healthy. His lips were breathing softly on mine. His arms around me were comforting and strong.

I was surprised at how much he wanted me. And I pushed away from him a little.

"I can get in big trouble doing this with you, right here." I said to him. "You know girl's get arrested and fined all of the time for this kind of thing right here!"

He laughed a little at my remarks and reassured me he wasn't with any police department or undercover agents. He sat up and put his hands through my hair. I was liking his touch but was thinking about Nathan. We had barely seen one another in a few weeks and our relationship was still very much on the rocks. It was hard to say where that relationship was going. I didn't know what we were anymore really, and that hurt me, the not knowing.

I went to look out the window towards the valley and I spaced out into the hills.

"Come here and get close to me." He requested.

I went to the table and he put his hands on my shoulders and looked into my eyes with his. He began to undress me, and he told me again how much he adored the red in my hair, my skin, my smile. He stood up and asked me to sit on the table in front of him.

I did.

He began massaging my legs, and then kissing them with his mouth. He then picked me up into his arms and walked over to the wall of the room.

I was feeling shy, a little rushed or embarrassed, but allowing it.

I liked him and the sweet way that he talked to me. I felt small in his hands and he put my back to the wall and placed his open mouth on my neck, nibbling at it. It tickled me, and I laughed.

I let him love me. I let him take me how he wanted me right there and the pleasure from the experience was intoxicating me. I remember looking out at the misty valley while pieces of him pulsed inside of me. The green mountain and mist in the air pierced a memory in my eye and the moisture from our bodies touching

Jennifer Lin Phillips

created wisps of air between us.

Both of our lungs breathing life right there together. It was passionate, and it soothed my emotions that day. I let him love me right there, and although I barely knew him, it was what I needed.

We got dressed and said goodbye. He wanted to come and visit me again, before he left in a few days. And I said I was open to that. I walked him out and got ready for my next client.

About an hour later. The police showed up at the spa. They were doing a routine check and needed to see everyone's ID's. Karla, the owner looked at me and smirked. She knew my visitor and I had some kind of thing, something happened between us.

The men went about their looking around, talking with us, asking us all a few questions. They said they were simply doing the rounds that day to all the spa's and business' in the area, and then they left.

You could say I was slightly relieved after they left, and had been trying to act cool, calming the nervousness and shaking inside.

What a weird day this one had turned out to be, I thought. I felt thankful to be getting off from work in a few hours. I was ready to pass out in the satin golden sheets in the room I had been renting. After my short walk home down the canal in the cool island night.

I was ready for my day to end and still reflecting on the mysterious, passionate, challenging and dangerous year I was having. My Golden year, the master number of universal service. Is the universe in service to me? Or am I in service to it, I thought? How utterly strange that now felt to me.

My days at work were consistent most nights and busy. In my off time, I spent a lot of my energy hiking, going to farmer's markets, resting and swimming in the ocean. I swam a lot across from the hotels in Waikiki on the days that I had to work, to keep close to town.

I was halfway through a massage one day and working on a client when I heard a knock at the door.

Tap, tap, tap.

I perched my face through as I cracked open the door of the room. "Here, I got this for you. You should wear it." Said one of the Thai women as she handed me a pretty purple skirt with black lace lining the bottom of it.

"Oh, okay, thank you." I replied to her as I took the skirt and went back to working on my client.

Nathan was coming in to see me that night. How

Jennifer Lin Phillips

perfect the timing of her gift to me, I acknowledged to myself. I would wear the skirt for him! I tried it on and the size was just right, with the black lace dangling on my legs just above my kneecap.

I was now a little nervous and anticipating his arrival.

After riding his bike along the canal to the spa, he came in fresh and energized. Karla greeted him at the door and he came down the hallway to me, where I was sitting in the lounging room.

I jumped up to meet him. I grabbed his hand and we went to the room that had the two massage tables and the shower. We closed the door behind us. He smiled and grabbed my hands, pulling me in for a passionate kiss.

We looked out the windows to the ocean and he complimented me on my sexy and seductive look. I was happy to see him. I felt at ease with him there, like he had come to protect me and bring me his love too.

He undressed casually, smelling like hempseed oil and fresh island air. He then got on the massage table lying face down. I wanted to show him how good I was getting at massage and put love and desire into each stroke along his legs and his tan back. When he turned over, I kissed his lips and smiled down to him.

He asked me how things were going there at the spa and if I was handling all the pressure okay. I said that I felt like I was blending in well with the other ladies there and doing pretty good with everything. Although, I was obviously half lying. I had been faced with a lot of pressure from the men that came to the spa. Most of them single or divorced. Lonely, seeking touch and comfort, and often hoping for some sexual or erotic encounter.

I lied to him and said things were going well. I was trying to stay positive and strong, but the hours were rough, and I would leave most nights 2am and walk home by myself, in the dark city streets along the canal.

I did feel very different from the other girls there too, being the only white girl there at the time and would often hide out in an empty massage room and curl up on the table and sleep when it was slow. Or I would lie on the floor and get into my stretching or read some article online. I was wanting him to be proud of me and to feel reassured that I was doing fine. Plus, we had grown closer living apart. And we were saving still for our adventure to Kauai. With the cash I was making, we could make it there in another few months.

I continued to massage him. I took off my shirt to expose my breasts to him and he nuzzled in to love on me. He complimented me on the skirt and snuck his hands up inside it to caress and squeeze me a little.

We kissed a few minutes more and then he got

dressed, ready to ride back down the canal to his apartment. We said goodbye, and my heart felt eased by his company. My body stimulated by his appearance at the spa.

He texted me later when he got home that he was proud of me and enjoyed the session. He called me GG again, or Graceful Goddess and said goodnight to me. I went in the back room after receiving the message. I was in the room where I had seen him and where we had talked and shared our sincere love.

I was looking out past my reflection in the glass windows as the Friday night fireworks were being set off out in the distance over the dark, midnight ocean. I watched them fire and shoot up into the sky, with two very sleepy eyes, knowing I had maybe another six or seven hours left at the spa to go.

Chapter 8: The Dragon Under the Moon

It has taken me years to fully understand and process my experiences while travelling on the islands. It is now fall in Oregon of 2017. Halloween was yesterday, and I spent the day writing and working. I also lit a candle for my Grandparents and placed it by one of my favorite pictures of them standing together.

In Ancient times the period from late October to mid-November was known as Samhain and a time of death and transformation. Of honoring our ancestors, and in reference to the Goddess, it was a time of the crone, or wise woman.

I finished carving my pumpkin a few days before Halloween. I felt drawn to paint a dragon with elongated wings on rocks breathing fire and standing under a carved out full moon. The moon twinkled from the candle I lit from within the pumpkin. I painted the wings of the dragon turquoise greenish blue with soft pink creases and veins. The body I painted red, grey and purple and the dragon has small horns and whiskers. She was breathing fire and standing on dark grey rocks. The painting came out quite well and I felt surprised at what I had created.

Jennifer Lin Phillips

I have been working on this novel for maybe a week and was starting to feel uplifted and much lighter in my life. My health has even been improving by expressing myself and my memories on paper.

After creating the mythical dragon and absorbing its presence in my being, I knew something spiritual was happening. That night as I began to fall asleep. I could feel the weight and texture of the wings of the dragon I had just painted flow through me. The energy was light, delicate, webbed.

I also felt the dark grey rocks beneath the dragon. I was one of those rocks, my back curled over, like in the yoga pose child's pose. And it appeared that I was slowly emerging and rising, this dark grey being. I realized then that I had been hiding, curled into myself, and this releasing of my story and my life experiences was truly transforming me. I was merging and turning into the dragon, with fire in my lungs, ready to roar and share my truth.

Upon researching the lessons and teachings of this mythical creature, I knew it had shown up in my life as a power animal and had come to guide me.

I learned that among animal spirit guides, the Dragon is the most ancient and imposing. Dragon rules the elements and can take whatever form she wishes. Metaphysically this equates to the shamanic goal of controlling elements as well as being able to transform into various power animals at dream time. Dragon represents fortune, authority, growth, luck and development. The ability to rise over circumstances and see things clearly. Dragon symbolism and meaning also encompasses the primordial natural forces on all planes of existence, longevity and the most-earliest of magics, some of which have been lost over time.

Dragon spirit is drawn to people of intellect, dignity, contagious enthusiasm and authority. Dragons guide such individuals toward brilliance and indeed enlightenment. In the form of the fire dragon, the dragon teaches you to roar, finding your voice, being heard and truly understood. Fire dragons bring you lessons of self-mastery, creativity, mental keenness, alchemical transformation and leadership.

Its looking like the full moon this month is approaching, in fact it's in three days, but can be seen most clearly on November 3rd. I will light the candle in my pumpkin the following night, the 4th, the evening of the full moon in honor of the dragon. And in giving thanks to her for appearing in my life and swooping in to pull me out from under the rocks I had metamorphosized into, in order to keep safe.

I will continue to give thanks for this time that has come for me. The time for speaking my truth is here. In all its heat, its fury and it's danger. In honor of the dragon, I will let it be breathed out now from my two lips and my own very lungs.

Jennifer Lin Phillips

Chapter 9; Freshwater Pearls

I walked out from the elevator to meet Nathan in the garage below the condo I was now living in. He had come to deliver my fresh alkaline water in a nice 5-gallon jug with the name of his company on a sticker on the front of it. The water was silky, so good, and I thought it was sweet of him to make a stop just for me. To say hello, sneak a kiss and a short visit in the middle of the day.

Nathan's effort, as for being loving and sweet towards me had improved a lot. I knew it had been good for us with my absence at his place, giving more space between us and still we both held the romantic vision of us escaping to Kauai together in our thoughts daily.

He pulled in and parked across from the elevators and I noticed him parked there, as I walked out from the elevator doors. I walked over to the side of the door that his smile and face were beaming out the window from.

He was smiling pretty big, from ear to ear, and I could tell something was up. He looked down and grabbed an item from the seat beside him. I looked at him waiting to see what it was, and he pulled out a jewelry box. Opening it to reveal a freshwater pearl ring. The color was a glossy peach and I thought it was very pretty.

"Will you marry me Jennifer?" He asked me with exuberance.

I looked back at him with a mixture of embarrassment and complete surprise showing on my face. It was adorable of him, the way he looked at me with ring in hand, smiling. But it was so early on in our relationship and with everything we were working towards, and just now working out the knots.

It felt superficial honestly. It wasn't like we had weeks or months of an amazing connection, without extreme turbulence and some arguing. And, traditionally, the man, to show his honesty and sincerity, is supposed to kneel before the lady to show his respect, commitment and vow to honor her. That gesture, I thought, was a very symbolic act that spoke loudly of the sincerity of any man's request for a woman's hand in marriage. A lawful commitment, that I thought, shouldn't be taken lightly or in vain. Perhaps I was being too judgmental, but my instinct was warning me his request might be forced and a bit too soon.

"Wow Nathan, that's a very pretty ring! Thankyou. Where did you get it?" I asked him.

"I got the ring in Waikiki at one of those jewelry kiosks my friend was working at." he said back to me.

"Honestly, I am a little thrown off by your question and

Jennifer Lin Phillips

I think I need some time to think about it." I looked at him with care. "I love the ring and will happily wear it as a symbol of our bond and loyalty to one another." I responded in hopes he would approve.

He seemed satisfied with my answer, handed me the ring and then he opened the door to his van to get out. He began to unload the jug of water from the car, and we carried it upstairs to the room I was renting. Once inside the room, after setting the water up on the stand upside down to allow the water to pour out below, he grabbed me and began kissing me.

He shut the door to my room and asked me to come down for sweet potato soup that he would top with hempseed oil and hempseeds. It was one of his signature entrees and he would be making it later that night at his apartment down the canal.

We kissed some more, I agreed to his request happily and felt like things were returning to that gooey state of ecstasy and excitement. He pushed me onto the golden, satin sheets and made love to me with the sliding door open to the lanai.

The crystal blue of the ocean water, even as far away as it was, was lapping over me still, even more so while in his arms and passionate embrace.

That night I walked the lovely canal to Nathan's

apartment. I watched the groups and teams in long canoe's racing in the water. There were people walking, jogging, biking, and roller blading all along the canal.

Often, I would listen to Dr. Wayne Dyer, "Aaaahhh Meditations" and it gave me much lightness in my steps most days, while I walked along the canal to work. He was such an inspiring life couch and I had discovered him through Nathan. We both did the meditation together sometimes and would say the "Aaahhh's" aloud or in our minds, while we visualized what we wanted to create in our lives, now and in the future.

We could visualize whatever we wanted to bring into our lives. This process was a way of gaining clarity on our goals, and a direct way of remembering and maintaining focus on them with sincerity. It also pointed out the negative thinking patterns, and how often, most of us focus on the things that we do not want in our lives. And unconsciously manifest them into being. We ALL do this. But I was now learning, a few simple tools to keep my mind alert, and consciously partaking in the manifestation and co-creation of my dreams.

When I arrived at his place, he was working intently on the sweet potato soup in the kitchen. I loved his simple, nutritious food. After steaming the purple sweet potatoes, he tossed them into the Vitamix with some hempseed oil and we had a smooth puree to eat. He scooped the soup out into bowls, topped with hempseeds, and we took a seat at the table next to the windows.

Nathan had his computer nearby, and we searched on YouTube while sipping his soup for some enigmatic mantra music. We found an eclectic mix of Indian Mantras. In long, high pitch feminine tones. The mix we found was mostly Indian women singing sweetly, in that unique style that they often do. Long, smooth, streaming sounds came off the singer's tongue. Stretching and pulling on both ears of the listener. Swirling tones that seemed like they could softly extend for eternity.

The mantra we found to recite, I had heard and practiced many times. My favorite version is sung from a beautiful composer and singer Deva Premal. It was the Gayatri Mantra and is known to be the greatest of all mantras.

I wrote the mantra on paper and it read;

"Om Bhuur-Bhuvah Svah

Tat-Savitur-Varennyam

Bhargo Devasya Dhiimahi

Dhiyo Yo Nah Pracodayaat"

It was somewhat thrilling and heart resonating to be

repeating the mantra now with Nathan's help and added intention.

The mantra is not easily translated, but generally means;

"We meditate on that most adored Supreme Lord, the creator, whose effulgence (divine light) illumines all realms (physical, mental, and spiritual). May the divine light illumine our intellect." The Gayatri is the Mother of all scriptures. She is the embodiment of all Goddesses. Our very breath is Gayatri and our faith in existence. The Gayatri is a complete prayer for protection, nourishment and finally, liberation.

I placed the writing on paper on the front of Nathan's fridge for him to remember and to keep the energy from our chanting alive and still vibrating in his small place. We chanted and sang in the side room next to the kitchen, while noisy, dirty buses swung around the street corner, just outside the front windows.

We turned up the music and sang and chanted aloud together some more. We laughed and hugged and danced. I felt so close to Nathan that night. Our wishes were echoing in the particles of air all around us. I was feeling so excited now to be on this crazy journey with him and it felt like I could feel our dreams being illuminated by our hearts and minds, our two voices.

Jennifer Lin Phillips

Chapter 10: The Docks of Honolulu

I handed the lady across the counter my credit card. She handed back to me paper and a pen. I needed to fill out the pieces of paperwork with the schedule of when our cars would arrive on the other island. It was hot in the city that day and after all the saving and work that lead up to this moment, I was feeling exhausted and nervous. Although overall, quite eager and relieved to be leaving the bustling and tourist driven city of Waikiki.

Jeremiah, Nathan's neighbor and friend took us from the docks of Honolulu, where both of our cars had been loaded onto fairies, back to Nathan's apartment in the city. We had the cars sent over a few days in advance to make sure that they were there, ready for our use, when we arrived on island.

A few days later, Jeremiah drove us over to the Honolulu airport. We chatted it up a bit, and the conversation on the drive was energizing. I honestly don't think any of us could believe the big jump over and adventure was finally here. Jeremiah had been a witness to mine and Nathan's relationship. He lived in the cottage across from Nathan, and he watched us change and grow over the three months we had spent together in Waikiki. I think he sure was fascinated by

Sovereignty and the Goddess

our courageous next step onward.

Most likely, we were going to be seeing Jeremiah again real soon. He had a love interest on Kauai. They had been dating, hopping back and forth from island to island for almost a year. He assured us he planned on making a trip over and visiting us at the house soon.

We approached the airport with our bags, got out of his suburban jeep, and said our sincere thankyou's and fair well.

The flight over was maybe an hour between the islands. Nathan and I both sat in the airplane seats, holding one another's hands while squirming around for comfort in the tiny airplane seats. It was really happening. We were now flying high over the islands with sweet, yet nerve wrecking anticipation.

But for real? What kinda trouble were we getting ourselves into?

When our plane landed, we took a shuttle to the ferry dock to pick up our vehicles. We had rented a hotel room in Princeville, just down the street from the house we were planning on occupying soon. After picking up our cars, we drove to the hotel to unpack and settle in a bit.

Jennifer Lin Phillips

The hotel was really charming inside and the outside had a nice patio that looked out over birds of paradise. Large, vibrant, red and orange tropical flowers that are shaped like birds. Healthy green grass with fruit trees aligned all the outdoor patios with views of the ocean.

Inside was a jacuzzi tub and a big island themed kitchen that we could cook in. Delicious plumeria flowers scented the small cottage and were placed all over inside. We found them on pillows, the bedspread covering the bed and on most of the countertops. They were carefully picked and placed inside, all in effort to ignite the romance between us and entice our senses to open. It felt like we had taken a heavenly vacation already, where we found ourselves, somewhere lost in paradise.

Nathan grabbed his camera while I was just stepping into the bathtub. He filmed a short video of the bubbles filling up slowly in the tub around me. I was casually sitting naked beneath the sudsy water, grabbing a few bubbles in hand, blowing them in the air with my shallow breath and lips pursed enthusiastically.

We were in the mood to celebrate the very first evening of our voyage. Which had finally arrived!!

Nathan waltzed around the cottage in his work tie and boxers, and it made me giggle at the mood he was in.

Sovereignty and the Goddess

We had decided earlier to grab some food from the grocery store at the start of the evening. I drank wine on the patio in total bliss, while he sang and cooked some dinner for us in the island themed kitchen in his boxers.

The following morning, we said some prayers while burning some of the sweet grass that I had brought with me from Oahu. We asked spirit for protection and then drove out to that house across from the beach he had been telling me about.

We turned down the street to the house, it diverted left and began to wind around black jagged rocks, what looked like a secluded beach, and the vast ocean water to the right. We drove past a spot that had the perfect continual waves for surfing. With a handful of surfers on surfboards waiting for waves to ride out at the wave break.

We then passed by a sandy spot with big rocks and on his side of the van, driver's side, was the infamous island red dirt and a short hillside. The wide ocean opened before us as we turned the corner and you could see all the way down the coastline, sandy beaches, reef and amazing million-dollar homes along the shores of the blue island water.

Jennifer Lin Phillips

The house was just around the corner and we passed it to park down the street a little way. We got out of the car and walked down the very long hedge of blooming red and pink hibiscus flowers on the opposite side of the house.

The property was fenced in with a wide gate that was closed and that one could manually open to let cars in to park. To the right of that gate was a smaller gate for people to enter and we pulled the hook up from the latch and walked onto the property.

The entire property was very outgrown. Nathan had told me that the house was abandoned and had been for nearly five years. That was very clear to me now.

The wild grass and weeds were as tall as we were and although we could see the steps that lead up to the front patio and front door, it was too difficult to make out right away how big the property and surrounding land actually was. Or if the fence went all the way around the property.

Nathan cleared a path before me, and we walked up the very dusty front steps to investigate the window. The house was totally empty and very spacious inside with hardwood floors. We walked down the stairs to one of the two patios on the back of the house. All the doors were locked, and we weren't sure just yet how we would actually get in.

We went down the stairs and back to the outgrown

grass. What a mysterious property, I thought to myself. And what a dream it would be to clean it up, put some hard work into it, give it some love, fix it on up to our liking and call it our very own new home.

After pushing through yet more tall weeds we found the third patio that went up to two separate doors. The one to the left, we assumed, was the small attached one-bedroom cottage and to the right was a double screen door that led to a somewhat sunroom that was screen all around.

We decided to cut through the screen and unlatch the door, and as simple as that we had entered the million-dollar home.

There were two tall, glass sliding doors that lead to the kitchen and main room that we were now casually looking through. When we went to slide them open, they actually opened.

We entered the front room with hardwood floors that lead to an enormous kitchen with stainless steel everything and nice windows over the sink and back wall, that looked out over the backyard. We could see the fence now behind four towering Palm Trees.

The property was big, and we had a ton of work to do if we were going to make it ours. There was a bar through a door beside the kitchen. It had a long tall mirror with cabinets and tall windows looking out to the patio we had just entered from. Everything was

Jennifer Lin Phillips

cherry wood in the bar, and it was straight up gorgeous. The room we were in, led out to the side patio we had been on earlier, which was then connected to an office with another bar made from Koa wood.

I guess we hadn't checked it earlier, but that sliding door to the office opened and we were surprised how much of the home was unlocked yet also unoccupied.

Along that same patio was another long window that was connected to the attached cottage and you could see its kitchen and front room from the wide window. There wasn't any furniture inside anywhere. The house was pretty dusty and there was gecko poop and droppings everywhere inside. All over the windows, floors, cabinets, the bars, everywhere!

The geckos can climb just about anywhere, and they certainly didn't mind leaving their droppings behind, over and over and over, for five years continually.

Across from the kitchen inside was the main front room with tall, wide windows and two more sliding glass doors that led to the front lanai. The lanai covered the entire front of the house. The beautiful roaring ocean was just off the long front patio. Beside that front room was a long narrow hallway with carpet. We walked down the hall where electrical cords hung out from a few holes in the wall. It looked like some of the light fixtures had been taken. There were two rather large sized rooms with elegant showers and private bathrooms. Each room also with its four tall windows that covered the entire front of the room, two of which were sliding glass doors that opened out to the long front deck. Each room was finished in that dark cherry, wood trim, and was incredibly crafted.

There was an open space on the deck in the middle of it, just outside from the second room, where you could put furniture for lounging and it also had the view of the ocean across from the street. The master bedroom was the last down the hall and had the exotic bathroom and tub. There were six windows above the tub. You know the ones that are in many island homes to help bring the breezes in. They are glass island shutters that open and close with a small metal handle. And each window contains about 25 of those small horizontal glass shutters that make up the entire window with screen behind.

They can be a complete nightmare to clean, having to swipe and wipe each one, both top and bottom to get clean. I was looking at them and now fretting the work ahead of me. The gecko droppings in the bathroom and tub were awful, poopy. Black and white gecko poop covered everything, and it was so obvious to me now that those little island creatures loved the bathtub too.

Jennifer Lin Phillips

There was a two-person shower that was designed in all tile with a small bench to sit on and a small shutter to the yard below, just to the corner of the tub. Two sinks for him and one for her along a long bathroom counter and full-frontal mirror. Plenty of closets with fancy Koa wood doors and two tall skylights, one in the bedroom and the other in the bathroom area.

I remember taking a picture of myself in the mirror standing by the tub in that bathroom after months of being at the house. In the picture I was skinnier than I had ever been before in my adult life. I was most likely weighing in at 108 lbs. and I average between 120-130 lbs. I had red and blue roses on my silky shirt that I wore in the picture that day with short cut off jean shorts with holes in them. My red hair was combed out and wet from moments before emerging from the exotic tub. And my strong red hair had been thinning for months.

Everything was dirty, and like I said there was years of accumulated gecko poop, but things looked to be in excellent condition. The floors looked like they didn't have a scratch on them. It was pretty thrilling to be inside finally after months of planning and we were now trying to figure about getting into the cottage and getting a key made for the house. We walked down the back patio which had the screen doors we had first come into the house through. And we made our way down the outdoor stairs to below the house.

Sovereignty and the Goddess

"Oh no, so this is where the squatters were living and hiding out!" Nathan said to me as we walked under the house to the garage. He had mentioned to me that there was talk of homeless people staying on the property before we came to the house. There was garbage, clothes, food, mail, plastic bags, and an awful musky smell emanating from the open garage.

Yikes and yuck I thought.

I ain't going to be touching any of this mess, I was thinking to myself. But of course, I knew, that once we started cleaning things up, we would have to get gloves and attack the creepy, scary garage too. Yuck and Eeewww......I was at least relieved that the squatters appeared to be gone and wouldn't get in our way, causing us any more hassle.

A large, grey, Kane spider scurried across the room of the garage and we both jumped!

We started making lists of what we would need and who to call to get things turned on and in our name. Or in my name we had decided. Nathan didn't even have a real license or ID and couldn't get one since he had a felony for some unpaid ticket or something like that, from when he had lived in Florida. The only ID he did have was the one that had his picture and said that he was an official member of the Sovereign Kingdom of Atooi.

Jennifer Lin Phillips

After staying another night in the cute hotel that we had reserved for ourselves, we had decided that the inside of the house was really in good condition. There was obviously a shit ton to clean, and we were feeling excited and motivated about our next move. We arrived back to the house and had scheduled an inspector to come and look at some of the rotting on the outside of the house in certain areas. We met him early that morning and discovered some interesting facts about some of the insects and even those large Kane spiders that were well established on the North Shore.

We also decided that the best thing to do would be to get the water turned on, the gas for the kitchen and heat, and set up electricity. We hopped back in our cars and headed to the west side of the island by the airport to take on our next step.

When we pulled into Kauai Island Electric, I was nervous. Everything was going on in my name and although Nathan had been working on some official paperwork that helped to prove he was the new owner of the house, it was feeling like a pretty big risk for me. But in reflection, every step so far that had brought us to that moment had seemed right. And I felt like we were in alignment with spirit. The King had our backs about occupying the house and he was happy to have Nathan on island to work with him more closely on the Kingdom's currency and on some other things for the Kingdom, including building a website.

The lady at the counter was friendly. I gave her my ID and within 20 minutes everything as for power was turned on. We went to the gas company next, and then the water company. It was all actually pretty simple, although extremely daring of us. We were staying calm and step by step checking things off of our lists. It was looking like we were going to be getting things up and running rather smoothly and then we would have to face our next big challenges. We set up Internet and phone and Nathan was happy to put that in his name, since we didn't need an ID for those services.

With still $6500 left on my credit card after paying to send both of our cars over. We still had some money to spend, and we were obviously going to need to budget tightly with the amount of work that needed to be done, the people to hire for help, and then of course some furnishings. We only had a few things as for furniture and bedding.

I also had a Macy's card and Target Card we could utilize to get some sheets, towels, bedspread, clothes and kitchen things. We had my little vintage Mercedes with sunroof that I had bought from Richard, the owner at the Ala Wai Mansion condo, I had been

Jennifer Lin Phillips

renting the room from previously. And Nathan had his van.

I had packed up and brought a lavender colored and velvet purple chair that a lady gave me, after purchasing a few items from her art gallery, that was closing over on Oahu. It was a really pretty piece and then there was the painting from Violette. She was an elder I had lived with and cared for on Oahu back in my early 20's.

Violette was an incredible painter. And often during our time together we would sit, talk story, and paint. I would, brush in hand, abstractly paint scenes from my memory while listening to her for some of her exceptional tips and advice. Her family, the Hu family, was well known for their artwork and many of her family's paintings were in the Honolulu Museum of Art. She even shared with me one day some old articles to show me some of her family's history.

In reminiscing, Violette and I were such a fun, sweet team together.

Sure, it would take us three hours to walk around the block in the hot island sun. With her using her cane for balance in one arm, and linked in with my arm for support, in her other arm.

Often, we would go out on ventures to feed the birds or sit on a bench by the ocean to watch waves crash. I loved buying her pastries and sweets from the markets to bring to her and try to sweeten her up even more. Often, we would paint there in her kitchen with cockroaches running along the walls at times and she would tell me about the dark and the light, and the importance of the composition of the painting.

She was 97 when she finally passed away and I still feel her spirit watching over me sometimes.

She did reach out to me one day and whispered to me, while I was moving around Josh's apartment, off of Punahou and Beretania Street in Honolulu. I was most likely on my way to the beach on scooter that day. I was standing next to one of Josh's paintings of a man splashing in water by the front door, and I heard her call to me...." Mae-Mae" she said. Which means granddaughter in Chinese. I perked up with ears out to listen and felt her there close to me that day.

"Po-Po", I mumbled aloud back to her. Po-Po was her nickname, the name that I called her, and it means grandmother in Chinese. Back when I cared for her and she was alive, she told me to call her by that name.

It melted me really, my heart. And I loved her so much over our 9 months together. Funny how she used to give me advice and try to mother me. Her daughter, Henry kept telling me. "You gave her permission to do that, by allowing her to call you granddaughter and you calling her grandmother."

But I just couldn't break up that bond we had

developed. The love that truly existed between us. I remember soaking her feet at night. Washing them and giving her foot rubs and scrubs. And then smothering her old, wore out feet in lotion. I loved her that deeply.

I can still see her incredible heart glowing brightly through her eyes and smile. You know those ones that are never forgotten and always missed. She really was that special to me.

And I knew that she had visited me that day. She was there to let me know she was near and quietly watching over me. And probably always would be. For a grandmother never forgets her granddaughter.

The painting I now had of hers, that Josh had held onto for me for years, was titled "Thorny Hills" and was beautiful. A scene of a tree with rocks and a path that looked thorny and a little rugged. I knew it was perfect harmony and that the title was consistent with the thorny road that was to come. I was thankful to have the painting with me and was really hoping to have her Grandmother protection around me still too at the time when I needed her most.

After buying some cleaning supplies and renting a carpet cleaner, we headed back to the house to get started on our big turnover. We began in the kitchen so that we could start cooking right away. I started on the tub in the master bath and was anticipating soaking if not that night, definitely the following night. I scrubbed the shower also relentlessly and wiped down some of the tall windows in the master bedroom as well, to clear for the view of the ocean.

After putting in a few hours, the night was closing in on us. We had plans to stay over that night in the house and sleep on a little mat that Nathan had with him. We brought some blankets and we both were able to use the amazing shower before lying on the thin foam mat on the carpet.

It was rather sophisticated to have my toiletries on my side with my very own sink and Nathan with his, mostly hemp products on his side. After sliding into the covers, each of us, music and a DJ could be heard coming from the house across the street and down the corner a little way. The music was coming from a wedding reception on a property that had small cottages for gatherings and parties.

It felt so ironic. Like the music was playing just for us. And we laughed towards one another and hugged a little. It was a special welcoming for just us two! And the happy music echoed down the silent street of million-dollar homes, charming us.

Jennifer Lin Phillips

Chapter 11: Tiki and Alii

We awoke the following morning and the moisture from the North Shore air was bringing volume and buoyancy to my full, wavy hair. We were going to need some help with the enormous yard and with cleaning up the dead leaves on the towering, giant palm trees. Everything was so over grown, and each plant had practically grown into one another, like a green grassy web covering the entire yard, at 5 feet tall or so.

We decided to look on craigslist to find someone willing to help us clear everything up in the yard and we were going to need some powerful tools to accomplish such a daunting task. We also found someone who could power wash the house at a reasonable cost and that would need to happen once the yard was finished. There was a weird grey color covering the entire house and it smelt pretty musky. Especially on the screens of the house, and on all of the windows and doors.

The yard took a few days, three or four to clear everything and then we began putting the debris into piles to take to the dump. Some of the piles and large leaves we just hucked over the back fence and onto the city land. The land around the fence was kept up by the city, mowed continually around the property and the small pond adjacent to the house. The land was green and gorgeous and lead up the valley to a few neighbors along the tiny canal. I pictured us exploring together up the small hill in search for fresh coconuts on trees.

With the grass and weeds all cut down now, we had put everything into piles all over the yard. There were many of them and it was going to take us some time to clear everything. I was feeling itchy on my skin from the dead leaves and grass. Especially after cleaning an area by the garage of many smaller dead leaves and foliage. I was starting to break out a little in red patches a bit on my legs. But I was very sensitive to certain things with my fair skin and knew everything would clear up after the work was done. I was also going to do my best not to touch anything with my bare skin, only with my gloves on.

Now that we were doing the work needed to be done to take ownership of the house, we decided it would be a good idea to get a few dogs that could help protect the property and warn us of any trespassers.

We took a trip back to the west side over to the animal shelter. The lady inside was incredibly friendly and told us about two brother doggies that she thought we would resonate with. They were a mixed breed of Pointer and something else, we couldn't determine the other breed. They just happened to be two peas in a

Jennifer Lin Phillips

pod who moved in tandem together, but with completely different personalities from one another. One of the dogs was very nervous, proud and strong. The other was friendly, happy and welcoming. They were very close in age and similar in size. But the nervous one had a chest and posture that stuck straight up and out, just like a champion.

Nathan and I agreed that we wanted to take the dogs home with us. We handled the necessary paperwork for adoption and paid the fees. We then loaded the dogs into his van and then headed home with the two brother dogs. It appeared we were starting our little family together, and our time so far on island was proving to be both thrilling and flowing quite well overall.

When we got back to the house, we let the dogs run free in the yard. We fed them food and treats that we had purchased at the store on the way home. The dogs seemed to befriend us right away, but the strong and nervous one was still protective of his space, wanting to make sure that we were indeed trustworthy humans.

Nathan and I went back to cleaning yet keeping an awareness on the dogs in the yard. We discovered that the stronger dog was also a great protector of the property. He began right away letting us know if anyone was walking by or if there was an unusual sound resonating that he had picked up on.

Nathan came into the bathroom where I was still scrubbing gecko poop from tiles. "I know what we should call the dogs Jennifer! Let's call the happy one Tiki and the mighty one Alii". He said to me. The word Alii in Hawaiian translates to royalty or the hereditary line of rulers of the Hawaiian Islands. I thought the names were clever and very fitting for the two brother's and I agreed upon them enthusiastically.

Nathan went back down to the yard where the dogs were, and I could hear him singing songs about the dogs of royalty while he was dragging large leaves across the yard and cleaning up the property. He sang about the two brothers, who were here to protect the sacred temple. I laughed to myself at his wittiness and was feeling relieved to have the dogs with us now. I was also thankful to be providing them with a new and safe sanctuary. Nathan spooned hempseed oil and olive oil on their food to give them extra healthy fat for strength and shinier coats.

The next day, upon waking, we noticed the dogs were gone. We both panicked a little and went searching for them down the street towards the park and campground. We walked all the way down to the campground and still no Alii or Tiki. We took the beach back to the house instead of the street and walked along the row of elegant homes. When we got to the beach that was very close to where our house was, we

Jennifer Lin Phillips

saw Tiki running in the sand. He ran up to us and jumped at us, hyper and energetic. He had obviously gotten a large dose of the negative ions off the water and was ready for some play!

Nathan and I followed Tiki halfway down the beach, but we didn't see where Alii had run off to. Tiki began splashing in the water and swimming a little as if to tell us of his brother's doings. And then we noticed him. His brother, the mighty Alii, was swimming frantically far out past the reef and break.

He had managed to swim all the way out to the waves beyond the reef and was tirelessly pacing, swimming back and forth. He had so much energy and anxiety, and you could see it coming off of him as he swam and splashed around, still pacing in the water.

We watched in amazement and laughed out loud to one another. That dog really was the chief! And we felt lucky to have him with us, both dogs. But we were going to have to figure out how to keep them contained and not bothering any of our new and wealthy neighbors. We took Tiki back to the house and patiently waited for Alii to return wet and sandy about an hour later.

Chapter 12: In Malie's Arms

I've been allowing myself to process the range of emotions I have been feeling lately. The weather has changed dramatically, and being mostly alone, living alone for another year, is getting harder. I'm pretty much single and have been since Nathan and I broke up five years ago. I have done some dating since then, but circumstance and choice has kept me mostly alone. I have continued to adventure, to travel and experience. I have had some pretty wonderful times here in Oregon. Getting quality time in with my sister's and my six nieces and nephews has been my main priority.

I always knew that the death of my Mother had fueled many of my travels and so did my desire to escape the alcoholism on my father's side of the family. I decided, at 21 year's old, I would leave on my first big trip down to Sacramento to visit cousins, and Auntie's on my Mother's side. I left on July 4th, Independence Day, and drove with the sunroof down and the wind in my hair that summer's day. I said goodbye to my grandparents and father, and a few other relatives. I made sure to kiss them goodbye at the pool party they were throwing for the Holiday. My incredibly beautiful Grandmother, wearing a classy and vintage purple suit, looked radiant at age 74. Her and my Grandfather both

Jennifer Lin Phillips

sipping their traditional gin martini's that day. I knew I needed to make peace with them. But the pain from my childhood, the fighting and abuse between my parents, had been clouding me much of my life. I had to understand why I had experienced so much suffering. And my journey began with tracing the roots of my mother's family. I began my journey south, driving down to Sacramento and stayed with my cousins.

Tamie, my favorite cousin on my mom's side, had babysat me and my sisters and taken care of us a few times during her visit's to Oregon when I was a girl. It was exciting that I was going to be staying the summer with her and three of my second cousins.

I remember Tamie saying to me one day in her home my first week in Sacramento...."After you get past the blues, you enter the mean reds" and we talked a lot about the confusion in our family. She had pictures of Aubrey Hepburn on her brick artsy wall and some of her own artwork too. She was an artist and wrote for the Sacramento paper. She was known for her one-line drawings. Which were intricate pictures that were done in marker without picking the pen up from the paper. She gave me one of her drawings that summer. It was of a nude girl with red hair and cowboy boots on. A red leaf covering her yoni. It was very fun, sensual and sexy, and also quite suiting for me.

I spent the summer there, but my health was struggling. I was not eating well, nor did I really understand nutrition or how to feed myself. Even at the age of twenty-one, I was desperate to find balance, wisdom, truth. But I found myself in a house that partied most weekends and drank alcohol often. It seemed like I was more confused than ever but was still thankful for the time I got to spend with my cousins and family.

Admittedly so, this was not the best way to go about leaving. But I just left one day. I wrote Tamie a note that I wasn't feeling well and that I was sorry but needed to leave. I packed up my car while Tamie and everyone was at school or at work and I just left. I was heading back up to Southern Oregon to Ashland where I had some girlfriends and had gone to school a few years back. Ironically, it was the town both of my parents met in, and where I spent a year in college.

I had a bright green, granny smith, apple in my car and some spring water when I arrived in town. I headed out to a spot, on the outskirts out of town that was very isolated. It was a spot along the river, near Applegate Lake, where I had camped once before with my other cousin Keely and some friends, back when I was in college. I fasted that night and slept outside by the rocks and water. The weather was getting cooler, but it was where I wanted to be that night. I felt safe sleeping alone under the stars, I knew Spirit would

Jennifer Lin Phillips

keep me safe and protect my lost and wounded soul.

The following day I went back into town to wash up and explore. I slept on Faith street the following night. And the next day met up with my friend Kirsten from Alaska. From there, I was taken in by three beautiful girlfriends. We shared from our hearts, we slept together sharing our dreams, and we would gather often to dance and cook healthy meals together.

So much of my travelling has been in pursuit of coming to grips with just what happened to me as a child and girl. How could my own Mother leave me? And what had my sisters, me and my father put her through? Why did my dad choose to continue his alcohol abuse and why did he marry someone who possessed the same alcoholic tendencies? Was my Mother's death my fault? Like my own Dad yelled at me one day when we were fighting, and he kicked me out of the house? Where was there a safe place, beautiful and new that didn't have the stench of empty bottles?

I found so much ease in newness. I could create with my will power something new and desirable every single day. It was miraculous to me that the intelligence of the universe was speaking to me in color and was calling me home. I soon realized that the stars and moon were my Mother and the sunshine my Father. The "Son" of the Father. I felt like I had stepped into grace and harmony and was excited and confident that spirit would guide me and keep me safe.

I travelled like that for years. I travelled all over the islands. I began on Maui at 23, with $350 dollars to my name and a few friends I had met at a full moon party. Within a few weeks I was living in remote Hana. I was perched up in the tropical rainforest out past 52 waterfalls and had my camp set up with my very own pool and small waterfall. I would play my cedarwood flute at night under stars and glowing hillsides, that I had purchased at the Portland Saturday Market. The flute smelled like fresh cedar, it was in note C, and had a small carved bear tied in with a leather string up towards the mouth piece. In Native American Folklore, the Bear represents the nurturing energy of the Mother.

I was camped out and staying on Uncle Eddie's land in Nahiku. Everybody called him "Uncle Eddie" and he called everyone "Sweetie". He was Polynesian, and in his 80's. And even in his 80's he took me hiking with his machete looking for wild pigs. I camped on his land for a few months. And in trade we would cook together, and I would scrub his back with a washcloth while he was in the shower. It was so cute some days. I would be cooking in the kitchen, and he would yell out to me, "Okay Sweetie, I am ready!" And I would go in and wash his back.

I remember when I got my first centipede bite in the

Jennifer Lin Phillips

middle of the night while staying at a friend's house in Hana, I called him. He came the next day to check on me. I told him I chopped that centipede right in half with a big kitchen knife. I was so pissed that critter had bit me like that while I was sleeping soundly. I figured I had taken on the powers of that centipede too. Now that his poison was in my body and he had marked me with his tiny fangs. Well that part of the experience seemed pretty cool to me at least. And I had also gotten my quick revenge on the creepy creature.

I knew this last trip to Kauai this past July of 2017 that I was still processing the sadness, confusion and grief from losing my Mother to Breast Cancer. I awoke one morning sobbing, and in the dream, I had been juicing and in the company of some healthy island folk. It was surprising to me to feel the grief in my dream coming up into my lungs, I was surrounded by some people in my dream and I was trying to push my feelings down, trying to contain my deep-seated grief out of embarrassment. When I allowed myself to feel it, it poured out from me in waves and woke me up with dripping wet tears, streaming down both of my cheeks. I spent that morning crying and drowning my face with waves from the ocean. It took me a good 40 minutes, jogging, crying, breathing, swimming, before I emerged in balance. It was surprising to me, that nearly 24 years after my Mother died, this deep grief was now surfacing.

Last night, I cried too. It's now early November and like I said the rains have been falling here in Oregon. It's been cold and grey, and I wake up alone almost every day to make my green tea on the stove.

She was holding me in my dream last night. Maile, one of my Hawaiian female clients that I had met just a few months ago on Kauai. I knew it was her with her contagious smile and laugh. She was smiling so big, holding me last night and although I was sobbing in her arms, I was smiling with her. The fat on her body was like jello and I fell into her. I was so happy to have landed in her loving arms and the fat on her body was like a pillow comforting me. It felt like our bodies had merged into one. I whispered to her that I was sorry for crying, but I was still sad about my Mom's death. She just kept smiling and holding me, and the stars from the sky that night and morning were beaming from Maile's soul.

Ironically, after writing this chapter in my book, I got up for a glass of water and checked my phone for messages. While writing I heard a few beeps go off from my phone, alerting me of messages coming in. One was from a new client of mine here in Oregon. I checked what he had written to me and it read, "So I had a first last night...."

Jennifer Lin Phillips

I wasn't sure how to respond, or if he was going to tell me something that I really was interested in knowing. I do receive a lot of attention from my clients at times, and a lot of it gets draining. A girl can only handle so much testosterone in this business I tell many of them. I responded casually..."Oh?"

He replied right away, "Yes, I had a dream of you."

Now I was definitely not wanting to respond, but he had proven to be a good and respectful client. I was even teaching him Kundalini Yoga and we had opened up to one another about some things in each of our lives that were hurtles for us that we were still overcoming. I asked him how the dream unfolded somewhat hesitantly, and he responded in kind, "Yes, you were holding me in my dream, and it felt like we were inside of each other. You were just smiling there, with your arms around me, and it felt very healing."

Wow, what synchronicity. I was pleased by his dream and that he was willing to share it with me. It was fascinating to me to receive this kind of confirmation of love being exchanged. I mean moments before I had just finished writing my dream of being held by Maile. The dreams were so incredibly similar that I had to trust that there was a spiritual shift and some kind of awakening happening.

I felt happy that I was able to be there for this man and new friend of mine. I was thankful that my spirit was somehow able to transfer the loving energy I had received to him in the exact way that I had received a soulful embrace only a few nights before. He too had needed the same love I had just received. I smiled inside at the work being done by spirit and felt a deeper trust in the web and mystery of human connectedness.

Jennifer Lin Phillips

Chapter 13: Moori Comes to the Island

The rains on the island had been coming down for weeks. Nathan and I had officially been in the house for about three weeks when his best friend Moori decided to make a trip out to see us. He was visiting with one of his friends from the LA area and came to assist us with some official paperwork for the house.

Our first visitors had arrived, and we had accomplished so much at the house already. We set them up in the rooms down the hall from the master suite, on mats on the floor. We were still working on getting furniture but had found some amazing pieces at the Bamboo Works in town.

We were also needing to get the power-washing done on the house and work on those huge piles of debris in the yard. But it was time to celebrate a little with our friends and complete some necessary paperwork for the house.

Nathan and Moori worked relentlessly on the paperwork, while I made sure to hit the local farmer's markets for fresh food to have around. I made a pesto sauce with local macadamia nuts and local basil. I cooked and made sandwiches. Everyone was well fed, nourished and hydrated with fresh island fruits like lilikoi, papaya, soursop, and guava.

Nathan and I were still in honeymoon mode and the feeling between us was romantic and sweet. I remember lying on the floor in his office listening to the men talk paperwork and laws, when Nathan jumped up and tromped on down to the yard. He came back in with a plumeria flower for me and placed it behind my ear with a smile. The men looked at me curiously, as I blushed fiercely with shyness entwining with joy. They complimented me on my exotic island look. How sweet it felt to be a tropical island girl.

A few days into having our guests, some men with paperwork from Bank of America showed up outside of the closed gate. The dogs barked loudly to warn us of the visitors and Nathan rushed out to see who they were. They said they were from the bank and ready to start working on the home to clean it up. They apparently had a lean on the house.

Nathan grabbed the paperwork from them and ripped it in half right in front of them. He showed them his paperwork as the new owner of the property and firmly asked them to leave.

I was scared and shocked by what was happening in front of me. Nathan came inside pumped up and went over to Moori to tell him what had just happened. Moori said with what we had there was nothing they could do. They were one of three banks that had leans

Jennifer Lin Phillips

on the home and it would be difficult for any of them to take ownership of the house with us there now. Nathan and Moori then retired to the office to continue their research and to figure the necessary steps to keep the banks off the property and off our backs. It was hard for me to follow them in that process mentally and for the most part I just listened and allowed them to do their work.

At night and at the end of the day, we would sit for dinner and discuss the work they had done that day. Moori was also a member of the Kingdom, and Nathan asked him to marry us on the beach over dinner one night. As he grinned at me. We laughed about it and how perhaps it was a bit too early, but the idea sounded romantic.

Often, we would put on YouTube videos of Alex Jones or Kevin Trudeau and listen to them talk about the US Government and how the rich were breaking laws and plotting against most of the middle and lower-class citizens. I was taking a lot in that I had never heard before. Yes, some of it sounded hysterical, but I just listened and tried to process everything I was learning.

After about one week of the men being on island, I broke out bad in a rash on my face. I had bumps all around my eyes and even after a few days it wasn't clearing up. I had been wiping the outside of the house trying to clean it and had come across some musky smells. We discovered that day that the house was covered in island mold, and then noticed it on all the screens and many of the trees in the yard. It appeared we were up against more than we had envisioned, and I went to the doctor to see what some possible solutions could be.

The doctor was hesitant, but he gave me a cream for my face and I later found out that the cream had steroids in it. I used it around my eyes and the bumps seemed to clear up instantly. Only to reappear again the following day, just like the mold was now every few days in the shower. My health was starting to suffer, and I felt helpless to my surroundings.

I phoned a friend that I had met through Richard at the Ala Wai Mansion, who had just recently told me of how she was healing her body through the Gerson Therapy Program. We had discussed her and her partner coming to the house and turning the house into a retreat center for Gerson Therapy Patients. The therapy was known to heal many illness', including Cancer, Kidney Stones, Diabetes, and even Melanoma. I got the instructions for the treatment and began right away. The therapy was intense, requiring lots of green and carrot juice, and 3-5 coffee enemas per day.

After a week of being on the therapy my skin was clearing, although I still needed the cream for my eyes. I began to glow from all the juice and enemas but

Jennifer Lin Phillips

noticed my hair and body were both growing thinner. I continued with the juicing and cleansing while Moori and his friend were on island. I wasn't going to give up on my health, so I stayed persistent and consistent with the regimen daily.

The men were enjoying the warmth of the island and had even made a few trips out to visit the King to talk about future plans for the Kingdom. We all went out to visit the King one day together at his house, on the west side of the island. I got to meet his younger daughter that day, and her and I buddied up almost immediately. It was exhilarating really, all of us sitting together, such different people and backgrounds. There was quite a blend of cultures in the garage that day and we were all merging, sharing ideas and mingling together.

The Hawaiian Flag waved in the wind just outside the garage door. I met the Queen that day and I thought her presence was strong. I told her that I make jewelry with the Niihau shells and that I had the perfect set for her. They were elegant earrings with peach pearls strung on the ends of pink spiraling shells. I thought the Queen was very beautiful with flattering Polynesian features. I had Nathan give her those earing's a few weeks later and she said she wore them and liked them.

Sovereignty and the Goddess

The King and Queen's daughter and I played and laughed a lot while everyone talked politics that day. She was around 8 years old I believe. We all walked around back to the backyard area and the King showed us his back room, in a separate building. It had a lot of unique art pieces on the walls, including an intriguing piece of the Goddess Pele. The Queen swept up incense dust into her hands from the table to clean it, and the King began explaining to us some of the stone tools that he had in the room that day.

One was an old piece used for defense and also punishment that the older tribes used in battle against enemies. He laughed out loud as he swung it, "This one is used for the head of your enemy." He said. That made me a little nervous, but I could tell he was trying to mess with us a little.

I glanced at the picture of Pele again and it was really pulling me in. She had red hair in the painting, and it was flowing down from both sides of her face. It represented the volcano and the two streams of lava poured out and down from the strands of her long red hair. Pele is the Goddess of fire, lightening, dance, wind, volcanoes, and violence. Her poetic name is Ka wahine 'ai honua, or the woman who devours the land. She is known to be both a creator and a destroyer. I later made a shrine to her at the house. And had pictures of her in frames. I placed shells, flowers and offerings to her daily, and I believed that when the

Jennifer Lin Phillips

wind blew a certain way, that she could hear me.

One of the artists of the artwork that the King displayed paintings of in his art room, happened to be there with us that day. He had made most of his artwork out of the house he had lived in. There was a hurricane on the island back in 1992, Hurricane Iniki, and his house was demolished. I think he was from Australia, and his artwork was really impressive. He included in the painting's the energy from the Aborigine culture and he was merging that with Hawaiian and Polynesian culture also. When I admired his paintings, I could hear the beat of the drum coming from them, pulsing through painted canvas.

A week later Nathan picked up a handful of paintings from him, and we had artwork for the whole house. It was perfect, and even connected us closer to what felt like our purpose was there on the island, being in support of the Kingdom.

Everyone returned to the garage, and me and the King's daughter walked out to the grass by the plumeria tree to continue playing. The tree had the beautiful white and yellow flowers and there was a small hill beside it. We exchanged flower's and giggles and she asked me to roll with her down the hill sideways on the grass.

I had been missing my nieces and nephews for months.

As we rolled sideways down the hill, white and yellow plumeria scents trickled into our noses. We poked at one another and giggled. Although I enjoyed the company of the other's there, the hostility in the garage was so thick. This is where I really resonate, I thought that day.

In play, in the garden, with flower's releasing intoxicating smells and vibrant colors. Enjoying things of beauty, like a child. Like an innocent child of the dear and loving Goddess.

In the mornings, Moori would take a short walk down the street we lived on down to the campground. He had made a few friends with some locals who chose to live on the grounds in tents. Moori had such a nice humanitarian spirit, and I could tell he had a compassion for pretty much everyone.

He was sort of a Rasta, with long dreadlocks and he wore colorful clothing. I remember sharing food with him one day, and he talked about how he still was connected to his ex and felt obliged to care for her. He felt it was his duty to continue to love and support her. He hinted to Nathan one day the importance of giving back to the ones who give their all to you. With Nathan's overconfidence in himself sometimes, I think it came off like a lack of understanding in the web and connectedness of all things. He had a very

Jennifer Lin Phillips

Narcissistic side that was deeply eccentric and that many people intuitively picked up on and mistrusted.

I was trying to refrain from judging too much at that time, I was more just taking it all in. My sense perceptions were on high alert however at the amount of newness I was experiencing, and I was still very much in survival mode.

It was time for Moori and his friend to leave. They packed up the car for the airport. Moori was hoping to return to the island one day with his ex and his present girlfriend possibly. With his aging body, he needed the warmth. And being a member of the Kingdom, Hawaii was a perfect place for him to retire. Nathan and Moori talked about securing a house for him and his family too. And also, a bigger house for the King and Queen. Once things with our house were well underway, that would be their next big project. We took them to the airport and they loaded the plane back for LA.

It seemed like there was a lot that transpired in those weeks with them on island. And it also felt like the honeymoon faze between Nathan and I had ended. We were settling in more with a routine, and I was still grasping for my radiant health. Nathan was happy to help keep me motivated with smoothie's and we ordered some fresh island fish for dinner's also. The Gerson Therapy was a lot to keep up on, but I was committed. Nathan even tried a few enemas to help flush his system as well and we found them both to be soothing and energizing to the body and mind. I was thankful for all of the friends we had met, and it seemed like the right support was showing up somehow at the appropriate times.

Jennifer Lin Phillips

Chapter 14: The Christian Family from the Farm

I was starting to panic a little about my reaction to the mold on the property. We needed to get the mold off the screens and the outside of the house immediately. We hired another worker we found on Craigslist who was handy with a power washer and we began the process. Once the work began, I started breaking out in bumps again on my face bad.

I did some research and discovered that the mold had spores that were released into the air whenever the mold was attacked or cleaned up. The mold spores were especially harmful to the lungs and I began noticing I was getting green phlegm in my throat and a seeping from my eyes. The power-washing took three full days and did a wreck in the master bathroom which was lined with the shutters and screens. I had to wipe up everything again, tons of dirty water had seeped in and I was afraid the spores would get into my face creams and lotions.

What a mess it all was becoming, but after much hard work and continual awareness on attacking that nasty mold, the spores in the air seemed to be settling and clearing up. I continued with my therapy and was somehow managing even with all the new spores in the air. I did my best to get out on hikes. And to rest at the beach across the street.

Or take a day trip to some beautiful beaches up North Shore. It was difficult to balance everything but what an adventure we were on. The house was incredible too and we felt like we were settling in to the neighborhood.

We had spoken to a few of the neighbors. A young man who worked on the yard across the street. He popped over to see the work we had accomplished and gave us some history on the neighborhood, the people, and the story of the house. He liked us, and we liked him too. It was feeling like we were fitting in just fine, and nobody really questioned us too much.

They believed that we had gotten a deal on the home because of the condition and necessary work to be done to a house that had been abandoned for five years. Our neighbors were thankful that the property was getting worked on and cleaned up. It was bringing the value back to the neighborhood and the horrifying story of the suicide and squatters was changing.

"Hi there! I walk along this beach to the campground to shower often. My family and I live on a farm down the road a little way. Can I talk to you about my situation and see if my family and I could come shower

Jennifer Lin Phillips

here at your house instead?" A lovely blonde woman said to me over the gate outside while I was picking debris up.

"Hi, yes, please come around to the side gate and I will let you in, and you can follow me to the guest room." I said back to her. There were five showers inside and even one outdoor shower below by the garage. I would have felt awfully silly denying her request that day.

"I've noticed things are looking really nice here now, and our farm has been flooded out for months." She explained to me as we walked down the hall to the shower.

"We are really struggling, my husband and I, and our three children. Can I talk with you about us helping you and you helping us? I bet you could use some more hands here on the property, but I congratulate you on the work you've done already." She reinforced her desperate needs.

I have always been a believer that when you help others in need, your chances of success and protection are greater. That has always proven to be a healthy and divine way to create contacts and relationships. And with all the work we still had ahead of us, five extra sets of hands could really speed up our progress in the yard. It sounded like it was just what we needed. The woman was very kind. She explained her situation at their farm.

The current rains had caused major flooding and had ruined a lot of their crops and the buildings that were there were now deteriorating. They were having to heat up all water from a stove for grooming and they were all growing very tired. She showered up and we talked about having the rest of her family come to use our facilities also.

The following day, two of the three children and husband came along with her. We discussed the work we wanted done. The piles in the yard we needed taken to the dump and help with getting some gardens going and a small garden fence made from bamboo. They all showered in the one-bedroom cottage this time, since there was so many of them. The son was seventeen, the daughter, twelve. They were an adorable Christian Family that lived on a farm with sheep, chickens, roses and honey-bee's.

With further discussion, and after they cleaned up, they asked us if we would consider them staying in the cottage for trade. They were desperate for a dry place to sleep. We talked it over briefly, and of course agreed to their request. We thought their presence on the property would bring joy, much needed help, and more of a feeling of togetherness and family around us. We met the middle child and daughter a few days later, she was fifteen and came over after a nice surf. The family, all five of them, crammed in the one-

Jennifer Lin Phillips

bedroom cottage that night, with warm blankets and warm spirits. We both, Nathan and I, felt really good about our arrangement with them and were happy to be providing them a healthy, dry place to stay.

The agreement was trade. No money would be exchanged. Only service. We helped them, they helped us.

I immediately took to Angela, the twelve-year old daughter. She was so much fun and talked to me a lot. Kai, the middle child was reasonably shy, and really loved her pop music, and getting ready in the bathroom to look pretty. Angela was more of a tom boy and could be found down below in the garage singing, playing with something or helping with the garden.

The mother sold homemade banana bread at corner stops along the roads in her free time for money and her husband did some work on cars when they weren't working on their farm. The teenage son built us the bamboo fence right away for our gardens, after Nathan and I dug up two giant squares of dirt in the yard. We weren't asking for a lot of their help immediately. They were tired and exhausted, and we wanted to give them enough time to rest before beginning work again.

It was about a month before Christmas when they

moved in, and we told them to stay through the holidays and we would discuss the arrangement after the New Year. I began working again doing bodywork and healing therapies. Nathan found me a massage table online from a local practitioner and I was able to support us with more finances. He continued his work on getting us a loan for the house and also kept up on miscellaneous stuff around the house, including the huge yard surrounding the property, and power washing the roof.

I began getting a few repeat clients and it was nice to have steady money coming in and new friendly faces. It seemed like we were finding a good balance as the holiday was approaching, but my health wasn't maintaining like I wanted it to.

I was still really struggling with breakouts from the mold and felt like my immune system was growing weaker. Even with the cleansing. And now with me pushing harder by doing bodywork and seeing clients, I felt like I couldn't quite keep up on everything.

Tensions began to grow with the family, being that everyone was crammed in a one-bedroom cottage, and we could hear them fighting some days. Nathan and I began fighting too. I was so incredibly stressed from being bombarded with these new symptoms and Nathan felt helpless as to how to help me.

My Grandfather had passed away back in Oregon, and

Jennifer Lin Phillips

we decided that I would go home around the New Year to see if I could heal better over there, back in Oregon. Far away from the scary island mold which was causing the horrible outbreaks, and who knows what it was doing to my blood, my lungs, and lymphatic system.

I phoned my Dad to ask if I could stay an extra week before the funeral to heal. He was worried about me, and of course wondering where my travels had led me to now. It was hard for him to keep up with me, and with all of the new things I had been learning, our minds and thoughts were on two completely different waves.

I pre-ordered some anti-fungal prescription, Nystatin, from a local doctor after telling her about my exposure and current condition of my health. They were spendy, but I was willing to try anything to get my body back on track. I spent Xmas with Nathan and we had our little Xmas tree with ornaments that Nathan had gotten for Me, Tiki, Alii and him. It was pretty cute. Our little family on the island together for our first island Xmas. We exchanged a few gifts, and Nathan even played some guitar next door in the cottage with the Christian family and sang a few Xmas holiday songs in good spirit.

A few days before my flight departed Nathan and I got into a good argument. He pushed me hard into the closet, threatening me with his words, and holding me up against the cherry wood door. This wasn't the first time he had threatened me like that or put his hands on me.

Our second month at the house he grabbed my throat real good and left a few scratch marks on my skin.

My opportunities as for getting out were few, since I had sold my car for the extra money, and we were almost always working on something at the house and were now relying only on his van now. Plus, with how the mold was affecting me. I wanted to get out as much as possible, and it was nice to have his company while out sometimes.

I had wanted to go with him on a trip across town and he wanted to go alone that day.

When he told me again that I couldn't go with him, I hucked a rubber ball across the room, not at him, but in annoyance and anger. He came at me pretty hard that day after that gesture. I was scared of him after that. But I had previously never trusted his outbursts anyways. He told me that he had pre-frontal cortex damage. Which is damage to the front part of the brain.

A really bad accident when he was 16 left him with the damage to his brain. I think he was even in a car chase

Jennifer Lin Phillips

with cops, driving like 90 miles an hour or something crazy like that, in the brand-new Camaro his father had bought him. He spun out of control, crashed pretty bad and ended up in the hospital nearly dead. His legs had screws in them, really deep scars and he complained of pains and aches in both of his legs quite a bit. The damage to his brain, he said, caused severe nerve damage and his ability to refrain from outbursts and reacting poorly to stress was severely weakened.

The nerve damage was so bad he would ask me not to move or touch him if we were cuddling in bed. It was such a weird feeling for me. I was afraid to stroke his chest or caress his arm. I felt like a corpse sometimes and my fear would creep up inside of me that he would jerk quickly if I moved or he would grab my hand and ask me not to move, with annoyance.

Anyone who knows me, knows that I am a total sweetheart most of the time. I am compassionate, generous, hard-working, and would do just about anything for someone I Love.

However, I am also known for being sharp at times, and expressive of my feelings. Even if they have tinges of anger attached to them or hostility. If I feel it is justified or needed to get my point across or my feelings heard.

I usually only act this way after I feel like my feelings have not been heard, or if I feel like I am being ridiculed or taken advantage of. I understand now, that this anger that comes up inside of me sometimes is also a warning to me. That perhaps this person I am dealing with isn't sincere. Perhaps they aren't really considering my feelings, they aren't being thoughtful or keeping things equal as for compromising.

You could say that I was ready for my trip back to Oregon to see most of my family. Including relatives coming from out of town from Chicago and LA. My favorite auntie from Malibu would be attending the funeral also, and she was always someone I felt inspired by and whom seemed to understand my journey and my struggle to heal. I boarded the plane for the mainland a few days after the New Year.

Jennifer Lin Phillips

Chapter 15: Turning Purple

My Dad picked me up from the Max train station in Beaverton, the town I grew up in. I had taken the train from the airport and was relieved and happy to see my dad in his full head of thick, white hair, pull up in his SUV.

"Hi Dad! Happy New Year! Thank you for coming to get me. It's nice to see you." I said as I kissed him on the lips. My family was like that. Very affectionate most of the time as for kisses and hugs.

"Welcome home Jen. It's nice to have you here for Bopa's funeral. I hope you start feeling better soon." He replied.

Bopa was the nickname for my Grandfather, and he was one of the most handsome and sweetest men I have ever known. He sang to me often as a child and continued to hum and sing to his many grandchildren even as adults.

At his 92nd Birthday Party at Morton's Steakhouse downtown Portland, I still sat on his lap while we took photos, playing with his hair and pointing out the thin spot on his very full scalp of white hair to him. That was our little game and what we always joked about together.

Out of everyone in my family, My Grandfather judged me less than anyone. He always respected my choice to be me and welcomed me into his arms with an incredible warmth and truly non-judgmental and genuine love.

We got back to my dad's house. The home my mother had helped design the interior and lived in only a few years before she had died in her and my father's room just up the stairs past the chandelier. My step mother was home and there was still a warmth from the holiday season just ending. I said hello to my step mom, gave her a hug and kiss and then set up in my old room, the room I had spent a few years in back in High School.

Oregon was so wet and cold, and I knew in a few days that I would be missing the warm ocean and breezes quite a bit.

The following day I picked up my prescription from the emergency center. I was eager to try it and see if I could get these nasty symptoms reversed. I had lots of bumps under my skin on my face, and you could tell there was some kind of infection going on.

Both my father and step mother made comments about my weight and were hoping I would put some fat on while in town. I told them I had been juicing a lot, and yes of course they were very skeptical of the

Jennifer Lin Phillips

health routine I was on to heal.

The medication was a nightmare!! After one day, my entire body literally turned pink and purple. I read the treatment and just what the anti-fungal drug was doing to my insides. I learned that the drug entered the body and began punching holes in cells as to kill the fungus dead. I discovered however that the new powerhouse cell entering my bloodstream and body was not cell selective.

Meaning that these new defenders went around punching holes in my good cells as well. My fighter cells were being attacked also, and this did not seem like a good thing to me. I also learned that the reason my body turned purple was because too many of the fungal cells were dying at once, and upon entering my bloodstream, the now dead cells were poisoning me.

Two hundred dollars for this?! I thought. What a waste. I threw everything away the next day and was going to research some more alternative therapies.

The following day Nathan had phoned me to tell me that he had finally received the power bill. Three months at the house and we finally got the bill. It's hard to remember now why it took so long to get the bill. We had a P.O. Box set up in town.

I think somehow the bill had gotten sent to a previous

address or something weird like that. Because the actual house we were now living at didn't receive mail or have a mailbox. The amount was quite a bit for three months. Something like 1700$, and they were asking for a new deposit on the account, in the amount of 1000$ because we hadn't paid a dime and were three months past due. I was blown away at what the cost to live at the house was. And thought maybe some power was leaking from somewhere.

We didn't even have a dryer for our clothes, and we both were very conservative and didn't use the lights very often. Only a few lamps or kitchen lights for late night dinner in the evening time. And the house was practically empty. All the power-washing had taken some power to run for sure, but 575$ per month?! Wha?!! Nathan was pretty nervous about the amount and said his dad wouldn't loan him any money right now.

We got into another fight over the phone.

We hadn't made up since our last argument on island and were still not getting along very well. We both really didn't like one another very much at that moment. I thought about what to do and decided to phone one of my new clients on Kauai. He had a very successful business over there. He was a pilot on island and did tours for visitors in small helicopters. He was well established on island and his company was well known and busy. He had been coming to see me once

Jennifer Lin Phillips

per week for a few months before I left. Each session was two hours, and he felt a real bond and friendship with me. I asked him to help us, and if he could loan us the money and get us out of trouble with the electric company for now.

It didn't take much convincing, since he was such a giving person, deeply compassionate and really loved my company and my touch. He made a special trip to the electric company and paid the 2700$ bill for us. The agreement was that I would pay him back through sessions. And it would take quite a few to get the balance back to zero, but I was thankful for his help and willing to do whatever I could to secure a place for Nathan and I to live and work from.

Even if that place was making me ill.

My options seemed limited and I had already invested so much in the property. I was really hoping that somehow things would smooth out. My health would kick into full gear, Nathan and I would return to loving one another and we could continue our adventure on the island and with the property. We were still holding the vision to sell the house and split the money and give a third to Moori and the Kingdom.

After the relief from the electric bill getting paid, I decided to refocus again on my health.

I discovered an old remedy. A remedy that an African American and female doctor, with a PHD and practicing in the U.S. had exposed to the public. She had been practicing for many, many years. She was in the business, and the business was selling as much medication and prescription as possible. She said the medical industry is corrupt and that she got paid to pass out prescriptions to patients.

She even received bonuses for that and was also often questioned and harassed by the companies and/or hospital if they noticed she was handing out less and less of them. She explained in many of her talk shows that were now being broadcast on streamed radio from Panama, where she fled to after the government tried to sue her and take her license away. She explained alternative remedies to her listener's, and she also exposed the medical industry for what they truly are. They are a business, and their income relies on the public being sick and addicted to medications.

Her remedy, that she had discovered, from speaking with her grandmother about health, was her grandmother's secret for maintaining health before the pharmaceutical industry even existed. What she had found was indeed profound. I am pretty sure that almost everyone has heard the term, "A spoonful of sugar helps the medicine go down." Well, that catchy phrase and song was sung for a reason.

The medicine was pine tree oil, or turpentine, and was taken with a few cubes of sugar, a spoonful, every so often, or few months. This folk remedy was used for aches, pain, infection, parasites and sickness. The oil is derived from the pine tree and is now sold in hardware stores as turpentine and considered to be dangerous. It is in fact very potent and dangerous if you are exposed to it in large doses or if it has gotten in the eyes or too much on the skin.

I decided to buy some and try a spoonful with sugar. This was so interesting to me, I thought as I took the oil with sugar, and pictured Mary Poppins singing to the kids she was babysitting in the playroom in that scene of the movie. She was giving the kids medicine and I think it was the same scene where with the energy coming from her hands, she was opening drawer's and putting toys away and clothes. I think even the kids got that power somehow in that scene as well, perhaps after taking the medicine. Hhhmmmm.....

I felt fine after taking it. I seemed to warm up, the oil got my blood going and I liked the piney taste with sugar. I had told my step mom what I was doing and asked her not to worry. It was late, and I then went to sleep. After a few hours of sleeping, my dad rushed into the room I was sleeping in. He was yelling at me to get up and come down stairs. I woke up alarmed and a bit frightened by the sound of his voice. Oh no, I thought to myself, what's up now? It seemed like every time I stayed at my dad's a big argument would ensue.

I hesitantly walked down the stairs in my nightie. When I reached the bottom of the stairs, he laid into me.

"Jennifer you have no idea what you are doing to yourself! Look at you! Your cheeks are sunken in and you are not looking well. I just phoned medical emergency and the lady told me it is very dangerous to ingest turpentine into your body. Are you nuts?! How much did you take and where did you hear about this?" My father questioned me.

I explained to him my sources and that it was such a small amount, not to worry. He continued to yell at me anyways. I was standing in my pjs shivering in the cold night's air. Couldn't he tell I am trying to recover and don't need him yelling at me, weakening my immune system even more? I had taken the oil hours ago and was fine. I felt fine. He began cursing me out again, "I heard you on the phone with your boyfriend on Kauai. I can't believe the way you talk to him. What is wrong with you?"

It wasn't like I could explain to my father how Nathan talked to me or how he treated me. He wouldn't have liked what he heard, and chances are he wouldn't have believed me anyways. My father held the position throughout my entire life, that what happened to me was always my fault. Even when the old vintage Mercedes car he bought me shot a rod a few months after owning it. I had just taken it to get the oil

Jennifer Lin Phillips

changed. He blamed me. It was my fault. My step mom later told me, it was his poor choice in purchasing a car like that. I was 19 years old and didn't have a clue about cars. I took the blame and tried to learn and feel my way through life. My father didn't understand my creativity either, and most of the time he would say things like..."Oh, that's just Jennifer. She is different." I felt really blown off by my dad emotionally. But he was always the first one to come at me when things weren't going as planned in my life, or I was struggling with something and needing a little help from him.

My father said a few more very hurtful things to me that night and called me a really degrading and horrible name, which I won't repeat here. A five-letter word that rhymed with More, Galore, Store and Door. Mmmmhhhmmm......not very nice. I couldn't believe my dad looked at me that way. I really felt like he never even saw me. He saw his projections. And just because I didn't live the conventional life of getting married, having kids, adopting some horrible habit, like drinking every night and making sure to have a home to do it in, did not make me an outcast or a failure. I asked him if he was finished and if I could go back to sleep please.

I went back upstairs and got into bed. I was frazzled from all the yelling and name calling. My dad has said some hurtful things but what he had just called me was the worst yet. I sat in bed thinking of how years before, about seven, my father and I had another falling out and he had never fully forgiven me since then.

We have had a few pretty good arguments before, and between my two sister's and me, there was almost always one of us he wasn't talking to at a certain time. I thought about the time my older sister had told him that I had been sexually molested at a young age and that I thought maybe it was him who had molested me. There wasn't anything I could do to prove the assault that I felt in my memory and in the cells of my body. I had a memory of being sexually abused and when I went to see a psychic, two, they thought perhaps it was him. I told my little sister and she told my older sister. And five years later, after I had made my peace with all of it, my dad calls me and is outraged.

My older sister had just been sexually assaulted by a long-time family friend and she thought it was the right timing to tell my dad about my thoughts of him. The thing was, I wasn't mad or hurt by my dad. I was over the memory I thought and had moved on. Until Bam! I return from Kauai the first time at 25 years old and this whole drama unfolds.

And then the threatening calls from both my dad and my grandmother. It felt like my back was on fire after taking the call from my grandmother one night. I told

Jennifer Lin Phillips

her that I didn't think my father had molested me, but with psychics telling me it was his fault what was I to think. It wasn't like I was going around telling people. I was trying to do my own healing and understand what had happened to me. I phoned another healer and psychic that I had heard of from a friend, the next day, and he confirmed it wasn't my dad, but it was his fault for not protecting me and my personal space. There was a lot of drinking going on when I was a girl and I do remember lots of people over and late-night parties. All I was doing was facing a memory I had and simply trying to heal and understand it all. But like many victims of sexual abuse, no one believes you and the victim is often the one blamed.

I stopped talking with my family back then, because all they were doing was attacking me. I just went on about my business that year at 25. I had just gotten back from my first trip to the islands. I went along living in my apartment in SE Portland and got a job across town at a night club, that I rode my bike to and from over the Burnside bridge at 2AM. I then transferred to a 1920's vintage building as a property manager. I bought a junkie car for $300, but the color was kind of golden and I liked that. A few months later, we all forgave one another, and we celebrated Christmas at my Dad's.

What a Xmas that turned out to be. Everyone was

drinking and celebrating, but tensions were still pretty high. I remember having some red wine and a few Bailey's and coffee drinks. I ended up going home upset and left all the gifts my family had bought for me at my dad's, most of which I never received after that. That hurt a little, but it was fine by me, I was not that materialistic anyways, especially at that time in my life.

So, after the gifts had been opened, it was my little sister's turn to take her jabs at me out of nowhere. She made some snide remarks, I reacted and then everyone seemed to come at me. My family was still upset at what had transpired only a few months before and being the black sheep in the family yet again I just left, hurt and upset. And as I slammed the door to my dad's garage I screamed, "Sure, Merry Christmas! Do you even know the story of Jesus? Do you even know what he represented? He was a healer and he taught people compassion for your brother's and sister's.
And look what happened to him. He was crucified and hung by nails on a cross by the public.
Congratulations and thanks a lot for reminding me the meaning behind Christmas and the story of the son of God, Jesus. Merry Christmas and goodnight." And I drove home.

It wasn't until ten years later when I went to Maui for the second time for a visit that my sexual abuse was finally confirmed. I ended up staying at a woman's home who sold crystals. Many crystals, and they were

Jennifer Lin Phillips

beautiful all sitting out in nicely open boxes on her lanai. Her name was Skye, and she was a very sweet woman. She attended healing circles on the island and invited me to go with her to one. I was happy to and very excited to meet the other's on island that were in the healing circle.

The teacher and leader of the group was an Asian woman, a very successful and attractive woman with a very big loving family. I noticed many pictures of them around her office. She was also a chiropractor and did these healing circles maybe once every other month. She had a nice big diamond ring on her finger, and although she practiced the healing arts, she seemed conservative. The technique she used is known as Cellular Regeneration Technique. It is a reading of the pulse.

It was my turn to sit in front of the fifteen people in the circle that night and I was eager to. I sat beside her and put out my two fingers just on top of her two fingers, and she read my pulse and response to her tapping. It was interesting. She would tap a few times on my fingers and read my response. The first thing out of her mouth was this "A case of Sexual Abuse." She then went on to read the very long list of the trouble in my body that were symptoms of the abuse that I had. The list continued...." weak lymphatic system, toxic liver, kidneys, poor blood flow and circulation, lung issues, mood disorder, etc....." I cannot remember but it seemed to be longer than anyone else's in the room that day. I was shocked. And it was true, I had suffered with my health my entire life. I was very sensitive to alcohol too and could only have a glass maybe two without feeling the toxic effects. I felt myself that night tap into my energy field and acknowledge the abuse that was there that I was forced to suppress. Waves of warm, hot even, energy came off from my body in the circle that night. Finally, I didn't have to feel guilty for being sexually abused, like it was something of my own creation. It felt good to have the confirmation after so many years of getting blamed for my memory. It was odd to me the amount of trouble in my body and my mind that that experience had been causing me over the years, and I knew I had a bit more healing to do.

After acknowledging to myself my own suffering and why my dad was still so mad at me and had practically disowned me over the years, I went to sleep. I slept in the room that I had slept in on my sweet sixteenth birthday, the same year I was crowned a princess at homecoming in High School. I took a deep breath and fell asleep. To this day I never brought up the sexual abuse around my father, nor did I tell him that it had been confirmed on Maui yet again. I knew he didn't care to hear about it, "Oh, that's Jennifer, there she goes again."

Jennifer Lin Phillips

The next morning after getting up from bed, I took a poop. And it appeared there were in the toilet, a few parasites in there. It felt a little symbolic, considering my experience the night before. I did feel a little better than I had ten hours previously. But there was no way I was going to continue that pine tree therapy in my Dad's house anymore. Not with the way my dad had reacted the night before.

A few days later at my Grandfather's funeral, I gave a eulogy and read a verse from the Bible that my father had asked me to. I read it in the church that both of my Grandparent's had sang in for forty years together.

My Grandmother played the organ there too, and I had many fond memories of attending sermon with them there. The Church was beautiful. A tall triangle roof, long elegant wood isles, and colorful stain glass on all the exterior windows. It always was a special place to me. While reading the verse my father had chosen that cold January day, I felt the sun peak in on my face through one of the tall skylight windows as I spoke. I got the chills and felt the Holy Spirit enter me and I spoke with ease and confidence. As I walked down the aisle afterwards back to my seat, a few of my relatives smiled at me warmly and I could tell that they had been touched by the presence coming through me.

Sovereignty and the Goddess

My father thanked me for my performance afterwards in his car as we drove to the cemetery up Skyline Blvd. The same cemetery my mother, brother and grandmother were buried in. He said he was proud of me and that I did a nice job reading. I was glad that my father was happy with me, even though our beliefs were so vastly different. I was glad that, even if he couldn't understand me, that I could at least meet him somewhere in a space that he felt he belonged in. I loved my Dad, and felt compassion for him, his losses, and his struggles. I did not like to see him suffer in any way throughout our life experiences together.

And if I could be humble enough to meet him there, on his side of the road, where the grass grows in patches for him around picket fences. Even if I belonged in a field that smelled like hay and dusty horse's hair.
Even if I was wild and he was tame. Even if I could look at my experiences and really review them, while he turned his head to the nearest distraction. Even then, I would meet him. I would stop in hooves for a moment, and refrain from looking, from bucking or galloping off and around. And I did, I did that again and I did it for him often. I did it for another few days while in Oregon, and then it was time to head back to the challenges of the wild, wet island.

Jennifer Lin Phillips

Chapter 16: Repaying the Debts Owed

When I got back on island, Nathan picked me up from the airport wearing a white t-shirt, smelling like the usual hempseed oil and it looked like he was growing his hair out. His hair had been balding some on top for a few years, but he could still grow it long, from about mid scalp. I liked his hair better short and slightly buzzed. His energy was anxious that day, but honestly, he often was.

We drove to Lydgate Park and he got out to harvest some coconuts on trees on the side of the road. He had purchased one of those climbing belts and was getting really pretty good at climbing with it. It was so refreshing to drink that coconut right there on the side of the road, and I smiled at Nathan's spontaneity. Maybe we would start getting along better, I thought, as I sipped sweet, fresh, water from the top of the cracked coconut. We drove back along the Kuhio Hwy to the house. The Christian family had moved out while I was away. They had a month or so off as a good break, and it was time for them to start rebuilding things at their farm. We arrived at the property, and when I went inside, the energy in the house was extremely chaotic. It seemed like Nathan had been creative while I was away, but the worry there he had exhausted from his being was present and I could feel it thick in the air throughout the house. Honestly, it made me a little nauseous.

I found a sage stick that I had on site and began to burn it and chant to Goddess Durga. The Protectress. You chant to Durga when calling upon divine energy or shakti, in request for that force to be used against negative forces of wickedness and evil. Goddess Durga is considered to be the combined forms of Goddess Kali, Goddess Saraswati, and Goddess Lakshmi. Durga literally translates as the one who is "unbeatable," "invincible," or "unconquerable."

I began to chant the Om Dum Durgayei Namaha mantra. The mantra translates as "Salutations to She who is beautiful to the seeker of truth, and terrible in appearance to those who would injure devotees of truth."

I spoke with fierce tone and intention as I walked around the house swiping the burning sage stick in the air, up then down in circles. The smell was soothing to me and the smoke always cleared the negativity from the air and space. I had used this practice for many years, and it had always proven to be a successful technique of mine. I intended for the space to be protected from danger, intruder's, and for the paperwork on the house to clear successfully.

Ensuring our safety on the property.

Jennifer Lin Phillips

After a few hours of allowing the intention, sound and vibration to wash over the home and land, I felt the ease return to the property.

I decided to sleep in one of the guest room's down the hall. I wasn't eager to be close to Nathan after all the fighting. He barely even thanked me for getting my client to pay our 2700$ electric bill for us. After a few days of sleeping on a thin mat on the floor with a few blankets, Nathan came in to me with a written note and apology for his behavior.

He had written up two pages of apology for attacking me and signed it. I thought his apology was well thought out, and we decided to make up. He slept with me in the guest room that night, and we both decided we would be more comfortable and warmer at night with our combined bedding. I moved back down the hall to the master room with him the following day.

I set up my Hematite crystal set around our bedding. I had maybe fifteen small and rounded, hematite stones that I used for protection and positivity. I thought it was really quite pretty seeing the glossy metallic stone lined up around our bedding, like a dark silver shield. I knew I was connecting with the core of the Earth, which is made up of the stones Hematite and golden, sparkly Pyrite.

I began working again. And most weeks brought in enough money for us to cover our bills, buy a few things for the house and eat. We decided to rent the cottage to a young artist who had a son. A single mother who created beautiful blankets, crafted in vintage Hawaiian style. Her name was Leah, and she sold her craft at the local farmer's markets. I remember visiting her there one day up North Shore at the market.

She even took me to Secret's Beach once in the morning on a jog together. She practiced her ballet techniques in the long stretches of sand, while I got deeper into my hatha yoga poses.

Often, I would go over to say hi to her in the cottage or to see if I could do anything for her or her son. We began doing trade for bodywork. I remember her saying to me one night while she was massaging me, "This is wonderful being the giver, your inner Angel comes out through your hands. Or she would say, "I'm really feeling my halo doing this work." I totally understood what she was saying and had felt a similar feeling many times before.

The flow of compassion can flow from the giver to the receiver, and it ends up healing both parties involved with its potency. I told her she was welcome to use our bath tub in the master bath anytime she needed to, but she was hesitant to come into our space too much. Being that she was the other female on the property

Jennifer Lin Phillips

and most likely didn't want to cross any lines somehow.

It was fascinating feeling her work in the cottage on the sewing machine, weaving her blankets most days. Sometimes it felt like she was a spider in there, weaving her web with her fingers and her thoughts. And on the days her thoughts were turbulent or negative, wow, you could feel it on the property, and somedays I felt the negativity come at me. I was processing her thought process at times, being that she was there on the property a lot working and weaving from home, and I was working on things just next door.

I began to understand that she was envious because of the nice house we had, and she was a struggling single mother. I just tried those days to give her the space she needed. I had plenty of work that was needing my focus anyways.

I began working to pay back the loan amount from the electric bill. My client who loaned us the money was married and rather troubled in his relationship. Him and his wife had three adult children and they both slept in separate rooms at night. Like many relationships, after the boxing ring of life gives you a few too many blows, you retire to different locker rooms to clean up and bandage your wounds.

My client wrote poetry and did photography in his spare time. He brought some of his poems in for me to read. He told me he was inspired again by me and he began writing poems again after being dry for many years. We had a nice relationship and he was respectful. Although, sometimes he would reach out and grab my leg with his hands and stroke it a little. This of course made me quiver a bit. I didn't like it when men I was not in a relationship with touched me in any way, and I usually cut it off right when it started. But since he loaned us the money without hesitation, I felt this was a different situation, and I granted him a few strokes of my leg here and there.

Most of the time, I would walk around the table out of his reach, and work on some other part of his body, if he tried to touch me. It wasn't that I didn't like him. I liked him a lot and admired his endurance in life. I felt compassion for him and knew he needed some love, and I thought it was good for him to feel the days of his youth return a little. Plus, I liked his character and his honesty in our conversations.

One day, while in a session together, a song we both liked came streaming through on YouTube. We both sang the song together in the room that day, and the energy we were creating felt righteous and uplifting.

One day he brought to the house some crystals for me. One of the pieces was rainbow hematite. Hematite looks metallic, dark grey, and shimmery. This particular

Jennifer Lin Phillips

stone resembles the colors that a rain puddle reflects after some oil from a car has mixed with it accidentally. It was iridescent, and was shaped like a castle with long, vertical ridges around one of the edges, making the castle shape look like a semi-haunted yet mystical palace.

The types of birds that would fly and swoon over in flock's, hovering over such a palace's walls, can you imagine?

At a later session, he also dropped off a Pu'akenikeni tree for us to plant in the yard. Those flowers bloomed a firm white flower that turned orangish yellow, the scent they exuded stuck around in the inner passages of your nostrils, warmly taunting the mind to unravel slowly in pleasure.

Nathan found a spot to plant the tree, by the outdoor shower, and along the fence towards the front stairs of the house.

One day, my client offered to fly Nathan and I around the island in one of his small planes, his treat. That trip was hard for me to handle, being that I was in the back of the small plane, where most of the turbulence is. I chewed and sucked on ginger candies to help with the nausea the entire two hours of the trip. We were able to view many remote parts of the island in such a short flight.

Upon flying back into some lush, deep valley, we ran into some rain. I remember when he captured the picture of the beach that our house was on from high above in his plane. Later when I reviewed the picture, the line of the reef almost brown in color, jagged and was very noticeable through the blue waters. There were portions of water too, in the photo, that were a pale, greenish blue. The perfect shade of tropical.

I had been up one night, drinking chicory tea with milk and honey and set myself up on my massage table with a handful of crystals of mine. I laid on the table with my sarong over my naked skin, with the crystals placed on each of my chakras and holding a few crystals in each of my hands. I began doing mantra to Green Tara.

I even had done a drawing of her a few weeks prior and hung it on the wall in the kitchen. Just across from the big shrine I created on the corner of the long granite countertop, which was intriguing to many of our guests.

I placed many shells I had collected from the beach across the street there at my shrine, and some shells I had collected off the vibrant beaches up north shore. I placed too some of my crystals there, with particles of sand scattered on the granite from the shells I had brought in.

I had some pictures I had printed up placed there also,

Jennifer Lin Phillips

which I would use colored pencils to sketch on and over. Most of the pictures at that time were of Anandamayi Ma. I printed up many pictures of her and had placed them around the house. Anandamayi Ma was an Indian spiritual leader. She was described as "the most perfect flower the Indian soil had produced." And her joyful and blissful state could be felt by everyone. Her half grin and subtle smile with meditative eyes captivated me. I was enamored with her presence so much, and I really looked up to her. Not only was she peaceful, but she was incredibly physically gorgeous as well.

I placed her pictures there around the house, so as to protect us and remind us of peace and tranquility, with her soft smile and motherly grace.

That night while lying on my massage table, I continued to repeat the mantra to Green Tara and while entering that twilight space between dreaming and waking, I felt her presence near. The room was a bit chilly, with only the screen-door closed that night.

But I loved hearing the sound of the waves from the ocean across the street and let them in often while meditating. The blessings from the Goddess were felt that night, and after a few hours of trancing out in deep tranquility and surrender, I walked the long, dark hallway to sleep next to Nathan.

Some nights Nathan and I would listen to the sound of

the OM or even the sounds of deep space music. I remember smoking some herb with him a few times at night, and while the OM was playing, I would stretch and move about on the floor getting deeper into the rhythms of my body. Every movement I made was electrifying and intuitive.

One night while meditating together in our room with the skylight, I felt my spirit climb a long rope that was attached and tied around the full moon up in the sky. I climbed up to the moon there in my mind, that you could see through the triangle skylight window just above us.

I had entered a deeply creative space and felt the images were magnificent and other worldly in my mind's eye. My spirit had no boundaries and could do whatever she desired.

I was preparing for a crystal therapy class that I was going to take on island and had three books to read in preparation for the week long class. I remember reaching a point in the book about going through the black hole of our mind and existence. How at a certain place in your life, you leave the shadows and fears behind in search of expansion of being and light, newness.

And one night while playing the OM in our bedroom, I felt that experience quite vividly.

Jennifer Lin Phillips

As all of the darkness in my being came to the surface, I was literally pushing through it while orbiting and breathing there in my mind. The OM was just streaming aloud, and I was pushing through the darkness and it was miraculous to see me passing through it, spiraling there into open dark space.

On another day I was listening to some music in the room where I practiced massage. The music being played from my computer began to skip. It was odd how it was happening and while listening to the sound that was now coming through the speakers, I could hear the word "Athena".

I knew that this Goddess was trying to make her presence known to me. I did some research and discovered that she is a Goddess of courage, wisdom, inspiration, civilization, law and justice, strategic warfare, mathematics, strength, strategy, the arts and crafts and skill.

I noticed in the images I had found that she had flower's strung in a circle around the top of her head and her hair was auburn.

Wow! She even looks like me, I acknowledged. I continued to read about her and learned that she had no mother and was born through the skull of Zeus, the Sky and Lightening God. I spent many days and nights channeling and humbly trying to connect with many deities and teachers. I felt ignited by their unique gifts and wanted to have them near me when I needed them.

I was humbled and felt so blessed that this new Goddess, Athena, had found me and channeled some of her gifts to me.

The following day after channeling Athena, my client who loaned us the money showed up for his session. I told him what had happened to me and he laughed at my creativity. I mentioned to him that chances were that he was connected to Zeus and had come through for me like a father in the past few months.

I told him that I had also just noticed the statue and fountain of Zeus with his long staff just up the street in Princeville, a few days prior. I told him that Zeus displayed a Protector's quality and bursts of golden thunderbolts came from his staff.

I said to him that day...."Hey, that's like you, riding in your helicopter day in and day out, giving tours of the island. God of the Sky above the sea. You possess a protector's energy and send positive golden lightning bolts across the lush island land." He giggled at my imagination that day. But I knew it had to be true.

The next day he sent me a picture and text message. In the message was a picture of a long golden airplane

Jennifer Lin Phillips

that was on the runway that morning. The same runway that his helicopter's take off from and land on. He said he had never seen a golden plane like it before, and we both were astounded by the synchronicities.

Our house on the North Shore was so quiet at night, but during the day if you hung around the house too much, could drive one mad. Roosters sounding loudly every hour, and with the amount of high-end homes on the block, with big outstanding yards, lawnmower's and weedwhacker's went off for hours every other day.

Some days I felt like I was gonna lose it with the amount of annoying sounds and frequencies on that street. Plus, I had only a few friends on island and Nathan was still working relentlessly on getting a loan so that more work could be done to the house. His effort in trying to get the leans off the house had gone nowhere. His work with the Kingdom was going okay and they managed to get a spot on the local radio talking about the coins and the currency. And the possibility of a future bank off shore.

I was really proud of him and his work that he spoke about that day on the show.

But that night I had a dream that was revealing. I was becoming quite intuitive with the little distractions around besides the noise. My clairvoyance was strong and one day, I even felt the bird's wings soaring and flying just around the corner at the Kilauea lighthouse. I was meditating quietly in my room and I just felt them, swoop in there and right through my mind. I felt like I was really tapping into the power to hear and see, and I felt I was opening to the messages of the sea, the sky and the land.

That night after Nathan's talk about the coins and the currency broadcast on the community radio, I had a very auspicious dream. In my dream the coin with the King's image on it was spinning.

It spun like that for a few seconds and then flopped head's down. The dream was insightful. And I knew right then that the coins and the currency for the Kingdom wouldn't make them much money.

I had this intuition that we should focus some of our energy in other places, to give back to the Hawaiian People. It did seem ludicrous to me in some way's to be still focusing on silver and gold, when silver and gold was what had stolen the land from the Hawaiians to begin with. And who knows how long it would take to build an offshore bank.

I asked Nathan the next day if we could talk to the King's cousin about planting fruit trees on his land. And if we started now, in 5-25 years there would be an abundance of fruit and work for the struggling or homeless Hawaiians. We made a few calls, but even

Jennifer Lin Phillips

with acres and acres of unused land, nobody made a move as to develop it for sustainability or for food.

Although the King and the Kingdom were making a lot of progress, gaining attention, receiving donations and support. There was still a lot of work that could be done hands on, to support the people on island.

Chapter 17: Full Moon Party to the Goddess

I had reached out to an Ex-boyfriend I had a year and a half previous back in California. He was a chef and we spent a few year's together back in the redwoods there in Cali. The area was incredibly gorgeous, and we spent a lot of time exploring on his old cop motorcycle.

The smells out there were invigorating. Bay trees infused the moist air and acres of vineyards and breezy lakes could be seen all around the area. It was a deeply sensual and romantic time in my life and I spent a few years there with him.

I had contacted him to ask him if he could send me the boxes of jewelry, I had stored at his mother's house in Washington State. My own Mother's jewelry was in those boxes, the things she had left me after her passing. He said that he would reach out to his mom and ask her to send them soon.

The box arrived a few weeks later, and although they had not been packed well, I did receive many of the pieces of jewelry I had remembered wearing that were from my mother. I loved the pink sapphire ring with the golden butterfly etched into each side of it. And there were some jasper and obsidian stones that I had never really noticed before.

Jennifer Lin Phillips

The box was pretty much a mess and one of the Opal diamond earing's was missing from the pair of two.

The reason that I had asked Derrick to send me my mother's things was well, because it was about time that I had gotten them back, and I was wanting to be in possession of my mother's diamond wedding ring that my father had gotten for her. She had left it to me in her will. My mother wore that ring all throughout her adult life until she died, and I wanted it back in my possession.

It never arrived. The ring was not in the box.

I emailed my ex and asked him about it. I asked him to ask his mother if she had seen it. Some excuse about house cleaner's and I kind of figured someone had pawned the ring for money. I let it go. My mother was gone anyways. What's her diamond ring going to do for me? I was now living in a 4-million-dollar home across from da beach and felt like the karma of that was a lucky success. So, I had won anyways.
Although I had considered selling the ring myself so that we could do more work on the property, while waiting for the loan to come through.

A few days later, on the day of our full moon party in honor of the Kingdom and the Goddess, I did ceremony for my dead mother. I put on some beautiful music and chanted, sang and danced that day in the kitchen while making ginger snap cookies with chocolate chunks and green salad with quinoa for the party that night.

This time, I was singing to White Tara now, and asking for the safety of my Mother's spirit.

I found an old picture of her wearing a wig lying on the blue floral couch we had growing up. She looked radiant and her smile, oh my gosh her smile.

I took the picture of her in my hand, while still singing sweetly, out to one of the garden's below on the anniversary of her death and the same day as our party. I sang, and I ripped the picture up into pieces and I cried. I kept praying for her safety and scattered the picture around the red dirt in our garden that day like ashes.

It was a special moment for me, and I felt that even after 20 years of her being gone from me, I couldn't remember if I had ever really prayed for her safety like that.

I then pictured her on a canoe, crossing over somewhere beautiful on the land that I was standing on in my garden. The land that was once a canal that lead to the vastness of the ocean. I peered down at the ripped-up pieces of picture with her incredible smile beaming up at me and sang. I sang and hummed for her safety and thanked the God's and Goddesses for listening to my prayer for my Mother. I especially thanked White Tara for the song I sang was to her, and

Jennifer Lin Phillips

I went back to the kitchen to prepare for the party that night.

We had invited a few of my new clients, the Christian family, Leah, who was renting the cottage from us, and a local guy who did work on the house across the street.

The food turned out great and there was a lot of interesting dishes to be eaten that night. I had even purchased a few bottles of red wine for the event, and people showed up just before dark. I was disappointed that Leah had decided not to come. Besides me and the mother from the Christian family, the guests were all males. It was a small friendly gathering anyways, but I would have liked to have had Leah's support that night and the energy from her son there also.

She was protective of her son, and in some ways, it was good, but I remember a few times him sneaking over to see me and say hello. I could tell he was nervous his mom would come home and discipline him. Sadly, she turned out to be pretty jealous of me.

One of Leah's friends had shown up that night. He was the reason she did not make the party. He had come to me for a session once and then asked me to go hiking with him. I told him that I couldn't and that I was with Nathan, but it wasn't like Nathan took me anywhere or on hikes in his free time.

Daniel was very attractive, and he surfed. I could tell he had a little crush on me by the way he gave me an incredibly warm hug and smiled at me. Him and Leah were just friends she said, but since he met me, he had lost interest in hanging out with her. I didn't want to get in between them, but with Nathan busy all of the time and us bickering and fighting constantly, I pondered going out on a hike with him perhaps.

- Leah didn't want him at the party and so she no showed the event. It made me a little irritated that she was hiding out next door with her son and wouldn't even make an appearance at our first party at the house.

Everyone had a fun time, and the worker across the street brought a friend, who Nathan and I befriended immediately. He made his own cannabis oil and he was really into the Crystalline and the Goddess energy I had ignited throughout the property. We all talked a lot that night, we ate some more and then sang some songs together.

We had candles lit by the bar next to the kitchen and talked story again. Then we ended up on the front lanai that night that peered out towards the moonlit ocean. It was getting late and people said goodnight, each person taking off in their own direction towards wherever home was.

After the party Nathan gave me a hard time about

Jennifer Lin Phillips

something.

I can't even remember now what it was about, but we got into another fight. I was so irritated at the tension at the house now, now that our guests had gone home, and I screamed towards the cottage and to Leah that I wanted her to leave.

We had been friends for months, how could she not have an appearance at the party, my party, in honor of the Goddess. I told her so many times what a Goddess she was and the amazing qualities as a woman and a mother she had, why couldn't she see past things and be a sister to me and be there? Nathan ended up taking some things out on me that night, and then I took it out towards her.

The next day she told me she had heard me, and we both agreed that she should move out. Our friendship had changed over the past few weeks and with only three of us at the house, we all needed to live in harmony and collaboration. I was honestly really pretty mad at her, how she had changed and handled herself on the property.

For weeks she made more of an effort talking with Nathan than with me. Even after I reassured her, I wouldn't go hiking with her friend. I had only seen him for a massage session. I was hurt that she had blamed me, and it felt like she was trying to make me jealous and come between Nathan and me. I was honestly starting to wonder if maybe she was making passes at him behind my back. I needed our friendship back and yes, I guess in reflection now maybe I shouldn't have invited her friend Daniel to the party, but honestly with the way she had been acting lately, chances are she would have found another excuse not to come to the full moon party that night anyways.

The next day, I moved back into one of the guest rooms. The one with the bright salmon pink bathroom and skylight. I had a new project ahead of me. I was going to paint it blue and add golden butterflies and flowers. I reached out to the guy across the street working on the house next door.

I asked him if I could borrow his ladder.

And with the paint's that were around in the garage, I got started right away.

Leah moved out a week or so later, and we placed another ad to re-rent the cottage on craigslist. The man who made his own cannabis oil, called me to set up an appointment for energy work and said he had some nice crystals for me. He told me he thought we could use all of the positive force and power at the house and on that land that we could get.

He showed up a few days later, with three very large and sparkling amethyst crystal rocks. They were powerful, I cleansed them in the ocean right away. He had given me a handful of smaller crystals too.

Jennifer Lin Phillips

One of which was celestite and a connector stone to the angels and celestials. I was so thankful to him for bringing us his set of crystals that he no longer used.

He was a very generous and kind man. We set up a session for him and he also began helping us with projects at the house. He even got Nathan a job doing yard work down the street at a lady's house who taught yoga some days. Although Nathan and I were on and off again, and I was still struggling everyday with my health and the mold at the house, it seemed like we were in right timing. And even with much struggle, we were surviving it.

Chapter 18: Big Waves

Later that week, I met a new client. He turned out to be the Producer of Ziggy Marley's music, and had a fancy house down the hill across from Anahola Beach park. We became confidants and good friends quickly.

I trusted him. And after building our connection, I mentioned to him how we had really acquired the house and what Nathan was doing for the Kingdom. I really felt a spiritual kinship with him, and he seemed to somehow show up for me at the most perfect time.

After working relentlessly on the bathroom, I had finally finished my work on the cool blue color and butterflies. I tried my honest best, to just work, see my clients, and stay away from Nathan as much as possible during the day. Although at night and morning we still ate together.

This worldly and somewhat evolved person showed up and gave me much strength and insight. He was very mad at Nathan for how he had been treating me. I brought in most of the money for our food and bills and he wouldn't even take me anywhere besides the health food store. It was driving me crazy, how he completely ignored my needs and I was literally working myself into the ground.

I had gotten very strong in my arms, but as for weight

Jennifer Lin Phillips

there was not an ounce of fat on me.

I had numerous people on some of my Facebook posts ask me what I was doing to get so strong, and how in the world was I getting that thin?! People were worried about me, but I just blew them off with my excitement about the new fascinating experiences I was having, which in all truth, wasn't exactly a lie.

I had pretty much lost my cute Phillips booty and perky, freckly boobs from all the cleansing I was doing. I was still jogging down to the canal some days, to feel the breeze in my hair and release some of my stored anxiety. But my mental wellbeing was fading, and I felt like a machine most days. If I wasn't working on the house, cleaning mold, finalizing some project, or working on a client, I was trying to recover at the beach or resting.

Honestly, the sounds from those rooster's got to me some days.

I could hear Nathan below the house punching the hanging bag with his boxer gloves, like a boxer. And some day's it felt like he was thinking of me when he swung his arms, kicked with his wounded legs, and made contact with that bag down there. It felt like he was psychically and mentally attacking me. And energetically, I could feel it. Even if he was physically taking it out on that dangling bag downstairs. I could feel his anger and his aggression being directed towards me some days, and I was starting to lose my sanity.

I had mentioned to Nathan for a few weeks that my mental wellbeing was fading. Especially being so isolated on that part of the island. Most of the people that lived on the block, honestly, used their house for a vacation or a retreat. One day, I marched down to the weights where Nathan was working out one afternoon and I had a fit right there.

I began screaming at him, "Why won't you take me anywhere. You do the same thing, day in, day out, at the same time every day and it's driving me crazy. You have no spontaneity in your routine, and you refuse to acknowledge that I have some needs in this relationship too." He looked at me annoyed and smirked a little. I grabbed one of his longer metal bars with weights on it. I tossed it in the air and with my right leg, I kicked it.

A giant gash and bruise appeared instantly on my right shin next to the bone there. I could not believe what I had just done to myself.

The feelings of neglect had finally gotten to me and I unleashed all the anger from months of being ignored. Close to six months at this point. With blood trailing down the skin on my leg and this newly wide-open wound, Nathan helped me upstairs to his bathroom. He had some of those temporary tape stitches and we

Jennifer Lin Phillips

applied a few of those after he cleaned me up.

I was crying, and the pain was intense. We were able to bind me up without having to go to the doctor. I could've easily gotten stiches that day, probably twelve to fifteen or so.

Over the years I have had a handful of people ask me about it, just what that long, elegant scar is on my right shin and just how I got it. Of course, I must utter a lie. A surfing accident, I reply. I banged up my leg pretty good on the reef one day while trying to surf, big, big waves.

I limped down the beach across the street to sit on the sand across from the house. It had been a few days since my self-inflicted injury and my mind was not in any better of a place. Nathan had some compassion for me I think, but he still wasn't willing to alter his behavior at all. He carried on with the same routine, and I continued to seek help from outsider's and new friends.

I ended up at the farmer's market in Kilauea town one evening. A young man new to the island began talking to me as I examined mangoes and star fruit.

"I could live on this stuff. What incredible gifts from

the land." He looked at me and said.

"I know," I said hesitantly, "I am at the farmer's market's every single week. I just rotate which days and market's depending on the food I am most in need of at the time. Most week's I go to two markets, and that way I am always stocked up on the fresh island fruit and veggie's"

We talked on the edge of the market that day, while snacking on juicy items we had just purchased from the street vendors. He told me how he had just arrived on Kauai. It was his first time here and he was doing some work on a farm in the area. He had bought a car right away and was using it to sleep in.

We seemed to have a lot to talk about, and I was enjoying his company, both of us sitting on the sidewalk, observing locals passing by with baskets filled with fresh local foods.

I mentioned to him the house where I was living, and I asked him if he wanted to stay in our front room for a few days. Maybe he could help with our garden, since I was still healing up from the gash on my leg, and pretty low energy. He agreed, and I brought him back to the house to meet Nathan.

He helped me with the food I had just bought from the market and we walked into the kitchen.

When we walked inside the house, Nathan was just

Jennifer Lin Phillips

coming in from his office to make dinner. I introduced them, and I could tell Nathan was slightly annoyed at the presence of our new guest there in our house. We had re-rented the cottage to another woman, she was a little older and Buddhist.

Nathan certainly liked being the Alpha male on the property, I could tell.

But honestly, I needed the presence of another man around with the way that I had been feeling lately.

I also felt like it would balance the energy on the property a little bit, and hopefully bring more peace and accountability to the house.

We agreed that he could stay in the front room for a trade. He needed to help us with the yard some and on keeping the gardens watered if I was not around. He agreed, and although he wasn't at the house much, accept for in the morning or later in the evening, I felt calmer with him there.

Our new guest didn't keep up his end of the deal that much. And when I went into his room one day to see what kind of condition it was in, I noticed beer bottles and garbage in the closet. I asked him to clean his mess up and please do what he could for us in the yard. I could tell his energy was spent on the farm he was working on down the street and I was trying to take it easy on him. But an agreement is an agreement. And he was using our power, water and home without a single dollar spent.

The lady in the cottage moved out, and I spoke with a nice man on the phone about renting it. The cottage was for him and his girlfriend, she was coming from New York soon. The gentleman that phoned me was on island, and we decided to meet later in the week. I could sense a kindred spirit with him immediately over the phone that day and I was excited about meeting him.

I thought it would be great to have a young couple on the property with us. And perhaps we could mingle and share meals together. I was in desperate need of some female friends too and I was hoping this girl and I would bond up together.

Jesse, the man who had phoned about the cottage, came to check out the rental and property. I remember his beaming smile and the necklace he was wearing that day. I asked him about the coral symbol that was strung around his neck and he told me it meant "Free Spirit."

He was very positive and had magnetic, loving energy. He was a contractor and did physical work on homes in the area. He had lots of tools and the power to help us at the house. He had also been on island for many, many years. He seemed to carry the gentle spirit of Aloha with him in his smile and in his gestures. We

Jennifer Lin Phillips

agreed later that week that him and his girlfriend could be the new tenants in the cottage.

We signed the necessary paperwork to secure the cottage for them, and then we said our goodbye's. They were scheduled to move in first of the month, and there was maybe ten days left in the current month at that time.

It seemed like things were coming along well, but tensions were still high at the house. I slept in the middle room with the butterflies and Nathan, the king of the jungle had the master bedroom still. I could tell that he was pissed at me for allowing the guy in the front room to stay at our house.

I remember walking into his office one day, while he was sitting in the bamboo chair, I had bought for him at his computer. I brought him some juice and mentioned to him that it would be nice to get out this week. The positive energy and spirit I felt from Jesse was inspiring and I wanted Nathan to feel some of the vibe. He ignored me, my request, and turned his back to me to begin work again on his computer.

I lost it. I grabbed one of the stools by the bar and threatened to throw it through the mirror across from the counter of the Koa Wood Bar. I hardly doubt now that I was going to do it, but I never got the chance to find out, because he tackled me. He tackled me, and then picked me up. After picking me up and over his head, I remind you, I was down to maybe 110 lbs., he threw me on the ground just about as hard as he could.

I landed strangely on my hip and back and felt right away that something was terribly wrong and that I had cracked something. Maybe a rib. I asked him to stop while I gasped for air and he acted like he was going to grab my hair and continue to beat me. I asked him to stop again and said this is serious. He let me go, and I got up somehow and went to lie down in my room.

When I got up from resting. I was light headed and needed some water. There was a very sharp pain coming from the left side of my back and I slowly and carefully walked down the long hallway to the kitchen. I passed the room the guy was staying in, and noticed that he was out still, working on the farm.

I poured some water for myself from the alkaline machine, grabbed some fruit and slowly walked back down the hall to my room to rest some more. I fell asleep, exhausted emotionally from my week.

My shin on my right leg was still healing, and the sharp, intense pain coming from the left of my back was serious. I let the air from the ocean in through the screen door to comfort me and I drifted off to sleep, hopeful that my dreams would hold me safely somehow.

I stayed away from Nathan for a few days. I was in a lot

Jennifer Lin Phillips

of pain and could honestly barely move about the house. I tried to shower myself and dry my naked, injured body, but couldn't reach the drops of water on my legs.

I rested for a few more days and avoided everyone at the house.

The next morning, upon rising, it was the third day after our nasty, big fight. The sharp pain was intensifying still, and it was signaling to me that my condition was not getting any better. I stood up in the t-shirt I had slept in and I felt quite weak and unstable. As I looked out towards the ocean outside the windows in my room, I noticed that my senses were fading. It seemed that there was a loud ringing starting to appear in my ear, my head became fuzzy and I reached out for the wall to stabilize myself. I honestly felt like I was going to fall over and die right there.

I steadied my weight on the wall and walked down the hall in my t-shirt to the front room next to mine, where our guest was staying. He had stayed over last night and was just getting up himself. I knocked on the door and said to him through the door, that I needed his help. He hurried to open it and I stumbled into his room weakly.

My vision was starting to fade, I felt light and tingly all over, and my skin was becoming cool and damp. My eyes started to roll back into my head. I was going to go unconscious soon I was aware, and I fell right into his arms. He held me there upright for a minute, as my spirit decided to re-enter my injured body.

I looked at him in his eyes as he steadied me. I apologized to him for needing his help, and he smiled and reassured me it was his pleasure. We got me down the hall, to sit on the bench in the kitchen and he phoned 911 emergency. Nathan had left early that morning, I think he was doing some yard work down the street for a little extra cash. And we waited for the ambulance to come.

When the fire truck came, I was still in my t-shirt, sitting casually on the flat of jagged rock that lined the long stairs to the front door. I was still not moving around all that well, and although it would've been nice to freshen up and put more clothes on, I didn't have the energy or consciousness for that right then.

A group of about ten firemen jumped out from the fire truck and there was one police car. They greeted me warmly and swiftly and asked me what was wrong with me.

I was still gathering my strength and trying to relay my story to them. A few of the firemen were local boys and actually quite charming. The smile from one of them made me blush. As if I wasn't feeling light headed enough. I tried to maintain my composure and I was talking low and shaking a little.

Jennifer Lin Phillips

"The big dog Alii side swiped me in the yard the other day while we were playing," I said to the firemen. "Him and the other dog play hard out there in the yard sometimes. He was sprinting by me and accidentally slammed into me. The collision twisted my back pretty good and I fell. It has been a few days, and honestly, I am surprised at the amount of pain that I am in. I almost fainted and that is why we called you."

One of the firemen knew the history of the house and he questioned me a little about how we had acquired it. I told him a few things that satisfied his curiosity and they asked me if I needed the ambulance to get to the Emergency Center across town.

I had health insurance, but it wouldn't cover the cost of the ride. So, I asked the guy staying with us if he could take me there instead.

He agreed.

I said farewell to the row of cute island firemen, and one of them helped me into my friend's car.

While driving down the road that our house was on to the Emergency Center, we passed Nathan heading back to the house. He was walking and he waved us down to talk to us. As he approached the passenger door window where I was buckled in and sitting, he looked at me with fear in his eyes.

I told him where I was going.

Sovereignty and the Goddess

He looked at me with a question pouring from his expression, and I looked back reassuring him that I didn't get him into any kind of trouble. The ambulance left our property a minute before we did, so it was safe for Nathan to return home now.

When we arrived at the Emergency Center, there was only a few people in line ahead of me. The doctor saw me right away and I was laid out on a stretcher beside him. I told him that I was in a great deal of pain. He decided that I needed X-Rays to reveal just what kind of injury I had.

The process of taking those was almost unbearable, barefoot, piercing pain shooting up and down my spine and half naked in the cold room.

The doctor didn't believe that my injury was too serious, because I had waited three days to come in.

I reassured him my pain was intense and that I was scared that the injury was bad. After reading the x-rays he came in to tell me the results. He had my x-rays scanned onto a CD for me to have. He handed me the CD and said that some pretty good damage had been done. I had a fractured L4 vertebrae, and that meant that my back had indeed been broken.

He told me how tough he thought I was for taking that much time to finally get in to see him for some pain medication. And I smiled at his humor. I left with a month supply of pain medication and was hopeful the injury would heal quickly.

We drove down the long winding highway back to the chill of the moldy house. What was I doing to myself? What was happening in my life, and what was going to transpire from the current situation we were all in? I asked myself as I walked up the front stairs of the house.

I walked in the front door and all I wanted was to sleep and to rest. To eat, shower, take some pain medication and sleep in the room with golden flower's and insects with wings.

I did just that.

I slept, I read, I prayed, I burnt incense and candles, I healed, I cried. After two weeks, I stopped taking the medication, I could feel the toxicity in my blood, and it made me feel sick.

I was irritated that I couldn't go running and had never been bed ridden in my entire life. I was used to being active. And it was those activities that I turned to in order to stay vibrant and healthy. My back was healing slowly, but I knew that I couldn't keep poisoning my blood with the medications that I was on.

I stopped taking them. A few weeks later I was back to running again and working on that house.

Chapter 19: Auntie Angeline's

I cruised by the green, jagged hills in the small town of Anahola.

I was heading to my favorite spa that was located just down the street from that soul igniting mountainside. The mountain was known as the Mystical Goddess and one could gaze at it while casually reclining in a lounge chair from the outdoor deck of the spa.

I had been in the routine of making my way down to the spa to steam and scrub nearly once per week after settling in a few months on the island. The spa was called Auntie Angeline's and had been around for some time. The founder of the spa, Auntie Angeline, had passed away and her granddaughter was now in charge and running the outdoor spa.

The granddaughter was Hawaiian and very close to my age. She practiced Lomi Lomi there, behind the curtains, in the main room some days. The spa was recognized for the amazing four hand Lomi Lomi treatments, and I almost set an appointment for one, one day.

The granddaughter was outgoing and sweet to me. I felt a kinship with her, she always made time to greet me warmly with her fresh island smile. Most of the

Jennifer Lin Phillips

worker's there were women, and the spa was known for the beautiful singing of Hawaiian chants in the steam hut.

The girls would come in the hut dressed in casual outfits, shorts, skirts, t-shirts, that would then get damp from the amount of steam being emitted into the air.

The ladies would bring in a jar of pink salt that was sourced from the big island mixed with a little clay. There were two massage tables used for scrubbing, and the recipient would lie down nude and receive an amazing scrub, from head to toe, front then back. It was really quite healing to be sung to in those sweet, sacred female tones, and I loved every second that I spent there.

I received a scrub from one of the ladies there only once and I deeply, deeply enjoyed it. There was a hose in the steam hut that one could use to wash the salt off and the seats one sat on. The water was cold, which I liked in contrast to the hot steam.

Most days that I gathered myself at the spa, I would pay for just the salt, so that I could do my own scrub while stretching and breathing in the steam. This routine of mine really kept my health in check, especially with everything I was up against at the house. It was a way for me to connect with some other women in a tranquil and healing environment too.

There was a stack of Angel Cards in the changing room, and it was so refreshing to draw one for myself each time and read what message was meant for me right then. And whenever I heard the singing there from the women, cooling waves of peace and love would wash over every echo of a wound in my heart. I would leave feeling fully soothed. It was no wonder that the Mystical Goddess mountain just above, was hovering over the spa grounds and keeping eye on all of us there.

I cried there too somedays. At my life. My stresses. My situation with Nathan. In the shower, red faced and pink, I cried for what I was going through.

I wanted to connect deeper with those ladies at the spa. Maybe get together with them outside of the sanctuary there. But I was so worried that they would see me. Really see what I was going through, and also up against. And the last thing I wanted was to taint the peaceful retreat that I had found for myself there. So, I went back weekly or so, and I kept quiet, I kept reserved.

Instead, I bathed in their presence, their voices, and in the rise and fall of the wet purifying steam.

One of my newer clients lived just down the hill from

Jennifer Lin Phillips

the spa by Anahola Beach Park. His name was David and he had an intriguing life to me. He travelled often and had many kinds of friends and I think a big family.

Some of his connections were musicians who had become famous and one day when I went to do an outcall at his gorgeous house on the beach, he showed me the studio where he recorded music for some of them.

Ziggy Marley was one of the most famous of his clients, and that impressed me. Oh, how I loved Ziggy's music. I first started listening to his music back when I lived in the redwoods in Cali and would go jammin' in my car. Driving from lake to lake, looking for secret spots to swim in the area.

I even wrote a brief paragraph about one of his song's "Rainbow in the Sky" on my Facebook intro about myself. In the intro I referred to the fact that most days I was aware of those rainbows in the sky and could usually be caught on a wild chase for the next one.

It was odd to me that this chance meeting was bringing a lot around full circle for me. And I thought it was incredible how we really can create so much with our mind and our vision if we imagine for ourselves what we want, and what we believe is possible.

David and I became really pretty good friends, and I

felt like I could talk to him about most anything. We laughed one day when I said to him that my auntie back in Malibu was famous too.

She is a model and actress and "she married this one guy," I jokingly said to him. "She ended up marrying this one famous singer. I think he is pretty well known for some of his songs," I said coyly to him. "You know that one singer who sang 'Born in the USA,' and he was known as 'The Boss,' or something like that."

His mouth dropped, and he laughed at me. He knew my auntie too and some of the work she had done. Those little things made our friendship real.

I think he was pretty impressed when I told him about my most inspiring auntie's wedding to the famous singer out in the country back in Oregon in the 80's. I told him that the tall and handsome stranger had asked me to dance during the reception at the house there far out in the Oregon hills.

I remembered getting up and dressed for the wedding in the middle of the night. They were to be married in the church my Grandmother played the organ at, which my Grandfather sang alongside her, at midnight. Being married at midnight would hopefully throw off the nagging photographers and the press. They had been camped out on my Grandparents front yard all week. With my Grandmothers sense of compassion and humor, she went ahead and ordered them all

Jennifer Lin Phillips

pizzas one night. Not exactly the quickest way to get them off from practically camping out on the lawn. But no doubt a signature move by my beloved Grandma.

I went to the wedding tired and wiping the sleep from my little and inexperienced eye's. I think I was about seven years old back then. After the ceremony we all drove in cars along windy roads with light brown and lime green open fields.

I remember the Cinderella slipper's and vintage wedding dress my stunning auntie wore that day. I watched as helicopters flew above, creating wind and loud, circular sound up above the house.

We had been followed. Perched up there with their camera's, hoping to catch a photo or two of the famous newlyweds and their family.

"Can I have this dance?" The singer said to me with a grin.

Oh my gosh, really?! He wants to dance with me?! Everything felt like a dream, and I looked to my mama for her approval. She nodded towards me and I took this enchanting stranger's hand. I looked up to him pink cheeked, wearing my blue Oshkosh-begosh overall's with pink bows on them.

"You are such a little Butterfly." He said down to me as we danced. He held my tiny hand and we turned in circles there together in the room.

A butterfly? He thinks I'm a butterfly, I giggled to myself. What a charming stranger I thought. And I continued to bounce around the room that day with rosy cheeks and blue and pink wings.

I did what I could to help David over the few month's that we held sessions together. He was struggling in his personal life too. Our time together was supportive and comforting for me. We both were needing some healing and there was a gap in both of our lives that was somehow being filled.

I remember when I was preparing for the crystal course and was really getting into the readings. I felt the crystals inside of me very strongly some days. And with the crystal blue ocean water so close to me, I could feel my essence metamorphosing.

One day I heard the name Calista, it felt like it had been given to me from somewhere. The name sounded like a higher version of me, my crystalline self.

I remember telling David about how it felt like that part of me was deepening and coming to life inside of me. He kind of laughed at me a little about my new name, but he still listened to me. Chances are he

Jennifer Lin Phillips

probably thought that I was losing it, being that I was so isolated on that part of the island each day. Dealing with the chaos of organizing the house and keeping things running smoothly. As well as the chaos in my relationship.

Perhaps Calista was the name of my alter-ego, that I was merging with and just creating.

David had some interesting things happen to him too throughout his life. He told me over a session one day how he had been struck by lightning a handful of times. Something like two or three and he had recovered from the injuries each time. He had even shown me pictures of the physical transformations he had to go through and the trauma.

I was wondering what kind of electricity was coming off him at this point and how could he draw such a force to him magnetically so many times? The experiences he had were indeed something supernatural and out of this world. And just what kind of superpowers had he developed from them? I thought......Hhhhmmm....

I had finished reading the three crystal books written by Katrina Raphaell, in preparation for the beginning course at The Crystal Academy of Advanced Healing

Arts. I loved learning about the crystals, the techniques used for healing, and the names and properties of them. I thought it was pretty cool too that the founder of the Academy started the school on Kauai and was now teaching courses worldwide.

On the morning of the first day, I pulled up to the house in Princeville, down the street from the water fountain of Zeus, and parked along the driveway. The house was modern, set in a nice neighborhood, with big flowering trees out front. I knocked on the door a little nervous to what the day would be like. A middle aged and incredibly radiant woman with tight curly blonde hair appeared in the doorway.

"Hello, my name is Tanize, and I will be teaching the course this week. Please come in." she said to me.

She was wearing a long gown and lead me down the hallway to the back room. There was an alter along a narrow table and a picture of the second book's cover in a frame. As I entered the back room with a long couch and fireplace, I immediately noticed the tables filled with thousands of crystals in trays.

I looked around the room to see a giant piece of Selenite beside the fireplace, a silky white colored stone with thin vertical layers. The amount of charged energy in the room was powerful, and I took a deep breath allowing the force to penetrate me.

I walked over to the trays of crystals and became

Jennifer Lin Phillips

illuminated from being in their presence. They were reflecting their light and color to me and it was remarkable trying to take their power in, both visually and energetically. I was a little overstimulated, but I didn't mind it.

My vibration was rising, and it felt like my body was becoming lighter too just standing there next to all that energy, color and light.

Bloodstone, Green and Pink Tourmaline, Lapis, Malachite, Azurite, Chrysocolla, Gem Silica, Citrine Quartz, Black Obsidian. To name a few of the crystals in the room that day. I was drawn to all of them and was eager to learn more about them and how to use them for healing. I had a few wands back at the house that were my very favorite pieces so far. One clear quartz, one Rose quartz and an incredible Amethyst wand that was nicely carved into a perfect point towards the top.

My clear quartz piece was placed at the top of a copper pyramid that was six feet long on each side and came to a point in the middle creating a triangle. The copper pyramid was made by a friend I had made on island, and it was sitting in the yard with my clear quartz wand directly at the point at its center.

Nathan and I, along with the friend whom had made the copper piece, did ceremony one day, and Nathan placed my clear quartz wand at its peak. It was a pretty special day, and I loved seeing the copper piece in the yard since then. I visually connected to the copper pyramid that held my wand that day from the class just up the street with my mind's eye.

Then I dazzled about, circling around the new colorful stones and gems there in the room.

There were three people in the course, including myself. A woman had flown in from New York and a man from New Zealand. They both seemed to know a lot about crystals and I picked up immediately from the woman from New York how to create a more holographic crystalline grid to use for setting my intention's into form.

Tanize was a healer who had come from Brazil. Many of the crystals were from there also. She would fly back to her homeland and collect the crystals from shops there. Whenever she flew back home to Brazil, she would get flooded with people wanting healings from her. She did the therapy for many year's she said, travelling back and forth until eventually retiring from healing and focusing solely on teaching the courses.

There was a ton to learn, and I took notes throughout the day so as not to forget the steps and procedure's to performing the healings. I was nervous to give them, but also nervous to receive. What would come up for me? The alcoholism and abuse in my family? The sexual abuse? The abuse from Nathan?

Jennifer Lin Phillips

I was taking a lot in right away, so I made sure to rest a lot back at home after the day had ended.

By day two I believe, we were already giving healings to one another. My first healing that was given to me was by the woman from New York. During the healing she placed different stones around me and many of them on my naked chest. I felt beautiful like that, lying there in the skin Goddess gave me, with crystals, an array of colors, shapes, and subtle light beaming off my body. I became very telepathic during the healing's too, and I could relay back to the woman doing my healing the color of the stones that she had just placed on top of me or near me.

It was amazing how much of a channel I became of the crystals and I think both Tanize and the woman from New York were impressed with my natural ability.

We discussed the cover of the second book that was written by Katrina, the founder of the Crystal Academy, that had been framed and placed on the alter. While Katrina was printing the cover, something weird happened to the illustrated drawing and picture of the crystal. It came out that the image of the crystal with background was printed a double image. Meaning that the image was cut perfectly in half down the middle, creating a mysterious and perfect mirror reflection on the cover of the book. The image was speaking a story to us, but just what it was, I was going to have to unravel somehow.

Over the weeks after the class, I saw so much in the image on the cover of that book, that had been created accidentally.

Including waterfalls, images of golden grasshopper's and flying colorful light beings. I felt like another world was trying to show itself through this strangely printed image. And I began to think of insects differently from then on too.

The color and perfect symmetry that insects portray in their bodies reminded me of the crystals. And I felt like the two kingdoms were speaking similar languages, although the words were spoken in form, shape, color and perfect symmetry. Like sacred geometry or something like that. It was fascinating too that insects could be found trapped inside of crystals and rocks. Their shapes being preserved for eternity. These two kingdoms were closely connected to one another, and obviously illuminated everything around them.

During the course, one day that week, I remember being overwhelmed by the feeling of water pouring out wildly and loudly.

I was tuning into a large body of flowing water there that day. A power source on the planet. I knew after

Jennifer Lin Phillips

some reflection that I had tapped into Niagara Falls. Wow! I must go there one day. What a source for pure energy and mana.

Ormas energy is what I have often heard it referred to as.

Powerful, lightning bolt force so strong that you could sense it miles away. I honestly had a gift for that. I could find the Ormas energy while on trails. And most often the source would be flowing, nourishing, rushing pure water.

Niagara Falls must be one of the most powerful sources on the entire planet, which is why I could hear the water pounding from there telepathically that day.

I thought about it later too. That the amount of color, rainbows, and light prisms that those waterfalls emit when sunlight beams through. Can you imagine? Can you imagine what that world looks like to an insect flying around there? And imagine the different kinds of bugs and insects drawn there, to the colors, the rainbows, changing with the time of the day, as the sun around the falls rises and sets.

What kind of world is there, beneath and around the clean, flowing waters? What kind of world do we really exist in, I thought? And seriously, just what has man done to it? Hhhhmmppphh....gross.

Sovereignty and the Goddess

Tanize and I did a trade during the course of the week. She permitted me 150$ worth of crystals and I would give her a two-hour session the following week back at the house.

I was so excited to have the new crystals to work with and use in my own healing. I got real intimate with them right away and was especially drawn to a piece that resembled a white and grey mountain with some pale blue clusters. Turned the other way, a white and grey heart.

About a year or so later, in my travels, I took that piece up to Mt. Hood in Oregon and Mt. Shasta in California. Mt. Shasta is known to be the root chakra of the planet, and it felt grounding and special to have that crystal with me there when I went camping by the mountain one year.

And, at my friend's cabin by Mt. Hood. I would place the crystal in the windowsill, and it would make a perfect mountain shape just below the actual mountain, Mt. Hood, perching up above the dark green trees down the valley outside the cabin window.

Everything was so symbolic, and I felt in perfect synchronicity somehow.

Tanize came the following week for her massage, and she gifted me a triangle rose quartz piece. It was

Jennifer Lin Phillips

perfect. I had mentioned to her about the copper pyramid and she brought the rose quartz as a gift to enhance the frequency there, and the energy of the triangle. It was very thoughtful of her and I could tell the piece was powerful. Rose Quartz is used for the heart chakra and unconditional love for others and for oneself. I gave her an energizing and healing two-hour session that day, and that was the last time that I saw her.

Chapter 20: Heading Home

Amazingly, we had things pretty wrapped up at the house now.

Jesse and his girlfriend after only a month of being at the house, moved on to another property with more privacy for them. I had finished the week-long crystal course and managed to heal up reasonably well from the serious injuries I had gotten over the past year. And Nathan and I had rented out all the rooms in the main house and of course the cottage.

Unimaginably, Nathan and I were sleeping together in the room with the golden butterflies, with the best sound and views of the ocean.

There was a passion and deep care that was there returning between us. It felt good. Consistent finally, now that the house was operating smooth. The coolness from the blue in the bathroom bathed us and our relationship was calm and creative for about a month maybe two.

There were young energetic couples all living at the house now, and there was a sense of wellbeing and aliveness. The renters were settling in, Nathan and I were taking a relationship course online, and with the money coming in now with the new renter's, we felt a

Jennifer Lin Phillips

moment of exhale.

Exhale. Exhale, exhale......

I had plans to return to Oregon for the year. I was missing my sister's a lot and it felt awful feeling like I was missing out on being in the lives of my nieces and nephews.

The nagging effects and symptoms from the mold were still exhausting me daily, and Nathan and I both thought that getting a year off island to recover would do me a lot of good. I could reunite with loved ones, deepen bonds there, reimmerse myself in the flow of the season's, and my favorite season, the vibrant Fall, was coming very soon.

Plus, I could return as often as I wanted. I could travel back and forth and have truly what I desired. I had worked incredibly hard for this and had created the very best of both worlds.

I now had a beautiful spot in the remote wild of the jungle, with all the beaches and exotic fruits a girl could dream of. And in returning to my roots, I could relax in the rain and the coolness of the city. Get my fashion on with loved ones, enjoy the vibrant flowers, markets, music and the more sophisticated culture of the incredible west coast.

I set my flight for early October. I was reflecting on my very challenging and difficult, yet deeply magical year. One full year at the house on Kauai.

Nathan and I agreed that I would return in a few months, most likely in January. I had one last warm, elegant, evening on the island. The warmth held me that last day. I was hesitant to leave it. It was scary to return to the cold of the city culture. Would it be dreary?

Hey, this is MY journey. I'm walking in grace. And I have nothing to fear, but fear itself, I thought to myself.

I said goodbye to all the guests in the house, exchanged warm embraces with Nathan one last time, and then boarded the plane for my hometown, Oregon.

When the plane landed that fall morning, I felt the density in the air. I was happy to be home, but oh my gosh, my first step from the plane was literally a time warp.

What dimension had I just re-entered? The subtle shift in the air. And the heavy medals in the air were thick, I thought, as I breathed in the Pacific NW city air.

Jennifer Lin Phillips

The rain had a way of bringing up the poisons from the ground, from the gasoline, the city water, the air, and pushing it right up and into the nose and through the layers of fresh skin.

Starbucks and Pete's coffee signs lined the airport halls.

A brewpub, gift shops with mugs and keychains that read the name, Portland. Yep, I was home. Oh, the memories of searching craigslist for jobs, trips to visit my mom's grave at the cemetery up Skyline Blvd., and of course, taking the Max train across town. All my memories were flooding me.

I was taking in a dense grey feeling, but I was still feeling happy to be back. Definitely, I was excited to see old friends, my family, and explore the forests, and of course the flower's.

Oregon is known for its flower's. The city of Roses. A beautiful, and charming city. A metropolis of diverse thinkers, entrepreneurs, free thinkers, hipsters and "Keep Portland Weirdo's".

Oh, I'm happy to be home, I grinned to myself, grinding my teeth a little from side to side slightly, top to bottom.

But, but, but what happened to my beautiful blue sky, turquoise water, sandy beaches and sea shells? I thought as I felt a little defeated.

I boarded the max with a handful of bags and my massage table in shorts and flip flops.

Thank Goddess for the sweatshirt I had bought at the cute health food store and market North Shore Kauai, Harvest Market. I quickly put that on over my head as the cool air from the open doors seeped in and onto the train.

My little sister would be meeting me at my new apartment out in the suburbs, Hillsboro, soon.

I managed to make two trips on and off the train to load my things carefully on and sat in the blue leather seat, window side, that was headed through downtown. It was foggy. Very cold and foggy for only a few days into the month of October. I phoned my sister from the train that I was on, heading out to the suburbs.

"Can you please bring me a pair of jeans, sneakers and socks?" I asked her diligently.

"Yes of course," she said. "I can't wait to see you. Amelia and I will be there soon."

I exited the train a half an hour later, and just barely was able to get my belongings off before the Max train doors closed. Whew, I'm here, I half giggled to myself in amazement at the journey I was still on.

Jennifer Lin Phillips

I was trying to locate on my phone, Google Maps, the new complex I was going to be renting an apartment from.

"Fuck," I said aloud to myself. "It's a block and a half away." I murmured and looked around. There's no way I am going to be able to carry all my things that far. The look on my face must've been revealing a sense of defeat, because the man beside me at the max stop asked me how he could help me.

"Two blocks from here," I said to him, and I pointed to the pile of my things.

What a gentleman. With both arms he loaded my stuff up. With our four hands we walked the sidewalk two blocks to the rows of beautiful Rudbeckia flowers. My favorite fall flower, yellow, black, cone shaped, firm and buoyant. The hedge of beautiful fall flowers aligned the front door to the office of my new apartment home.

"Thank you kindly for your help, sir!" I said. "You must be some kind of train angel......thanks again." And I stumbled into the office there with my things stacked up outside.

I signed the necessary paperwork in the office that day. I called to set up my renter's insurance and PGE, Portland General Electric account too before leaving there. I signed over to the Nexus apartments, my first month's check at a pro-rated amount. I asked if I could get some assistance to my apartment with my things, and one of the maintenance men loaded my stuff onto the cart outside and guided me to my new home.

My sister will be here very soon, I thought to myself, as I got some help with my things up the few flights of stairs and down the long-carpeted hallway to my new home. We opened the door to a modern living one-bedroom apartment. The view from the small patio, with black metal bars, was nice. A large grassy area with a trail around the children's park and swimming pool.

I noticed a firepit burning that cold foggy day out beyond my patio. It appeared to be next to the hot tub that was producing a little steam rising into the air.

My apartment was completely empty besides the bags and massage table I had brought in. I sat down on the carpet thankful to be home, safe and warm, and I waited for my sis and three-year-old niece to arrive shortly.

I knew I had a lot of work to do to get new furnishing's, and to get around town would prove to be challenging without a car. But being so close to the max train station was relieving to me a little. The weather was cold, but the air in the suburbs smelt fresh. One of my favorite markets was located just across the street,

Jennifer Lin Phillips

New Season's Market. And my favorite hot yoga studio was only a few blocks off the train stop down the road in Beaverton, Hall Street Yoga.

It's going to be a good year, I was confirming and trying to convince myself. I was acknowledging my success so far, already, just sitting right there on the open, bare carpet. That gesture alone is in fact a miracle right now, I thought contently to myself. And look, I'm here, I made it, I made it back safely home.

My sister and baby girl niece knocked on the door to my new apartment. I opened the door with excitement.

"Aloha Annie! Hi Amelia, it's been so long since I've seen you two!" I said to the two smiling fresh faces in front of me.

We exchanged loving hugs and kisses. And I knelt to give Amelia a shell that I had brought from the island. She grinned enthusiastically, taking from me the shell that I had for her, and the girls entered my empty one-bedroom apartment.

We talked and caught up a little by the kitchen. It was eerie not having a single piece of furniture to sit on in my new place, and I felt naked and vulnerable before them. My sister knew a little about the adventure and turbulent journey I had been on, and I think she was thankful to have me home safe finally.

Amelia marched around the empty rooms and had found my turquoise and malachite prayer beads sitting in the windowsill of my bedroom.

She put them on and around her neck, prancing around my apartment happily. It was sweet watching her wear my beads. The beads I had prayed with many times over the year and had even bathed them with my hands in the cool Pacific Ocean waters, along some of my favorite beaches.

I took my phone out to snap some pictures of her and a second later after capturing some poses and cutesy smiles, the beaded adornment broke.

She had swung her arms up wildly and the string connecting the beads had busted. She frowned with disappointment up towards me, and I could tell that she thought I would discipline her now. I just looked at her adorable face, and the few turquoise beads that were scattered on my new kitchen floor and smiled down to her.

"Wow!" I said to her as she stood there looking a bit helpless.

"It appears you wanted to bless my beads with your gesture. I will take those back now my little darling.

Jennifer Lin Phillips

Thank you for briefly wearing them."

She looked a little confused and squeezed the shell I had given her in her tiny hand.

"I'm sorry Aunt Jennifer," she said to me sweetly.

"It's okay babygil. Your essence is in the beads now." And I let her off the hook. I really did feel that day that somehow, she had blessed my broken prayer beads with her three-year-old joy and innocence. I felt closer to her then. And I kneeled to steal a hug.

A few weeks later, while visiting my little sister at her house in Beaverton, Amelia handed me a necklace that was strung with wooden brown beads that she had found somewhere. And this became my new set of prayer beads that I wore around my wrist some days.

I felt that her and I were bonded from then on. And we were.

She really loved my collection of crystals too. The pile of crystals was the first thing she would go to after coming over to see me. And sometimes, I would bring a few of them to her at her home, so that she could admire and hold them. She was immediately tuned in to their magic. And I could tell that she was able to absorb their healing energy.

She surprised me, when she intuitively placed them in

Sovereignty and the Goddess

a bowl of water and put the bowl out in the sunshine to cleanse them one day. A little fairy of the crystals. I was quite thankful to have her innocent knowing and her understanding of the beauty and power of such shiny gems.

A few days later, my older sister dropped by with her three kids.

I had purchased a bed, just the mattress, and it was lying brand new on my bedroom floor.

The group of them came streaming in to bring sunshine and brighten my day. It didn't take long for the kids to discover my new white bouncy mattress sitting lonely in my practically empty bedroom.

Naturally, they began tackling and jumping on top of one another right there on top of it. With mommy lying flat on her back, each of her babies jumped up, on and around her.

I laughed out loud at the act before me and watched them closely with sincerity and happiness. I went around snapping pictures of them laughing and bouncing around one another that grey, rainy morning.

My heart felt full.

It was amazing to be embraced by both of my sister's and their children that first week back in the rainy, wet

Jennifer Lin Phillips

city, that we each had grown up in together.

Their visits were very much needed at that time in my life. And I could feel some of my own baggage coming off me in the company of those kids.

I couldn't tell them. My sister's. I just couldn't tell them, there was absolutely no way that I would have the energy or time to express to my sister's the trying year I had just been through. So, I just bathed in their love, and in their lives as growing mother's. And I held those kids close to me and listened intently to what they had to say....

"Aunt Jennifer, Aunt Jennifer......" And they would pull and tug and poke at me. I could see the sunshine beaming from each of their eyes, and I could sense that I wouldn't be too alone and cold over the wet, drizzly winter.

I acknowledged to myself the importance of these people in my life. My beloved two sister's and the incredible children that they had borne. How fortunate and smart of me to rekindle the flames of our relationship that year.

It was a wise choice for me to return home to be near and with them.

Our relationships have each faced some rough times

throughout the years and chances were that they would face many, many more. But with the holidays approaching, I was looking forward to the warmth and togetherness, the yummy feasts and the festivities with all of them, my family.

Jennifer Lin Phillips

Chapter 21: Truth is, We are All Different

Well sure, it doesn't take a genius to assume that I was and have always been the black sheep in the family. Flying sheep. Sorceress. Rainbow Bright warrior. Whatever you want to call me. I was the different one, point blank.

Both of my sister's had settled down, married men that could support them financially as well as somewhat emotionally.

They had children, a few, and both of my sister's had never travelled too far from the Oregon border's.

I was the exception.

The rebellious middle child, the one with bright red hair, and the one who wanted to see and feel the world outside of my hometown and my family.

It's true for me, that it was hard to relate to my family through most of my young adulthood. I pushed boundaries with myself and I wanted to learn through my own experiences about culture, and about right and wrong. I craved newness, quality of living freely. And I think in some ways, I was admired by many of my friends for the adventures I had tasted, and the beauty

I had embraced and seen.

My two sisters, my step mom, and I all met at the Italian restaurant one evening, across from my new apartment. It was my first night out since I had been home maybe a few weeks. My older sister brought for me from my Dad's a box of picture's, art project's, and things that I had created when I was a girl.

I was being flooded with a lot of emotion and memories.

We all caught up that night over red wine and fresh fish entrees. My two sisters sat across from me and my step mom, and it was obvious the special bond that they shared. With both being conservative, Christian, and Mothers, there was no way that my rainbow loving, water seeking, free-spirited Pegasus self was going to have a chance against their similarities.

It hurt me how they would call each other "Sis" to one another, and I never heard them call me "Sis" in that way. I was the different one. I had always been, and now being back in their company was like smothering that truth all over me. Like how white pasta is smothered in thick alfredo cream sauce.

I know, they tried to listen and smile when I discussed some of the exciting times on the island that I had experienced. But I could tell they weren't really all that impressed.

I was different, and at that time in my life, it felt like they wanted me to know that.

It wasn't until three years after the Italian dinner that night, that some of my pain and suppressed feelings about my relationship with my sister's emerged from inside of me.

The raw feelings came out in a dream after I had partaken in a healing session with a friend.

My friend performed a tuning fork and sound healing therapy session on me. And before I could return the trade I buckled down in pain over the table. My stomach was cramping up so bad. The pain was fierce, intense, and I explained to my friend that I needed to go home right away and rest. Once home, I crawled into bed nauseous with a glass of water. I was in a lot of pain and was wondering just where the bloating was coming from.

That night I dreamt of my sisters. In the dream the pain came out of me.

The feelings of hurt erupted. For so many years I suppressed feeling different. I was upset about feeling like the third wheel in the group. And I don't think I ever felt understood by them. Honestly, many times it felt like they were purposely trying to make me feel like I was the weird one.

Well, in my dream that night, the trauma released itself. At least now, I was able to admit to myself, shame free, the suffering my relationship with both my sisters had caused me inside. I guess that I was thankful also to not be stuffing it anymore.

That was five years ago, and over the years, these things still come up.

I try to come from forgiveness and compassion, but many times I have felt belittled and unacknowledged in my relationship with my sister's.

"We are all Different," My older sister said to me on the phone yesterday.

I had to grin, then smile, half smirk and release in a deep sigh when I heard her say those words to me right then. I had only minutes before given the title to this chapter in my book. Oh, the synchronicity and the harmony in her words. I was being held in a moment of bitter forgiveness, and although strange, it was relieving.

I looked at the bold words on my computer screen, and somehow giggled a little at her perfect sentence.

I had called her. My older sister, Meg. I was talking to her about how I felt hurt by how my little sister had blown me off an hour before.

Jennifer Lin Phillips

It's Thanksgiving here in Oregon now, 2017. I just started seeing someone new and thought it would be awesome to bring him to my little sister's rather large house up the hill for the holidays. Thanks and giving. Celebrate togetherness and love. That's what I thought the holidays were about.

I got the "No boyfriends" response from my sister and that cut like a knife. What? Seriously? I honestly could not believe what I was hearing. Her house was big enough to hold a small army.

"No boyfriends." Ouch.

Today, this year, I am going on my 5th year being single.

I have never brought a boyfriend to an event at their homes. I would think my family would be happy that I like someone and want to bring him along. There is ample space for my guest and plenty of food. What's really the big deal?

So, now I get to go to the holiday alone, yet again....and talk with family members that have made me feel very uncomfortable in the past at times, many times. Yep, just me, Jennifer, with no one there for my support. That's how they are used to seeing me anyways. No kids. No dog. Just me and my travels.

That decline of my simple request, has literally been the essence of my relationship with my sister's many times.

I feel unacknowledged quite often, and I must exist and show up in their world under their rules every time. They cannot bare to exist in my world. To them, that is often the only way they can see it or relate to me.

Last night, after talking with my older sister about my feelings, I got off the phone and began more writing.

I felt listened to, thankfully.

My older sister had softened my heart a little.

My relationship with my sister's is always changing. It's always shifting over the years. Hopefully evolving. But as life moves forward. Things just keep getting stickier. I am learning that most relationships do as we spend more and more time on this little planet called Earth.

My older sister comforted me in my feelings, just like my little sister has done many times as well. Once off the phone I felt a bit better.

After writing, I put on my Mooji meditation and group satsang that I connect with a few times per week online.

While tranquilizing my heart and emotions with the satsang, resting there, in the Is-ness of being, I began to doze off to sleep. I sensed the presence of my

Jennifer Lin Phillips

mother close to me. It has been years since I have felt her that close to me, and I knew she had come to me to be with me in my moment of need and sadness.

I was so tired and felt drained from the emotions I had faced earlier in the day, that I could barely acknowledge her. All my excitement for the holiday had been stripped from me. I got up, plugged my phone in to charge, and went off to sleep alone in my bed.

Thanksgiving 2017 is today.

I am going to my little sister's house with a bottle of red wine I bought, an Oregon Pinot Noir.

The label reads Firesteed and has a black horse in motion on it. Seems pretty suiting.

I will play with my nieces today and can hardly wait to see them actually! I get to meet my sister in laws two beautiful Milano young girls also. I will go alone today, again, but proud. The lone wolf of the family.

Today is no different than many days I have experienced with my family and how I feel around them often. But it is just one day, and even if I must abide by their rather unthoughtful rules, I will show up with a smile and love in my heart. But inside, I still know and feel that I am not seen for who I am or acknowledged as an adult who should be allowed to bring a guest of mine to a family function. I am an adult and I have people in my life who care about me. "Don't you want to meet them?"

Sure, it's probably my fault, I always go for the guy who doesn't show up for me, takes from me and then abandons me. Only to show up later wanting another chance with me. But this guy wants to be here. He's here with a sincere heart.

Can't they just be happy I have a new supportive friend?

And so today, I will be the bigger person, and I will celebrate the holiday slightly irritated, and I will bring the bottle of wine they suggested but leave my guest and new friend at home. And I will show up like usual, alone and chin up, vibrant in spirit and face and very, very thankful.

When I had returned from my trip to the islands back in 2012, there was no way to foresee the types of challenges I would be faced with. I was not prepared for the years ahead, but was ready to take each day in stride, and continue to learn, to challenge myself, work hard and grow.

I was talking with Nathan on the phone that night that my sisters, my step mom and I all went out to dinner at

Jennifer Lin Phillips

the Italian place.

"I just cut people out, the people who are judgmental towards me like that, I scissor them out quickly from my life," He said to me.

He was kind of short in temperament, cutting me off from explaining my evening to him over the phone. I could tell he didn't really want to hear about my night with my sisters and trying to find an easy solution to my new dilemma.

Nathan was great at stuffing his real feelings. He had also lost his mother to cancer at a young age. In fact, I believe he was the same age as me, fifteen years old.

He was an only child. And he tended to have that only child syndrome. As for compromising and working on adjusting his stance on relationships and evolving them, I think he was used to just cutting people out and moving on with his life. Not needing to process or understand, just reaching towards something else. Something greater. I get it.

But is that really the way?

"Those are my sisters!" I said to him abruptly. "You don't just cut your sisters out of one's life like that. It shouldn't happen that way, and with me it is not going to. I will continue to be there for them, to learn from them, and to hope they learn from me."

We got into an argument that night.

And after that conversation, you know what Nathan did? He turned right around, and he cut me out of his life. He told me that he had enough of arguing with me and that we were better off apart. Barely a few weeks of me being back home and off island and away from the house I had just worked so hard on organizing for a full year. And Nathan tells me he doesn't want me to come back.

Maybe for a visit.

We had plans for me to return in January, and with the cold and wind and rain coming even more, I was going to need that return and break for myself.

The house was our project. I had worked just as hard as he had. And I was the one who had the idea to rent the house out, to have substantial income coming in every month.

And I made all the contacts and did all the work to make that happen.

We finally had the house running on its own after a year of hard work and struggle. It had been maybe three months of it functioning on its own and he tells me not to return! Wow.

I felt manipulated and was wondering if this was his

Jennifer Lin Phillips

plan all along.

Honestly, I was obviously still healing from the year that I had faced on the island, and so I decided to withdraw from him after that call. I was going to need all my healing energy to focus on myself and my health.

Maybe one week later, after I stopped using the cream on my eyes for the mold symptoms, I broke out in hives all around both eyes and a little on both cheeks. It was awful.

I did my research and discovered that the steroid cream I had been using for the entire year, had been suppressing my immune system. And therefore, my natural ability to respond and heal had been suppressed for a full year and was now able to finally respond. My body was trying to kick the steroids I had been taking out of my bloodstream and cells.

I was feeling pretty beaten up at this point.

No ocean, no car, no furniture barely, and now hives all around my eyes. Nathan and I were barely talking, and I was still facing a lot of struggle with my family.

Oh my. My senses were telling me this was going to be a challenging winter.

My body was still weak from the mold symptoms and

now I had to face yet another health challenge. From the research I gathered on other people who had used the cream and once stopped, it was going to take 6 months to a year to recover. No way, I just can't wait that long. I cannot have hives like this covering both eyes an entire six months, half of one year. Nope, no way.

Walking around in the cold like that for months, Uh uh.

I started up again right away on my Gerson Therapy Treatment, and the symptoms began to heal slowly.

I was building my strength and began taking clients again. I needed the money bad and had no choice but to work.

One of my clients really fell for me after our first session together, and he became a real support in my life that winter. He had quite a spontaneity about him. And he was kind enough to bring by groceries for me when I was too weak or exhausted to make it to the store.

When he took a few trips out of town for business, he let me use his car while he was away each time. With what I had just been through emotionally and rebuilding my health. I had absolutely no sexual drive at that time in my life.

Eric really resonated more as a dear friend to me.

Jennifer Lin Phillips

So that is where we put our focus. On our friendship.

We took hikes across town to Mt. Tabor Park and along some of the nature parks in the area. He was sweet enough to give me foot rubs sometimes on my couch after taking me to dinner. He was a positive person in my life and offered me a lot of love and support, and our friendship remains today, supportive and loving.

I put on my calendar a trip out to Hawaii that January.

It appeared to be good timing. Because once on island, I realized that I had a court date there at the courthouse. If I were to not show up, I could've been arrested.

It was accidental that I was on island at the same time as my court date, but I knew spirit was still watching out for me, even after all the trouble I had been through.

Nathan had been a real asshole the three months I was away. We had to re-rent three of the four rooms to other people, and it was no surprise that the people in the house were having trouble with him too. One girl, even called the cops on him. He scared the crap out of her with his moods and his temper, yelling at her down the hallway one afternoon.

He was a bomb ready to go off most days. But from an outsider, all you could hear was the slight noise the bomb was making; tick, tick, tick, tick, but one could surely sense the warning of danger coming.

I went to my court date, with red itchy eyes and the symptoms of hives around both of them. I was a wreck. And due for court. Wtf.

Yes, you could say that I wasn't in the best overall shape.

But I was thankful to be back on island even if for only a few weeks. I needed the ocean, to swim, bathe in the sunshine and lye my aching, tired bones in the sand.

Nathan drove me to the courthouse that day, and we had been getting along fairly well since I had returned. He even apologized for getting angry at me in the past and over the phone recently. And, somehow, it felt like we were rebuilding our friendship.

Oh yes, my court date. Why I was summoned to appear. Well, about half of a year previous, I had been speeding and I was pulled over by a Japanese Hawaiian officer.

Goddess was he intimidating. And proud of it. I think he got pleasure out of talking down to me with anger, rage, actually, underneath his fierce tones. He had the badge. Not me. And I'm a whitie on his island.

When I reached into the glovebox for registration and title.

Jennifer Lin Phillips

Well, of course, neither were there. Shit! I was in Nathan's van, and I had stopped paying his car insurance a few months before.

He never began paying it again.

As a member of the Kingdom, he thought he was above all of the government's laws and rules. And he decided to not insure his car or get it registered.

And he told me on the way to court that day, that "As a member of the Kingdom, they decide the laws governing their tribe, not the courts." I was pretty worried about the fines I was going to have to pay. But at least I was here. Showing up. No arrest.

Well, I got off that day, hands clean.

I mean, the ticket for speeding went on my record. But the other's about insurance and registration were dropped.

The state lawyer was kind to me and pulled me aside before my appearance in court. I told him my side of the story. That I did not know he hadn't continued to pay his insurance or to get his car registered.

The law state's that if you are driving someone else's car unaware of those things, you are in fact innocent of the crime. The lawyer in the room that day was very compassionate to me, and I know he knew about the

Kingdom of Atooi. I think he was part Hawaiian as well.

Nathan pulled him aside to talk with him and also tried to intimidate him. It reminded me of the time Nathan almost picked a fight with the guy working at the library.

"You wanted to fight the Librarian?! " I asked him that day. Because he didn't have an ID, so couldn't use the computer. Omg.

I was found not guilty for the charges and was very much relieved to be leaving the courthouse.

Nathan and I grabbed some lunch and pulled over near the beach at a picnic table to eat. It had been a long stressful day in court and the hives around my eyes were still bothering me. Nathan got up from the table we were sitting at, while eating, and went to pick a white daisy flower near the sand.

There was a little warm, breeze coming off the hill, just above the ocean.

We were sitting at a picnic table, at a beach park. He brought the flower over to me, just like he had, the first day he had asked me out. He wanted to make me smile.

Why did he just do that? I thought. Gosh, with all the abuse, the trouble, the hurt. Well, I smiled somehow. It

Jennifer Lin Phillips

worked.

And it was moments like that where his temperament surprised me.

How was he able to find that kindness and generosity in such a difficult situation?

Nathan had always had that side to him too. And, it was because of those little things that he did and had done for me, that I continued to care for him. And try to nurture still a friendship with him with the remaining energy that we both still had.

Beautiful and passionate Rachel was the only one left at the house, whom I had known three months before. Her boyfriend, Travis had moved back to Sebastopol California, and they were still working on their relationship, I think, from a distance.

Claire and her small family had moved out of the cottage and into a bigger home down the street.

The single guy, Walid, in the front room had moved out too. Most likely headed back to New York after his work at the hotel was completed.

It was so good to see Rachel again and I felt really embraced by her there at the house. I think she was happy to see me too. We shared from the heart, like always. And we talked about the struggles we both had experienced living on such a remote island. The isolation, the remote location, it had proven to wreak havoc and was hard on romantic relationships.

A few days later. That appeared to be true yet again.

I can't really remember now what happened to invoke another abusive response from Nathan on that short trip to the island.

But when I went down to take photos of the horses down the street, and a few selfies of me standing along the fence there, I noticed the purple mark on my lip. Maybe I had said something he didn't like. I was known for that.

It's hard to remember now even how I got the bruise.

I think he cupped his hands over my mouth hard and bruised my skin close to my lip, just above it. As I was trying to take a selfie there, with the elegant horses just behind me in the grassy field, I realized how foolish and pathetic I looked.

And just how pathetic the situation had really gotten. How stupid I had been to allow myself to be treated like that for a whole year. While I nearly worked myself into my own grave.

I couldn't believe what I had been through. How our island dream had turned into such a horror story. And now here I am, being abused yet again.

Jennifer Lin Phillips

Standing there in front of those horse's, those wild and beautiful creatures, who were fenced in yet ready to run free at any moment. I knew I had to return home and move out of the barb wired fence that was dangerous and holding me back, that I had found myself in.

I decided to change my flight the next day, and I cut my trip short. I was heading back to the safety of my own apartment back in the cold Pacific NW.

I decided that I would have to make trips to the coast out there even if the open skies were overcast most days up until summer. It was natural and important for me to stay in tune with the ocean, the air and the sounds of the ocean waves.

It felt good to be heading back home where I had managed to afford furnishing's, I had my old friend's and had also recently developed some new important bonds with people. I wanted to start out this New Year out right somehow. Whatever that meant at this point. Even if I sort of lost the house that I had been working so hard on for one full year. Even if that meant wearing boots in the snow instead of sandals on the sands for a while.

I think overall, I was gaining strength in looking ahead. I managed to feel excitement about the new season approaching. It was obvious too. That with all the abuse that I had faced over the year, I needed to at the very least, to feel safe in my own skin. I recognized that I was still on my journey. Discovering who I was, who I really am, and still learning after all these years to hold tight to ME.

Nathan took me to the airport a few days later, if not the following day.

We barely talked the short drive there along bright green landscapes. I would surely miss the beauty and warmth of the island, but I couldn't wait to get out of the car and onto the plane home.

The arrogance, hostility and negativity he exuded in the car that day was so toxic coming from him. I knew then he had some kind of personality disorder. Bipolar, sociopath, split personality, I don't know, but I did know that I could barely stomach him. And I was finally admitting that to myself after all the struggle that year.

I even admitted to myself that drive, how much I hated hearing the tones coming from his lungs and from his voice spreading his sickness and icky ill will everywhere.

I mean, come on. I practice sound vibration and mantra.

I had been practicing that therapy and repetition of

Jennifer Lin Phillips

sound for fifteen years. I know better than to allow myself to be in the company of such hatred, darkness and disgust.

Sound vibration is the art of honoring oneself through sound. Healing the heart and auric field, the mind, the emotions through sound. I know better, I thought to myself, and I can't let him poison my energy field anymore.

I boarded the plane with ease somehow and tapped into the real energy of the islands. The mana of the people there, the Hawaiian culture, the crystalline rainbow energy that permeates the land. Yes, I know there is still a real fight on island, the battle for Sovereignty isn't over just yet and that fight is very real.

But I just let it go. I allowed myself to feel safe, relieved. I let myself fly over all the trouble and darkness that is also a part of the islands.

I could hear Bradda Iz's sweet voice resonating and vibing higher than the noises coming from below the choppers of the plane. And as the plane sped up along the runway to depart, I felt the true energy of the Islands there, the powers that really created the land, and I thanked Goddess Pele for having me again.

Chapter 22: The Blue Fairy

It has been very interesting really; new revelations and truths have been revealed to me since beginning writing this book about my travels and my journey.

I am fascinated by the instinct to seek, that is inherent within me.

My spirit knows, when and what to seek and at what appropriate times. This I know to be true through my seeking and understanding, but that does not necessarily mean that my journey will be easy. I will still make poor decisions at times, I will still have to grip hard and fight for my survival.

My Sanity.

It will still sting, as I grip and cling to those who do me harm. And, eventually, I will have to face the feelings of injustice, disappointment, by being let down by the people I am loyal to. Who Goddess knows I would give my life for and have. Whom I care deeply for, and for whom I naively trusted.

I do believe that spirit has always been guiding me to experience the deeper layers of myself, as well as the mystery of the worlds around me. This has all been a

Jennifer Lin Phillips

process of learning, expanding my consciousness and my ever-growing awareness of true reality.

This is a Spiritual Book. This isn't just a story. This is my life. My experience's. And my experiences are rich. They don't make sense to the average person. Why is that? Well, because the average person doesn't think nor experience life for himself. He does so mostly through the layer's upon thick layers of societies influence and conditioning.

My very first experience with life force energy, also known as Shakti or Kundalini was at the ripe age of 19 years old.

Yes, I had smoked a little herb, boarded the train for the Portland Saturday Market with a friend and sat in a seat facing the opposite way that the train was moving.

There was something that happened to me on that train ride that changed my perception's forever that day.

Maybe it was the way that I was sitting on the train, the herb I had just smoked and the speed of the train on the tracks. But while the train was moving, I had an experience of merging with the Oneness around me, and I became a part of everything on the train.

Including the sounds, the train was making, wheels grinding on steel below, air swooping by windows outside, and the voices of all the people sitting on seats or standing in aisles around me.

This happened to be my very first mystical experience. And I remember exiting the train to the market in a trance, only to end up standing and staring at a tapestry hanging outside of a vendor's booth that read;

"I am not a Human Being having a Spiritual experience, I am a Spiritual Being having a Human experience."

And right there, my mystical experience deepened. Feet planted on wet sidewalk beside rain puddles, eyes staring into the tapestry in wonder like it was a portal reaching into the unknown.

I have had many mystical and kundalini life force experiences since then.

Including the experience of a thousand petal Lotus flowering at the top of my head and crown, as I emerged a flower opening under sunlight ray's. I felt sunlight all around me, coming down on me and bathing me to my roots. And I sat there blooming, enlightened.

I also once had my entire bodymind start to seizure while sleeping, only to merge with the sound of the OM that I tuned into there, unconsciously.

Jennifer Lin Phillips

I was able to tune into the OM vibration through the art of practicing my mantra. Grabbing onto the resonating OM, flooded my being with golden light. And I was turned into a vessel of universal bliss and golden liquid love energy.

I remember feeling that this energy is everywhere, and we can access it at any time. We just haven't found the awareness or accessed the tools within us to do so. That experience happened to me while I was completely sober, after falling asleep one day after caring deeply and selflessly for the elderly. I was around 28 years old.

This shifted me profoundly. I believe that I still carry this unconditional golden liquid love within me and can truly help activate those who are ready, open and aware. I also believe that because I have had these experiences that some people naturally feel the mana emanate from me, and therefore trust my sincerity.

One of my favorite Gurus of mantra and meditation lives in India. Her name is Gurumayi and she is followed by many. She describes this kind of experience as "grace", or "Shaktipat." When the disciple is ready and deserving, grace will shower its power over you. Sometimes at night before bed, I simply ask spirit to show me something new with humbleness and sincerity, and often times I will have some kind of kundalini experience or healing release in my dream.

After meditating on the energy in space for about one year, a pink orb, about to burst with incredible power visited me one night. I could feel it just along the right side of my bed. I was surprised by the visit and did my research but couldn't find anything. The following week I discovered from one of the groups I follow on Facebook, The Resonance Project, that these scientist's in Mexico are discovering and harnessing free unlimited energy in outer space.

Ha! About three years ago this all transpired. A pinkish ball of that energy visited me by my bedside, or perhaps through my meditations I had pulled a little piece of it down to me. It was a supercharged ball of energy, and I remember describing it to many of my peers as a force like hundreds of thousands of orgasms, all ready to explode.

But the energy was somehow contained in this orb, letting me know it existed, something great and powerful like that existed somewhere. Free super charged energy. Clean energy, so full of power, ready to assist us, human kind, in our transformation into cleaner beings. Not harming the planet and destroying its purity anymore and contributing to the extinction of many of the animals trying to live, survive and thrive alongside of us.

And why aren't these things a major priority on the planet? In government? Why has the entertainment Industry capitalized on human evolution? People would rather be dumbed down to their own power. They would rather live through some star, some fantasy of success rather than perhaps discover and be a part of something truly fascinating. We are powerful beings.... we just need to clean up the shit we keep dumping everywhere.

I smell money, greed. Dirty money. Germs are everywhere on that dollar bill, ewe, just eeewww. But we all want it and need it. What's wrong with this system that goes against nature? What is wrong with us for not rising above it, and why have we been continually blindsided and lied to?

Every year, I keep learning. It is somehow natural as I am drawn to the next subject of interest, looking for clues or my next healing.

While writing this book about my travels, I was revisiting the experience that I had over on Kauai with the crystals during the course as well as the revelations about the insects. Through my own work on my body, I have found some yoga poses to be deeply replenishing that resemble some of the postures that insects make, even with their hands in prayer often.

Sovereignty and the Goddess

Their bodies are so perfectly balanced, left and right side, brains in full alignment. I felt often, that these poses align both sides of my brain, and I would practice my mantra or hold a crystal or place them around me as I went deeper into the poses I was learning intuitively.

Yesterday morning, after allowing the energy from the insects back into my awareness, a beautiful blue fairylike being with wings was swooping near me in my morning shower. A surprise visit from this being delighted me, and I thought perhaps she had streamed down from the water to make herself known. Being that blue is often associated with water and I was bathing there before her.

What an honor, I thought, to have her say hello to me. And I went about soaping my body and relishing in the warmth from the flowing water. I knew that this fairy being presented herself to me because of the expansion in my consciousness and by acknowledging and remembering her kingdom. She was there to tell me that I was onto something and to keep seeking and believing in the mysterious kingdom of the insects and these winged, delicate beings.

Last night I did a search on google images for pictures of the fascinating insects and was soaking up their

Jennifer Lin Phillips

incredible shapes and colors, their big bright eyes and the iridescent waves of light that shines off them. Especially the gaps in the weavings of their wings, they capture then reflect very colorful light prisms As I crawled into bed to rest from my day, the colors and shapes of their wings were all around me.

They were covering my walls and ceiling and covering me like an intricate blanket.

I was lying beneath my velvet purple throw, and yet also being blanketed and protected by their majesty. What a source for healing and transformation I admitted to myself. And then suddenly the thick, dense, rainy and covered in heavy medal walls of conditioning started to weaken their grip on me. The same old music streamed to us, the pop culture, the television, the media. Each signaling to us what to feel and how to think.

Not that pop music and culture is bad, it's great in ways, it really is. The capacity for human emotion, the ability to dance, move and express is amazing. But in seeking healing and balance, another un-folding and discovery was changing me. And changing my cellular memory.

Those beautiful divine insects. Those wings. What majesty and exquisite beauty. Are they really speaking to me? Can their wings really protect me?

I was so thankful for this new discovery of mine and

knew that this year would be about regaining again that connection to the innocence and beauty of such a divine kingdom. Just adding more tools in my toolbox, each year.

New healing tools for me to turn to and absorb their energy from, after the conditioning of society is too much to handle and makes one sick. Beaten down, like so many of my friends, peers, and family members at times.

Trying to find a way to cope. To rise. To heal. These delicate winged beings, how light, how glorious and colorful they are.

I turn to the crystals, sound therapy, touch, yoga, mantra, travel, space energy, movement and dance, nature, animals, the herbs and mushroom kingdom and now the mysterious world of the insects. I am curious too, just what else they will show me.

After returning from the short and challenging trip to Kauai that January 2013, I began working hard again and meeting new clients. We got a big snow that year in the city which is rare, and it lasted nearly ten days on the ground before melting.

I watched the people playing on sleds in the grass just

Jennifer Lin Phillips

off the black bars of my patio. I still tried to go jogging in the mornings, which was amazingly fresh, so fresh and cold in my lungs that the air nearly hurt to breathe it in too much.

It took another few weeks for the hives around my eyes to go away, but after only three months after they appeared, they were completely gone. I knew it had to be all the juicing and enema's I had been doing to cleanse my lymph and my bloodstream.

Whew! What a relief to be on the road to healing yet again.

I was still learning what kinds of things would speed up my recovery and help with the positive bacteria in my body as well as being anti-fungal. I began taking a Medicinal Mushroom tea and tincture known as Chaga. I was happy with the positive effects on my energy level and was able to see more clients too with the increased energy.

I ordered my own dried Chaga from a distributor in Alaska and began making my own herbal tinctures with organic vodka and purified water. I would place my crystals on the jars and sing and do my mantra while the alcohol absorbed the properties of the mushrooms for 30 days. It was exciting to be learning so much and making my very own medicine for myself to take, enhanced with my own intentions and song placed within it.

I ordered small 1 and 2 oz bottles and began working on bottling the Chaga tincture once finished.

I could sell them and start my own business maybe.

I hardly doubt anyone charges their medicine with mantra, crystals and love. And the powers of the mushroom kingdom are still just being discovered by people. I was positive that the Chaga would move towards the right people, and it totally did.

Over the following few years I sold, did trade for and gave away maybe 200 bottles.

The potent medicine kept me well during the cold months and so many of my friends told me of the amazing benefits that they had experienced. The Chaga is an adaptogenic herb, which means that it assists your own body with adapting to the stresses in your life, whatever they may be. The benefits that people had told me they experienced after taking the medicine were all very different according to their individual needs at the time.

I began hiking up Mt. Hood and staying at my friend's cabin on Trillium Lake. One of my dear friend's and owner of the community spa in town allowed me to use his cabin when it was free. That summer he took

Jennifer Lin Phillips

me on some incredible hikes up Mt. Hood National Forest, and I even walked along the Pacific Crest Trail at times.

I was chillin' up at the cabin by myself one weekend, with the little dog I had rescued and named Walnut.

I was totally binging on YouTube video's about mushrooms and the power's they have and even the complexity of the mycelium, which is the roots of the mushrooms.

I happened to be binging on Paul Stamet's video's, the well-known mushroom King, and found him to be an inspiring teacher and speaker. I have enjoyed many of his talks on the fascinating kingdom of fungi. The mycelium, or roots of the mushroom, is one layer thick, and can cover an entire forest floor, unbroken.

On pondering the symbolism in that finding, later that night before falling asleep in bed, I realized something cool. The mycelium seemed to me, so very similar to the web of relations that humans have, like as in what the flower of life symbol represents. Even if a relationship has a weak root, a stronger root will branch out somewhere along the web to insure its nourishment and survival.

And so, the web carries on, forming new bonds intricately, and either deepening or weakening old bonds. One layer thick, unbroken.

Earlier that day, I had been out doing some mushroom hunting and found all kinds of beautiful varieties. In observing them grow, the mushrooms nearly floated from the ground upward, and the way they grew on trees was also intriguing.

Three or four or many more all clumped together, resembling shooting stars that had fallen there together.

That peaceful night on the mountain, before drifting off to sleep, the mycelium and web of roots beneath the forest floor spoke to me in silence. The cells of my body merged with the cells of the mycelium, and the unbroken web of streaming life force was moving through me and speaking to me.

It honestly felt like a river of an unbroken web of connected and healthy mushroom cells, was moving through me and talking to each of my cells, trying to harmonize with them and in turn teach them. The web was trying to heal my very own cells in my body and mind. I just allowed it to happen and was feeling so thankful and grateful for yet another gift from Goddess, from the mushrooms, and from grace.

I was literally delighted after the exchange, and thanked them, the mushroom kingdom, for blessing me with their knowing. Then I drifted off to sleep under the shadows of tall Ponderosa Pine trees. The fragrant patches of light green moss, and the soft

Jennifer Lin Phillips

sound coming from the creek flowing just outside the upper bedroom balcony.

And yet, another truth had been revealed to me.

Chapter 23: Pipi

I had made it through the winter. With the explosion of cherry blossom trees and piles of pink, wispy pedals lining the dark and heavy roots of trees, I knew that Spring was here.

I loved the colors in April, the yellows and pinks, the lilac, the eggplant and plum shades of purple. By May, while the rains are still pouring down hard, those few bright sunny days, call in the memory of summer.
The flower's in Oregon are truly a remarkable show. I was looking forward to exploring the varietals of roses at the Portland Rose Garden come summer.

Hot Cocoa had been a favorite varietal of mine one year prior, with chocolatey rose-pink pedals and a faint rosy, airy smell. I found it interesting that the roses that were incredible to look at, didn't have much smell to them. While the ones that were nice but not crazy fancy as for appearance, those ones tended to have the most exhilarating smells.

I compared my discovery to that of people and thought perhaps my findings could be true for them as well. Just because one may exude an outer beauty, does not mean that their inner world is rich, sensuous, and tasty. Some of those bruises and bangs we get along the way, make for juicier experiences, perhaps

Jennifer Lin Phillips

intoxicating character and a natural wisdom.

By May, I had a few reliable clients that would come by to see me.

One of my clients, Philip, was in his early 60's, and Mexican. He was tall, with an intriguing and bright smile. His humor was refreshing, and his love for the arts and music was stimulating to be around. He also had some of the best stories to tell.

"Hey Pipi, nice to see you!!" Philip said to me as I opened the front door of my apartment.

He was right on time for his two-hour session with me.

"Hello there Philip, please come in." I gestured kindly back to him.

What a smile he had. And laugh.

I think I made him laugh just by being me. Kind of naive, heart worn on my sleeve at times. And me, with my trusting and vulnerable nature. Even after everything I had been through. I guess one could say I was bullet proof. How I managed to get back up after every blow. And somehow, I didn't lose my innocence. I still allowed myself to be surprised by life.

However, my warrior's protective shield and boxing gloves were on and ready for the next predator or challenging situation. I was not going to allow myself to become a complete mess or sandbag in life. I had learned a bit through my victories and failure's, but yes, I still was learning.

As for some thing's I just had to learn by going through the experience.

Feeling like I was practically an orphan in my family most of my life, only pushed me in the direction of becoming more unique. More me, more different.

It is kind of funny now, looking back. I swear to you, I thought that I was an orphan when I was a very young girl. Some of those vulnerabilities, the confusion of not belonging in some ways still show up in my life.

Motherless, the different one. With little emotional support from my father.

It's true, when I was younger, I would tell my sister's, how I didn't think it was fair that Mom always told the babysitter to watch me?! How could she? I thought back then.

"See, I would tell them. I am an orphan. And I look like you guys, (talking to my sister's), because Mom and Dad took me to the orphanage one day. A little while later, they decided they wanted another child. They went back to the same orphanage and you know what, they accidentally picked me back up again. Can you believe that?!" I would say to them.

"They treat me different and it's not fair."

Jennifer Lin Phillips

I know I pushed my parents to the edge sometimes. I had a very curious spirit and wood often do things just to see what would happen. Like when I learned the word Jerk.

"Mom is a jerk, Annie." I said to her in the garage one day. I said it just to say the new word I had learned. I know a lot of kids do these kinds of things. Just to see what happens. Just to see if it really is a bad word.

Or, the time we were in the hot tub, my little sister and me. And the water was hot. I thought it would be interesting to get hot water from the sink also and compare the temperatures. Pouring it on my little sister's head was probably not the best way to go about testing that, but I had no idea it would hurt her.

You see common sense at a young age, can be hard to come by.

Honestly, I felt on my own at a young age, and I was afraid of my parents often. With the amount of arguing, and yelling and some physical abuse, I was very much confused as a girl.

My mother used to rush in, in the middle of the night crying and would put me and my sister's in the middle of the argument she was having with my father. And twice, I remember answering the front door of our home to see a policeman on the other side. The abuse between my parents was vicious and the abuse my sister's and I faced from both of them was harsh as well.

It was a lot for a little girl to deal with.

I still somehow did well in school, I had a ton of friends also and excelled in team sports. My parents although struggling were also amazing people, I loved my mother dearly, so much I would kiss her bare feet before going to bed sometimes and tell her about the castles I would buy for her once I could.

I honestly thought that she was the most beautiful woman in the entire world, and I would wonder if my friend's thought the same about their mother's. My dad happened to be my biggest support in the sports I played, and he was even my coach during elementary school basketball.

I can't imagine the kind of stresses my parents were under, but I wanted to help when I could. I even remember counseling both of my parents one day, standing by the screen door of our back patio around eight years old. Telling them that it was okay for them to get a divorce if they needed to.

I knew that I feared them however, underneath it all. Wondering, waiting for just what kind of situation they were going to put me and my sister's in.

So, in defense to the feeling's I had, I learned to create stories in my head. They are talking to the alien's and I cannot trust them, I would think.

Jennifer Lin Phillips

One night I was so afraid to go to sleep after watching an Asian fighting movie. Those star spears that they throw at their enemy. I thought for certain, my mom and dad would come in with a few, and spear me right there in my bed, some nights. How could I fall asleep? I would stay up, blanket held in tight, waiting, listening.

I'm sure I dozed off drooling in no time, pink blanket held tight in hand.

Philip was refreshing and intelligent.

He always had something new to share with me, and he often brought me gifts.

Maybe some fresh fruit from the Hillsboro farmer's market.

On one of his sessions with me, he brought me some long winter knee-high socks, a cute t-shirt, and a flavored liquor alcohol, I think it was called Vermouth. It was very warming and had a cinnamon spice flavor. He brought me three short story books too one day.

One of the books was about Pipi Long stocking. The young orphaned, independent, redheaded girl that I read about and watched the movie when I was a child. Everyone knew about Pipi and the house she lived in, out in the woods, alone.

The weird foods she would bake, and the animals that

lived with her. She even wore knee high socks, with a gap tooth grin like me I believe. She had an incredible imagination, and was happy on her own, living in the world of her own spectacular and creative desires.

It cracked me up when Philip began referring to me as Pipi. When he called me, he would say, "Hello Pipi, how are you?"

I think he only called me by Jennifer a few times, and it was usually the times he was scolding me or upset about something I wasn't doing or providing for him. Kind of how my family said my full name in that; you know you are in deep trouble tone "Jennifer."

The other two books that Philip brought to me was Pele, the book of the Hawaiian Volcano Goddess. The book told the story of Pele, her relationships with men and her sister's, and how she had created the land. I loved the part in the book when Pele beat 'Aila'au, which means forest-eater.

He was a fire God living on Kilauea, and he burned everything he touched. The two fire God's threw fireballs at one another, shaking the earth abruptly. And eventually the land became quiet again, because Pele had defeated him.

The final book was about a little white Scottie dog named Jennie, even spelled the same as my name, back when I went by the name Jennie.

Jennifer Lin Phillips

In the story, the dog left home on an adventure, and ended up in beautiful and strange places, sleeping in piles of leaves under Oak trees. It was a big venture for the small dog, and she got lost and came across some danger. The picture of the dog with her briefcase made me laugh. The story was adorable and short, and talked about how the little white dog named Jennie had built up much strength from her exploration of the unknown, but that the adventure had also made her appreciate the comforts of home even more.

Philip and I would talk for hours. His sessions were long, but we would go on and on about some exquisite memory he had, the updates on his family and how each of them is doing. Or a perhaps a music event he was interested in going to near town.

He was incredibly romantic and sensual, and he loved talking about the experiences he had throughout his life with different women. Not only the sexual side of these experiences, but how he felt emotionally before, during and after they had ended. He spoke of his marriage. How the relationship had changed over many, many years of being together, ending in a separation. And what to do next?

He would sit on the massage table with his hand under his ear lying sideways, and I would rub him down with oil and chat away with him. Some days, we had a few shots of the flavored liquor and I would bum a smoke or two off him.

The relationship was sincere and loving, and although yes you could say he had his own agenda. He was still respectful of me. Sometimes, he would plan for something sexy to happen between us. To see if it unfolded that way. And yes, me with my naivety, he caught me a few times, stunned.

"Try on the stocking's I got for you Pipi, I bet they are darling on you." He said after bringing me the gift one day.

"Well, they are pretty fun," I said back to him. "Okay give me a second."

I would play his game a little. It could be a little amusing, I thought, and I went into the other room to change. I wasn't that much of a modest person when it came to my body and being naked. I had been to many hot springs, spa's and even lived on an organic farm, where people walked around half naked in sarongs.

But this was different. And I knew the difference. I needed to be careful and keep my boundaries firm around men and the clients I was making, I confirmed to myself. But his gift surprised me, and I wanted to be a part of the fun a little, and not be a complete stiff either.

Jennifer Lin Phillips

I came back out in the t-shirt and stalking's he had bought for me, daringly, not knowing what to expect, but still aware of my boundaries. Guard up.

"Ohhhh, I love them on you. So cute. And you will have something to remember me by when I am away, and you are all warm over here." He grinned at me.

He had a charm that you can't really explain. His timing and humor, his laugh and gesture's, the way he shrugged his shoulders sometimes admitting half guilt, half innocence. How could you blame him, he would look at you with intrigue?

We took a shot of the Vermouth and he asked me to sit on the chair next to the table, so he could take my picture in my new outfit.

I crossed the room feeling warm from the heater putting out air, and the shot I had just taken. I went to sit on the chair, tossed my hair over my shoulder and smiled over to him.

He took a few photos of me and went to put his phone down. I sat there and peeked out of the window at yet another grey Portland day. At least it isn't raining, I thought to myself, and he walked over to kneel beside me.

He then put his hands on both of my legs, and he just looked up at me intently. I was wondering what his next move would be, so I stared at him with question, a little sternness in my eyes and watched him. He lifted my shirt up a little to expose my pantie's. With his hands now, he opened my legs softly.

I was still watching him. He then leaned over with his head and mouth and blew a few teasing breaths on the outside of my underwear there.

I laughed and pushed him away at his shoulders. I was shocked at his sly behavior, but because of our bond, I was also a little entertained by him. Embarrassed.

He knew that I wasn't interested in a romance with him, although we loved flirting with each other. I didn't want the situation to go any further, but his demeanor and charm had gotten to me a little.

I laughed at him again in disbelief and I was coming out of the feeling of slight eroticism and surprise that his gesture had left me in.

His pursed lips, blowing his soft breath between my legs. I think he could read it in my eyes that I was reaching my limit with our session, and he got up and dressed to go home. We said farewell that day, both slightly shocked and blushing quite a bit at the scene replaying in my mind and his, that had just taken place moments before.

The relationship with Philip continued to deepen. By the time my lease was ending, he was the first to volunteer his services to help me out of my apartment.

Jennifer Lin Phillips

I had just bought a new car and was not sure where I wanted to travel to next or how. I had my little dog, Walnut, whom I adored. He was by far the cutest and most loving dog I had ever had, a Mini Pinscher and Chihuahua mix.

Philip had offered to let me stay with him at his apartment until I found the direction, I wanted to head in. He had a spare bedroom and would make room for my company he told me.

I also had the ability to go up to Mt. Hood to stay some nights up at my friend's cabin, and soak in his outdoor custom-built cedar sauna, that sat beneath elegant towering pine trees. Between the two places, I felt that I had a few options for myself at least. Although the situation left me feeling uneasy and slightly awkward by not being in my own comfortable and protective space.

I just needed a bit more time to find my direction again and gain more clarity as to where my life was heading.

After a few weeks hopping between the mountain, the blue cold lakes of Mt. Hood National Forest and Philip's place, I planned a road trip with my dog Walnut.

We would travel back to Northern California to see if I

wanted to live there again, and we could round back up through the Mt. Shasta area and see the lake during the summertime.

Walnut and I prepared for our trip, I purchased camping gear and a little grill. I still had a little money saved from not paying rent for one full month. I packed my car up with gear, and me and my cute little Walnut, set upright and ready in the front seat by me, set out for our summer adventure together.

We took the windy and elegant HWY 101 along the Oregon Coast and slept next to a lagoon in the woods our first night. We drove maybe five hours and made it to the perfect camping spot. The nights were getting much cooler, being mostly past the hot summer days and into early September.

By the second day, we had reached the town I had once lived in, in the northern parts of California. Monte Rio and Guerneville. I had called my friend Ed along the way, and Rachel was also in the area not too far from where I was.

Ed was an old neighbor of mine. He was in his 80's and lived alone. He had an extra bedroom and I was hoping he would be happy to have me visit for a few days. We always had a wonderful time together. I remember he would call me by the name Redbird, and then he would point them out perched on apple trees in his flowering and colorful side yard.

Jennifer Lin Phillips

We had managed to keep in touch through email for maybe four years.

Back when I lived in Cali, I would go over to his place and we would go walking with our dogs underneath the cold shade of the tall, thick redwood trees. Gosh the air could chill your whole body, under the long shadows those trees created most days. It would be nearly impossible to warm up somedays. Often, Ed and I would go for some spicy lunch together and traditional chai tea with cream and honey at the Indian restaurant just down the hill from the beach. Or maybe we would spend some time shooting arrows at the target in his yard next to the T-Pee he built. Dead center. I hit that target dead center my first try one time. Sure shocked the crap out of the both of us that day!

He called me back from his phone, and he invited me to visit. I stayed a few days, and we took a trip to the beach again with our dogs.

The colors over the water while the sun was setting were beautiful that summer, and every summer. Warm pinks and yellows, vibrant creamy oranges dazzling over the ripples of water making waves.

My intentions in making the trip, were to try to get a feel for the area again. To see if it was a place I wanted to move back to.

I attempted to see Rachel, from Kauai. But she was

leaving on a trip out of state, and the timing unfortunately was off this time.

My little baby Walnut and I did another day of camping at the park over at Armstrong Woods. That place was insanely beautiful. Besides the group of pesky crows who wanted to devour the food Walnut and I had, the experience up there was quiet and peaceful.

I decided that I still loved the area, that was a certainty. But I had this feeling that I wasn't done exploring. I didn't want to settle down and move to the redwoods again, or just yet.

With as dirty and rugged the trip had been already, I couldn't stop thinking about the breezes and comfort of my second home, the islands. I hadn't been in the warm ocean water in so long. Well, it had been only under a year, maybe eight months, but it felt like an eternity, it really did.

Although I had been swimming in the freezing, icy cold lakes that were filled by melted mountain snow most the summer, my spirit was craving the sand and warmth of the ocean to bathe my ever changing and aching, yet youthful body in.

Walnut and I said our goodbye's to Captain Ed and began heading up back North. Eddy was given his name from when he was a Captain in the Navy and

Jennifer Lin Phillips

sailed boats in the open seas. How perfect for him to have a house in the redwoods just a few miles from that raging sea.

Walnut and I drove by vineyard after vineyard in the back country of Northern Cali. The area was unbelievably gorgeous, and it seemed like the vines and leaves would be turning color soon.

We were on our way. Headed up to Mt. Shasta area.

The lake was barely noticeable when we got there. With the amount of forest fires in the area, we were also facing a drought that year. It was too bad for me, I had not been swimming in that lake ever. I sure hadn't the memory of ever swimming there. Instead of camping and swimming, I continued my drive-up North. I thought we could sleep in a hotel and wash up in Ashland. The cute town I had once gone to college in.

Wrapping around a curve in the road, I turned on my blinker to pass a car beside me. Yes, I admit, there was a line of cars, one on top of the other, on the two-lane highway.

An SUV behind me, instantly siren's go on. What? An undercover cop is pulling me over for that little move?

People slightly cut one another off all the time, is that really a crime?

I could tell the officer was having a bad day, and when he came to ask for my license and registration, he could tell that I was running out of steam, dirty and ready to be somewhere still.

Yes, he was annoyed at getting cut off a little, but thankfully, he decided to let me go. I got a lecture about my careless driving. Although I had plenty of time to use my blinker and switch lanes.

I thanked him and was back on the road again, ticket free.

Woo-hoo.

I arrived safely in Ashland, incredibly fatigued from the long journey and tired.

My road trip would be coming to an end in the next day or so. My week-long road trip with one of the best travelling partners' I have had since then, loyal and loving Walnut.

We slept in a cheap, vintage hotel on main street that night, where street lights and head lights from cars turning swiftly around the corner peered in half the night.

The shower I had after unloading a few bags from my car was like streams of liquid heaven pouring on my wore out skin. I washed away the miles of travel, the

Jennifer Lin Phillips

dirt, and the toxic air from the highway off my skin and from the passages of my lungs.

I phoned Philip to tell him that I would be back in another day or two. I then snuggled up contently next to my four-legged little baby and fell asleep exhausted and thankful to not be feeling too icky and discouraged from the long, lone, full circle, highway journey.

Chapter 24: Andara's

I had only stayed in Oregon at my friend Philip's maybe another ten days. I was getting the urge to go. And feeling claustrophobic at his small two-bedroom apartment again. The weather was turning its usual shade of grey again too, now heading rapidly into the fall season in the Pacific NW.

I took Walnut up to Mt. Hood where he would be watched by a mutual friend in a cabin next to my friend's cabin on Trillium Lake. The fellow had a few dogs of his own. Including another female doggie, the same mix as my Walnut, Mini Pinscher and Chihuahua.

She was nowhere near as cute as my Wally, and she barked a lot at people. She was a very grumpy girl and untrusting of everyone around her. I can't remember now what her name was, but I think it was something snooty and edgy. She wore a scarf often and oh yes! Her name was Chihuahua, little Chihuahua girl, that's right! Ha.

I boarded the plane for Maui, and after much inner debate as to which island to venture to, Maui won the draw. I had not returned to Maui in about thirteen years. Not since my very first voyage over in my early twenties when I had lived in Hana and worked at the Hana Ranch Restaurant for a few months.

Jennifer Lin Phillips

I had arranged a room for myself in Kihei. Just up the hill from Kam 2, a very well-known beach in Kihei. The area was very active, the beaches Kam 1, 2, and 3 all lined along the main road and Highway, running through downtown.

There were many hotels, and condos along those beaches, but it was still very much a neighborly place to stay.

I was renting the room in a one-bedroom apartment from a lady in her mid-sixties named Skye.

She was very sweet, had much spiritual interest, and even sold crystals and Tibetan flags online mostly. She could play the Ukulele well too, and she tried to teach me a few times when she had the time and the patience for it. The Ukulele is not an easy instrument to learn, much, much harder than it appears. Your finger's need to be held in so tightly together while strumming, since the instrument is quite small.

After a few attempts at playing, I gave up quickly. I just couldn't quite pick up the art of playing all that well. And my fingers didn't like cramming in together like that.

Skye would be on the computer most of the day, working on emails, or learning something new. Usually of spiritual interest and inspiring for her mind.

On the day's we spent together, we would walk to the

health food store or to the beach for a swim. I enjoyed her company, and we had many wonderful conversations and even meditated together a few times. If my memory serves me right, we engaged in a few days of the Oprah and Deepak Chopra Meditations together, during one of their 21-Day Meditation Challenges.

She was very accommodating also, and allowed me to practice my healing therapies in the room I was staying in. At night, I would fall asleep in the main bedroom, and she would curl up on the futon in the small front room with a blanket, across from her well used computer and sleep.

Now being that I was on foot, I made some friend's quite easy.

One was an artist and painter, named Michael. His small, white truck had at least a hundred artsy, vintage magnets all inside the doors and the ceiling of the truck. We would meet for lunch or go to the organic market together sometimes. One night, we were drinking red wine on some hotel lounge chairs out on the grass, oceanside, watching the sun go down.

We spotted some of the migrating whales passing by out in the distance that night. It had been some time since I had seen the whales migrating and swimming. Not since my initial visit to Maui up in Hana. We

Jennifer Lin Phillips

watched them swim, leaping into the air, bodies splashing so hard against water. What an exceptional experience admiring them, a miracle it felt like. Catching a glimpse of them right there was pure magic.

Michael and I sought out some of the local art on the island too at times. Stopping in to a few galleries to view the latest island artist's work whom lived on island, or perhaps one of the other islands.

Michael was a painter too.

He gave me a small piece once, blue and red colors mostly, painted in thick paint. A few millimeter's thick coming off the small square panel, organic and abstract. I liked his work.

One day we watched one of the fieriest orange sunsets past the white sands of the wide and popular beach that we were on. The sky literally looked like it was set on fire that day. It roared with color coming off white and grey clouds.

We had planned a picnic that day. And indulged in some of the best swimming on the island there on that beach. The break of each wave seemed timed out just perfectly for floating and the waters were deep and clear.

Another friend I made on island was a lifeguard from

Brazil. He worked on one of the three beaches in my neighborhood in Kihei. Either Kam 1, 2, or 3, depending on his shift that day. He would watch me run, stretch, and prance along the beachfront, if he happened to be there on site when I was working out.

That's how we met.

I was running. He was watching from his lifeguard stand. I imagine he had met a lot of ladies that way. But I didn't care. He was outgoing, seemed harmless and held a sweet demeanor.

And soon after meeting, we were practicing and exchanging massages on the beaches somedays. Then we would end the treatments with some swimming together. With him being a lot stronger than me and being the gentleman that he was, he would carry my table down to the shoreline for our exchange.

We found the beach to be such a relaxing place for touch and therapy, with the charged ions floating by, and the soothing sounds of waves crashing upon waves, along the sandy shoreline.

I loved his foreign accent too. We had some great talks about relationships and living on island.

I remember an intense energetic exchange with him, sand all over me and wet from my swim, sun beaming down at me across the water, lighting up my freckled skin. The wind picked up through us, and we smiled

Jennifer Lin Phillips

and shared friendly glances towards one another. It could be so easy, to experience the feelings of pure love and beauty while on the beach some days.

And we shared a moment of that purity right there together one day on Kam 3, by the big black rocks with holes in them and fresh salt water pools.

I attended some yoga classes at a hotel just off the beach with Skye and met some more friends that way too. It was so nice being on island, and even without a vehicle, I was able to get into the local scene quickly with the friends that I was making.

I went to a healing circle with a nice group, where my sexual abuse was finally verified.

That was relieving for me, and Skye and I reflected together on the circle that night, and about the Cellular Regeneration Technique and its accuracy somehow.

I created many crystalline grids on Skye's patio there where I was staying.

She let me use her crystals for many of my grids and for casting out prayers set with my intentions.

I was eating so fresh, taking the bus to the markets, and marching up the long hill with bags of produce and purified water in my arms a few times per week. I was feeling amazing. Free, energized, strong, inspired. My flow was soothing. Just me, the warmth of the island,

and my intimate flow with spirit.

One challenging event that happened over my three-month trip is hard to forget. I was having a difficult time with the neighbors there living at the house right in front of ours. They were related to the owners of the small condo Skye had been renting for a few years.

The actual owners were in the top of the house, and a small family lived below. The owners above was an elderly couple. Below, was their daughter, her husband, and their two kids. Every night the father would jam his music so loud that literally my bedroom would pound and shake.

That was so irritating to me and I couldn't believe how rude he was to do such a thing every single night.

He would come home from work, turn on his music, start drinking, and then some fights would break out some nights between him and his wife.

I just couldn't believe he would do that to his parent's in law upstairs either. He wasn't even paying them rent, Skye told me.

He was surely paying them back with his attitude, behavior and complete disregard for their peace of mind. One of the elder's was even going through dementia. I just could not imagine what that felt like

Jennifer Lin Phillips

trying to live and function above all that fuss, loud ass noise and aggression. I could barely stand being next door to it. My entire nervous system was starting to feel shaky, intimidated and disturbed.

This had been going on for the two months that I had already been on island.

Finally, I had decided I was done with his complete lack of consideration and the amount of noise he was inflicting on everyone in the near vicinity. What an inconsiderate asshole. I marched over and knocked on the door.

The Hawaiian gentleman answered curiously.

"Hi. Good Evening. Can I ask you to please turn your music down? The noise is pounding loud in my place and it is pretty disturbing to the peace in the area." I said to him slightly annoyed.

"Hmmmpphh....excuse me? You want me to turn down my music?" He retorted, half-drunk towards me.

"Uuumm yes, if you could please do that, it is actually too loud." I replied back to him, sensing I was going to get yet another defensive response.

"Well, actually no, I won't turn it down, you Haole girl visiting from the mainland, telling me what to do?!"

"Ha!" I burst out in surprise at his attack on me.

"You jam out your parent's above you. And you sit around bickering at your wife in between pounding beers. You are no Hawaiian man, and in fact any intelligent and normal Hawaiian would be embarrassed that you were a part of their culture. Respectful Hawaiians don't act this way!" And I turned and walked away quickly up the stairs back to Skye's across from his front door. Thinking he may throw a beer can at me.

I was frazzled.

But I felt good about my strength to finally stand up to this man. No one else was going to. They would just let him walk around like that belligerent and aggressive.

Well, I decided enough was e-nuffff. And If I learned anything from my hard childhood it was to stand up for myself. To not care too much about what other people think. If it is possible, I stand up for what is right and for what is just.

Uh oh………Oh, man, he let me have it after that.

Threatening attacks were being yelled towards me through the screen of his house. I had no choice but to call the police.

The police showed up and they talked with him. They were compassionate to him really, I think because he was Hawaiian. Then they came in and asked me about my situation.

Jennifer Lin Phillips

After they left, they told him to turn the music down and that he was disturbing the peace. They asked him to apologize to me for his threats towards me. After they left, he did come over the next day to apologize.

His music stayed at a comfortable level for the three more weeks I was on island, and honestly his moods really changed. I think he needed someone to be a real witness to his suffering. I was, and I wasn't going to let it continue like that, poisoning everyone else around him.

He even started singing sweetly out loud at nights, and I know his parent's in law up above were thankful for the change in his energy and behavior. His wife still kept her distance from me but smiled a little relief towards me some days. I can't say if his attitude and better nature extended much longer after I left Skye's place and the island.

Chances are, he went back to being the person he was when we had that first encounter. People like that don't just change. They need therapy, and counseling. And they need to quit drinking for a long, long time, if not for eternity.

Skye had collected some fascinating crystals. My favorite were the Andara's that she had in her selection. They were glass crystals from around the time period 11,000-14,000 BC. They had been collected near Mt. Shasta area, which I found to be ironic that I was purchasing them all the way over on Maui, when I was so close to the area back home in Oregon.

I bought four of the Andara's, and the turquoise blue one I use today in many of my grids, has a beautiful transparent rainbow in it. The blue Andara is my very favorite, because to me it represents all the water on the planet. And when I use it for my latest intentions, I remember that, and try to invoke the flow from the bodies of water on the planet in my offering and in my prayer's. I invoke the water surging through me, cleansing my body and cells.

I ask often too, that all the water on the planet are cleansed and nourished and washed over with rainwater, to purify them for all of humanity. And for the animals and insects to feel the fresh cleansing also.

I celebrated my 36th Birthday on the islands, and I was thankful to have the majesty of the ocean to swim in and breathe next to for my very special day.

Philip, my friend in Oregon sent me two eye dazzling and incredibly fragrant bouquets of flowers.

The card on one of them read;

"You been selected as the Best Unicorn on the Maui.

Jennifer Lin Phillips

LOL."

Oh, he was so clever really. Showing his natural charm with good timing, delighting me for my Birthday. I read the card revealing a satisfying smirk on my face.

One could assume that he was missing me a lot, and even though he was frustrated by our friendship, he still showered me with his love. I think you can tell by now, that Philip had a crush on me and in some ways wanted our friendship to turn into his fantasies.

I did love his thoughtfulness about my Birthday, that warmed me, especially being away from all my friends and family that year. The bouquets were so pretty, and they brightened up the cozy space that Skye and I had been sharing for a few months.

I met Maya when I was out on a run one morning. He was a stand-up paddle instructor just down by the mall at a hotel in Wailea.

I would run the sidewalk that lined the ocean front condo's and hotels. I could run along the winding sidewalk for hours some days, feeling the breeze from the ocean nearby, and watching the hundreds of tourist's playing in the sands with their kids, either jogging themselves or taking pictures of one another by the ocean.

The area was very energetic, and I would beam and smile at everyone as I jogged by, getting super high on the vibe.

I was a little out of breath and had just made my way around the elegant church with stained glass windows revealing beautiful Hawaiian people in long gowns carved in color in the stained glass all around the building.

The church was surrounded by water, lotus flowers, koi fish, rocks and tropical plants. It was captivating me. I believe the building was one of the oldest churches in the area. And the water from the creek nearby rushed all around the intricate building.

I was done admiring the church and back on the sidewalk, after my little rest and discovery. I was gearing up to run back towards Kihei, when I passed by a young man standing at a kiosk.

"Hey, how are you? Would you like to try a stand-up paddle course here at the hotel? Are you staying nearby?" A very handsome guy whom resembled the presence of a movie star said to me, with his broad and gleaming smile.

"Hi! Yes, I am nearby, renting a room in Kihei for another few weeks. I would love a class, oh my gosh, I have always wanted to try stand up paddle and never have. Is it easy? I tried surfing a few times, and that nearly killed me. I hope it's not like that." I responded

Jennifer Lin Phillips

to him.

He laughed at me a little, and I could tell he was charmed by my response and high vibe. I was having a great morning run, and I know he could sense the endorphins coming off me.

"Well, yes, it is a lot smoother than surfing. You will do great. You do yoga, right?"

"Yes, I do. I have a reasonably strong core, I think. I could probably maintain my balance once standing, as long as the waves aren't too disruptive."

I got his card and his number and reached out to him later that day. We would do a trade for services he suggested, and I felt that was a reasonably fair deal.

He even offered for me to go diving for free as well, but I don't know, all that gear on me? Yikes. Now that seems a bit much and going down so low to the darkness. And the pressure down there? The pressure I hear is hard on your lungs, maybe your ears too.

I told him no thank you, that I would be happy to give stand up paddle a good try though.

There were maybe fifteen of us doing the standup paddle that day. After a short introduction, I asked him to take my picture doing the yoga pose Natarajasana, on my stand-up paddle. I held the pose in front of the blue ocean with slight breezes brushing over each shoulder from behind me.

That is one of my favorite pictures from the islands that pops up on my FB feed from time to time.

We all got in the water smoothly with the help from the instructors and we set off, bumping up then down in the reasonably steady waves. The wind was light, and I had a natural ability on the board that day. Maya was a great instructor and everyone in the class seemed to be learning rather quickly.

We admired our surroundings and paddled for an hour or so and then we gathered together as the class was ending to chat and share our experiences. Each of us still on our boards out in the water. Maya challenged us all to one last thing. A headstand on our boards. I accepted the challenge, butt in the air, legs straight, feet flexed, stomach pulled in, and then legs went up. I had managed a headstand, and they were counting, "One-one-thousand, two-one- thousand, three -one - thousand." The water rippled a little below me just enough to knock me over sideways and into the water. My first and only flop of the day.

We paddled in and took our boards back up to the hotel where they were being stored. Maya asked me if we could schedule his session with me the following day.

Jennifer Lin Phillips

I agreed, and then I walked the winding sidewalk back to my room at the tiny condo.

Maya pulled up to my place on a pretty, jet-black, and silky Harley. He was definitely an exciting person to be around, and I was looking forward to getting to know him better. I had only ten days left on island, so we took advantage of our time together.

The session went well, and halfway through, he asked to nuzzle me on my bed.

We cuddled and talked and laughed. He talked about his Ex-girlfriend and how he was still in love with her. Our time there together was intimate and sweet. I was surprised at how much he had wanted to share with me about his love life, and I could tell his heart was still hurting.

As we were lying sideways looking at one another and talking, he skimmed his fingers up the sides of my thighs. I could sense his intrigue. He pulled my pantie's down to look a little. The energy was sexy, and really good between us.

We were both curious about one another.

He just sat there for a few minutes, maybe ten or so, just casually touching the lips around my punanae.

He touched delicately and examined and played with them. He had no intention of trying to make me climax, but he was just trying to get to know me. Doing a little examination.

I loved it.

And I felt really comforted yet aroused by his fingertips. I liked that he didn't have the goal of making me orgasm set in his mind, and that he just wanted to feel me and admire my unique femininity.

On his motorcycle, he took me on some amazing rides around the island, and we even had a few beach days together. I liked visiting him at his place down the street. He had a private room in an elegant home, with an outdoor shower area.

He was a pretty hot lover, I'm not going to lie.

I enjoyed the glass vibrator he had and had never experienced that feeling before. I could tell he liked pleasing me, and that was electrifying for me. Not to mention the incredible feeling of riding on the back of his motorcycle and eyeing him through the shades of my tinted sunglasses. Dang, what a stallion! I would think to myself while hugging my hands tightly around his manly body and chest.

I did a crystal healing on him one day. And placed all my crystals, and new Andara's on his bare chest, covering and opening his chakras. He looked so lovely

Jennifer Lin Phillips

and illuminated lying there in peace.

He drifted off to sleep and I snapped a few cute pics that I made sure to send to him later.

I had an evening flight set and Maya was the one who took me to the airport. I decided to leave my massage table with him. With all of the travelling I had done in the past few years, my table had been through a lot.

I could order another one back in Oregon online, it was time that I got a new one to use for work anyways.

He invited me out to one last dinner with him, and I chose an authentic and lively Indian restaurant. I remember him drinking a spicy warm chai, while I sipped on a glass of white wine, Pinot Gris. We held hands the entire way to the airport, me leaning over to him, resting my head on his lap and shoulders.

He dropped me off in the evening time at the airport in Kahului just a few days before Christmas. I was looking forward to heading back home to the mainland, to Oregon, as the year 2014 was ending.

"I will try to come see you in Oregon soon, "He said to me.

We kissed sweetly and reluctantly said goodbye to one another. We had created a rather special bond in the last ten days of my island venture. I thought maybe I would see him again, and for the next few months, we managed to talk and exchange photos back and forth.

He never made a trip out to see me, I never pushed his visit. It was just one of those things.

And, about a year later, he ended up leaving the island and making a big move to Las Vegas. I really had no attachment to him anyways. I wished him well and was happily settling in to life again in Oregon.

Jennifer Lin Phillips

Chapter 25: Twenty Months

Last night while skimming the newsfeed on Facebook, I came across a Ted Talk on my friend Kelly's page. Her and her family had just made a winter trip to Maui and had pictures from Hana and Haleakala Crater. I was skimming through her fabulous island family photos when I came across one of her posts about the effects of trauma from childhood.

The title "Childhood Trauma Lasts Forever" caught my attention. Dr. Nadine Burke Harris gave a short speech about the dangers of childhood trauma.

She went on to state that abuse, neglect, substance abuse, and/or domestic violence by a parent is the leading cause of disease later in life, in children that are exposed. Losing a parent at a young age was not on the list, although divorce or separation was, but I can only imagine the effects that the death of a parent, could have on a child.

She went on to say that exposure to early adversity dramatically affects health across a lifetime. It affects brain development, the immune system and hormonal systems.

Responsible for this is the Hypothalamic Pituitary Adrenal Access, the brain's and bodies stress response system that governs our fight or flight response.

There is a release of adrenaline and cortisol when your body is responding to a threat and to stress. If this system is activated continuously, the response which is supposed to assist one in defending oneself and saving one's life turns to maladaptive or health damaging. Dr. Nadine helped to create the Center for Youth Wellness in San Francisco, where doctors have a protocol to treat, prevent and heal the impact of this kind of early childhood toxic stress.

I always knew that my immune system was weak from the types of things I was exposed to as a child.

This is precisely why I chose the healing path, even to be on it alone, with no one really quite being able to understand me, my call from spirit, or the acute listening I had to my own soul's work. Last night, I had a dream about my Grandmother. I have never dreamt of her before. She passed about five years ago, and I do think of her often with sweet love in my heart for her life, the way she lived. Especially how she loved.

Last night, I awoke to her shaking me. It felt like she actually was there in my room.

Gasping for air, I awoke with an energetic shaking upon me and the air right around me. It really felt like her spirit was there, shaking me widely awake.

Jennifer Lin Phillips

In the dream, I was living out some of my current and past relationship experience's. It appeared that I was in the room at my old house, the house I slept in during High School and that my mother had died in.

My Grandmother, grabbed me in the dream, gave me my little handheld radio, funny how we used to listen to those cute things before CD's, laptops, phones, or the new boom speaker's.

I played with my radio a lot as a girl. Dancing in my room with friend's or my sister's. Preparing for the school's talent show or singing along to some pop singer from the 90's, like Bel Biv Devoe or Mary J. Blige. Me and my best friends Christina and Jill danced on stage in our elementary school gym to that one song, "That Girl is Dope," sung by Bel Biv Devoe, shocking many parents and schoolmates with our stylish and ghetto moves.

Again, in my dream, she handed me my radio, and told me to leave, insisting that I go somewhere else, and set myself free.

She was pushing me through the window in my old room with my radio in my hand now, and I could feel the screen below the open window on my arm. There was an urgency there in her tone and the way she was nudging me out the window. I resisted her, and smiled, and felt the light around me. I connected with the beaming light there, and I expanded it around her and over me too. Like a giant halo around the both of us.

I told her that I loved her. "I love you Grandma," I said as I smiled at her and expanded deeper into the light surrounding us two.

I said it again, "I Love you Grandma." And although I was trying to reassure her that I was safe, with the presence of the light around us, she started to shake me, begging me to please go.

I awoke with the feeling of love in my heart that I feel for my dear Grandmother, and I was thankful that my love for her came through me and was relayed to her in my dream. But I also awoke with a sense of serious danger. She was warning me about something, and I couldn't help but wonder if it was in fact this book.

How will my family respond to me writing about them, or our deepest secrets, our darkness? How will my friends respond to the life path that I have lived?

Will everyone turn on me, blame me, and judge me harshly?

In the study of children exposed to childhood trauma, the child exposed often acts out in high risk behavior. In reflecting on my life, this has shown to be true in many ways. I have put myself in danger many times,

Jennifer Lin Phillips

but it was my belief in the light of protection that got me through into safety.

Is writing this book yet another rebellious act? A high risk? I believe there is no doubt in my mind that it is. I am exposing my life. I am sharing my struggle, my family's struggle. The poor and good choices I have made, and my darkest secrets. Why?

My life journey has been about healing. In writing this book, I am somehow able to rise above where I currently am in my life and understand why I have chosen in the way's that I have.

Will others be able to relate to me, to my life's journey? Will my experience reach someone else? Will the magic I have known and the gifts from grace have any relevancy in another's perspective or on this planet?

The wind is blowing hard today. I know things are stirring up in my life. Why should I continue to write? Why not just go back to living? To being happy and free?

I want that so bad, I do.

I have forgiven so many wrong doings in my life and returned to the place of love and light repeatedly. But I still struggle. I struggle with direction, and another ten months in Oregon this year, has exposed to me some long, dark, and harrowing shadows.

There is still so much darkness in my family and in my relationships. There is still a lot of darkness in the world, and in how we treat one another.

I am saddened by it, really. And it feels thick here to me, just like the grey sky does often in Oregon, day in, day out.

No wonder my Grandmother told me to run. I am a free spirit, and my journey has been about newness, beauty, creativity and rising above oppression.

Yesterday, on a short video on YouTube, the fires in Ventura California are raging bad. Oregon also has faced a lot of damage too this year along the Columbia River, where 20,000 acres were burned down due to a few careless kids and some fireworks.

The fires in Cali are horrendous, and so close to Hollywood and LA. Where much of the conditioning on the planet spreads out like, what would you call it, wildfire?

Why can't people think for themselves? Hellloooo? It's called intuition.

We have these incredible bodies and minds. Why can't people turn inward and discover the incredible gifts that are there? Einstein said that we are using only 10% of our brains. That's because the other 90% lies in

Jennifer Lin Phillips

our connection to the planet.

To truly loving and honoring one another. To honoring the animals, the insects, the plants, the water, the mushrooms, space energy, the ability to heal and move from within. And most importantly to free renewable energy. Which each of these subcategories truly represents.

The shooting of the fires in Ventura on film in fact looks like a blurp from a Hollywood movie. It's horrifying. A friend on Facebook had pictures of her horses that barely escaped the fires. That footage was some of the scariest footage I have ever seen on forest fires, with cars lining the highways in packs, driving many miles to safety.

Why am I writing this book? Is my insight and life even relevant?

I think it is.

I have struggled, but I have flown. I have risen above adversity and occasionally I have even soared.

I have tasted, and I have learned through my own experience's. I have found alternative therapies, I have shared them. I have healed in many ways and helped others to heal also. I have shared raw from my soul, and I have held out my hands to my peer's, to a stranger.

I have done my best to quiet my codependency's, and my only addiction is to be understood and to understand. (besides coffee, which I'm working on, and my vibrator, which you can't take away from me!) And of course, some negative thinking. But really....

Is that not success?

Twenty Months, I stayed in this complex, rebuilding my relationship's here with my family and friends. I befriended a young girl named Dominique with cancer at 23 years old. I learned quickly through her, the effects of childhood trauma.

This young girl had gotten a tumor in her brain, and one in her ovary. I met her through a dear friend of mine, and we became good friends. He had asked me to watch out for her, she had only six months to live.

That was the time frame that she was given.

I put her on my Medicinal Chaga that I charged with crystalline energy and prayers, to boost her immune system. And then I began crystal therapy and bodywork sessions with her. She had been through a lot of toxic stress and challenges at a very, very young age.

I had Dominique lie down on my table and turned the heat on in the room.

Jennifer Lin Phillips

I put a blanket over her nearly naked body. She was eager to try the crystal therapy and I answered the questions she had beforehand.

I then went about placing my crystals on her bare skin, starting with her first chakra. The first chakra is at the base of the spine, between the legs. If you are attuned to your own body, you can feel a warmth and tingling there. The colors on the first chakra are blacks and browns. Like the color of dried lava, dirt, sand, roots, soil. This is the core of the Earth, and the core of the person.

The second chakra is different shades of red, the center for the passion of the being, and his or her sexuality. The crystals really are amazing in that they work with that person's unique energy field and body. They are placed by me, but somehow unfold in flower and snowflake shapes, in perfect symmetry with that person's essence.

She was enjoying the process of healing that day, although she was a bit nervous.

After each chakra was arranged with the crystals, I would guide the color from that chakra through her entire body and her mind. I would ask her a few questions. Like how the energy felt with the crystals placed there? And if she could sense or see anything. I got to her throat area, with midnight and cool sky blues, and one of my favorite fairy size blue wands.

Her body was receptive.

All the crystals had been placed on each of her chakra's, and the last step was to guide golden light through her being and connect her with all her own unique angel's.

Honestly, as we went through each of her chakra's the trauma buried there, came to the surface. The healing session lasted nearly two hours, and there was a lot of pain and turmoil there for a girl of just 23 years old.

Fortunately, she had the ability to access a lot of magic inside and was able to utilize the world of her imagination for vision and healing. She went to hidden places within herself and reemerged a better version of her.

In the cold month of January, Dominique and I took a trip up to my friend's cabin up Mt. Hood to visit my doggie Walnut. We walked around Trillium Lake with him in the snow. The lake was silver and white, and all elegantly iced over.

We walked many miles around the lake on foot. I was so proud of her for walking in the snow with me, and I know she felt exhilarated and encouraged by our friendship.

Jennifer Lin Phillips

She told me many times that I was the most positive person in her life.

I did my best to help her and offer her love and support. I tried to show her a different view of the world and point her to her own power there, flowering inside.

Three years later, she is still growing and learning. She is engaged and doing fairly well. The Cancer is still there however, and every day is still a struggle for her. Although our relationship has faced its challenge's, I love here dearly in my heart and know the difficulties that she has been through. She is still learning to reprogram her DNA through self-care and her inner relationship with herself.

Chapter 26; We Lost the House

It seemed like there was rarely a positive phone call from Nathan over the three years we talked, after I had left the island. The first and second year when we spoke, our conversations were mostly about rental issues. Or the many reasons why he couldn't give me the full amount of my portion of the money generated from the house some months.

Because something on the house needed work, there were unexpected costs and upkeep, maintenance. All the reasons were legitimate, the house certainly was a lot to keep up. There were many needed repairs for a house that had been abandoned for five years. Mold issues, rotting wood and insect problems, grimy roof and gutters, a fence that was falling apart. You name it. I know that Nathan spent some of his portion on the house at times also. But there's no doubt in my mind, that with Nathan's character, he would be taking from my end before he would take from his own cut from the house.

And when the King asked him for a third of the income from the house, I was very happy to give it to him.

I wasn't sure why the King was so upset about us not telling him about the renters. We had worked on the house tirelessly for a full year, it wasn't like we were

Jennifer Lin Phillips

trying to hide it from him. But rather trying to support ourselves and pay off the money we had borrowed to do the work over the entire year.

I remember when Nathan phoned me that very early spring day in Oregon. The bite from the frost that winter was easing, and I felt like I was a tulip bud popping up from half frozen soil.

I was sitting in the sun, and there was a cool dampness in the air.

My potted plants were showing new sprouts, surrounding me. My cell phone rang, and it was Nathan. He usually did only call me when there was some sort of issue with the house or something he was up against with the King.

This time it was the King.

We talked it over and of course we were both happy to give the King a third of our profits from the house being rented monthly. Of course, that was not a problem. We had some steady money flowing in now, and some of our debt paid down. The King had his family and we were more than happy to help support them. He had backed us on getting the house in the first place and after the first few years, things were running quite well.

Nathan mentioned to me how the King had talked to him about wanting to cut me out of our arrangement.

But he reassured me that he wouldn't let that happen. Him and I went in on the project together as a team, fifty, fifty. It was our joint effort that allowed for success and he told me again and again, that to cut me out would be bad, poor karma, unjust and outright wrong.

Beginning of the New Year 2015, our third year at the house, Nathan phoned me about one of our mutual acquaintances, an ex-fireman, named Quinten. I had met Quinten at the house our first year there. He felt to me like an incredibly generous person. Huge heart, and he would come over to help us accomplish little tasks at the house or repairs. He was nifty with hands on repairs and you could tell he enjoyed offering his help to us often.

Nathan phoned me one evening to tell me that he hadn't seen Quinten in a year or so, but he was now renting out the garage, in exchange for helping around the property.

What a relief for Nathan to have the brotherhood and a set of extra hands on site. And Quinten had a place to stay. He was obviously in some sort of trouble, staying in the garage and all. I wondered what happened with the nice girlfriend he had talked about. The one he had shown me in the pictures of the two of them looking sweet together.

Jennifer Lin Phillips

Nathan mentioned to me over that phone call, that Quinten's behavior was a bit off however and that he wasn't sure what was quite going on with him.

Something about Quinten punching the air in the backyard beneath the trees and talking to himself.

Nathan sounded really concerned, and so I offered to pray for them and set up some more protection around the house. I did this often for the home, even from afar. It was a good way to put a strong aura up and to warn off any upcoming danger.

That night, after getting off the phone. I sat on my meditation cushion and began to meditate and bubble up a seal of protection around the property. I was sending good vibes and continued like this for a good fifteen minutes.

My legs were growing tired from sitting in lotus position, so I got up to get some tea from the kitchen.

I had a guest coming soon anyways.

I opened the two french doors from my bedroom to walk out into the open room. Upon exiting my bedroom, something incredibly scary and freakish happened. A wave of intensely dark, soul sucking, I would not bat an eye to say the words, hellish, demonic, and evil energy, rushed through my small apartment behind me.

As the demonic force passed around me in a wave, I cringed in horror and disbelief. After years of weird experiences of dealing with entities, either from people that were close to me, or from living in places where bad spirits roamed, this was the most horrific, and absolute proof to me that a hellish dimension exists.

I was in complete awe at the rush of nasty energy that swooshed by me. I went for my sage stick immediately. I burnt the dried, hand wrapped sage leaves and said more prayers to Goddess Durga for protection. I closed my aura and asked all the dark forces that I had felt to leave my space as well as the house on Kauai.

When my friend showed up that night, he was surprised at the tightness of my breath and my need to share what had just happened with him.

He didn't seem to be all that surprised at what I had just experienced and had himself been aware of supernatural forces that are not very pure in nature. We had some interesting talks that night, and the following day I phoned Nathan to reveal to him my finding's.

Nathan had decided to ask Quinten to leave.

It appeared he was on crystal meth and his spirit was gone, his spirit had been taken over. I wondered if he could even come back. After what I had felt, I honestly doubted it.

Jennifer Lin Phillips

It felt kind of like that time I had a dream about how a person actually goes crazy. Like looney tunes.

You know the ones, homeless, walking around talking out loud. Pointing at things, etc. When you are a sensitive empath and open spirit, you just learn these things somehow. You are a channel of both light and dark. I had to quickly understand how to harness the light, control or accept the darkness I had, and dispel the disgusting darkness that lives on many planes of existence.

Back when I was caregiving for Violette, her anxiety was overwhelming the both of us most days. She would express the same thoughts repeatedly. Fearful thoughts repeatedly thought and then expressed aloud. I sat her down to meditate. I mean really, she had made it so far in life, elegantly, beautifully. Her glow, her smile. Her light. But that fear, boy did it pick at her.

We cleared the air that day.

After meditating together for twenty minutes, we both took a nap. Completely exhausted from her mental state. I gave her a mantra and we both went to sleep in the middle of the sunny island day. Upon sleeping, I saw how a person can lose their mind from repetitive thoughts that are destructive and unhealthy. Like a switch being flipped. Once flipped up, from thinking too much fearfully, that's it. Gone. No more so and so.

I discovered that the soul sucking energy was real, and I prayed for Quinten's release from it. Nathan had asked him to leave. I don't know how he could come out of the horrifying state that he had entered in alone. I was hoping there was something more Nathan could do for him, but sadly, Quinten had made his choice.

And most likely, he had made that choice over and over again. Until that flip a switch thing happened, and the complete darkness overtook him. Pretty sad, pretty gross, pretty umm, well yes, pretty damn disturbing.

Well, I had been talking to this guy from Oklahoma online for almost six months. It was, it really was in my journal for nearly two years to plan a hot springs tour through the desert. Utah, New Mexico mostly, and make a trip to Idaho first to see my older sis and my nieces and nephews.

Our online chemistry was electric.

Even when we talked over the phone, David and I just had this connection. I felt like I trusted him and that he would be an amazing friend and partner.

He really wanted me to come visit him, and so I was convinced to do the trip. It was only another 10 hours'

Jennifer Lin Phillips

drive from New Mexico to Oklahoma, why not?

Honestly, I was comfortable now in Oregon. I was enjoying my relationships, I was feeling grounded for once, healthy and nourished. I had finally replenished from the island journey that I had set out on three years earlier. But, if you know me, I was also getting a little bored. I was just about ready for another adventure. I felt so stimulated by David. His pictures, his voice, the way he talked to me and the things he told me.

He called me by the endearing name Red Rose, and most nights, would tell me that he would meet me by the Oak tree to sleep under the stars. He was good with his words, romantic and made quite an effort towards me energetically and verbally.

And he seemed spiritual.

Nathan had finally gotten the electricity turned over into his name, and although I had been paying all the bills on the house every month on time those three years I had been in Oregon, Nathan insisted that I allow him to start paying them.

The one time that he wanted to pay them in the past, well, that had set us back two months. He had proven that he couldn't do it effectively or timely, and that he would spend the money on himself or his food. Who knows what he spent it on, hemp products? He was always trying to get more than his share from the profits.

I agreed to have him pay the bills, and he transferred things into his name finally.

A month later, late August, my lease was ending, and I had arranged to take my desert road trip to end in Oklahoma. I was going to tour the desert, visit some hot springs, camp and then cruise the long country roads where tumbleweed crosses highways in windstorms, and girl's in gas stations take your cash for gas, speaking with a twang and wide country smile.

I had everything arranged. A little money saved, a credit card on hand for backup and my plans for what to store and what to take. If things went well between David and I, I would just stay with him for a while. So, I was going to need some extra things, clothes, shoes, jewelry.......my crystals.

Nathan phoned me a week before my departure. He knew I was leaving on my adventure soon. I answered his call.

"Jennifer, oh my gosh. I have to talk to you." He said in earnest and out of breath.

"Hi Nathan, what's wrong, you sound in disarray?"

"Oh my gosh, you have no idea. I spent last night in

jail." He says, in heightened expression now. Fear coming in, desperation, and the sound of tears upon his words.

"I did, I slept in the jailhouse last night. They are taking the house back. The cops, they came to the door yesterday with paperwork. A three-day notice to vacate the property or be arrested, fined and put in jail. I laughed at them. I took their notice, and I ripped it up right in front of them. I was not going to leave my home. This is my house." He said.

"Oh my god, Nathan, that's awful, are you okay? "I replied to him in disbelief and shock.

"They arrested me. They handcuffed me and took me to jail after I refused the paperwork. The housemates are so upset. They cannot believe that I lied to them about the house. We all must leave. The King is so pissed at me."

"The King is always mad at you Nathan. Screw him. You did your best. It's okay." I tried to calm him down.

"I know, but this is my house. My dad's going to be so mad at me. I'm going to have to go live with him now and work off some of the money I borrowed from him for the house. And Alii, I have to bring him too. I must figure this out, how to get him on the plane. I don't have any money. And the renters are so upset, they are packing up all their things. We don't have the money for their deposits. I'm such a loser. I failed.

I'm so sorry Jennifer." He says crying now.

"I'm so sorry Jennifer. I tried so hard. We tried so hard. I'm such a loser. They can't take my house. I need to pack up my things. I don't have time, and the King, he's so mad at me. I can't believe this. All the effort we put in for nothing. It's all gone. It's all gone." He repeats aloud, sobbing and out of breath now.

"It's okay Nathan. You will be fine. You did your best, we did our best. Look what we risked and look at what we accomplished. The King got money for nearly two years from us. We helped him and his family. We gave people a place to stay on the most beautiful beach on the island, for cheap, in a resort style home. We did our best. It's okay. And now, now you have an opportunity to rebuild a bond with your father. You can learn some things from him and hopefully he will learn from you. I know how much you dislike the mainland, but after saving some money, you can go somewhere tropical again, maybe Fiji or Tahiti. You will be okay. Be thankful, that your dad is there for you, and that he is offering you a place to live and to work."

"I need to go. I need to pack up my things, and figure about the dog. I can't leave him. He's all I have. I'm so sorry Jennifer. We lost the house."

Nathan and I said goodbye heartfelt, and I let the feelings of what had just happened sink in on me. Well, it wasn't horrible timing, really. I had just paid my

Jennifer Lin Phillips

last month's rent and I was going to be heading out on an adventure soon.

I surely was going to need to figure about working sooner than I had planned, so as not to go under on my bills and hopefully not max out my new credit card. Nathan and I had almost paid off the credit card that we used together on the house. I had maybe one more year 'til that would be paid off, a year and a few months hopefully.

As I allowed the phone call and news to sink in, a feeling of disappointment, yet also relief came over me.

I was so tired of dealing with Nathan.

His anger, his mood swings, the way he belittled me and talked down to me nearly every time we talked on the phone. Accept for that one week where he visited me in my dream and then started calling me "babe" again over the phone for a few days.

That was two years after I had seen him. I guess he had finally had a change of heart. It was weird and so far out of the blue. I didn't know how to respond to him, so I just talked about the house. Then a week later, back to being a dickhead again.

I felt relief. The house was no longer in my name. And now, in fact, the house was no longer ours. I was free from the nausea that my relationship with Nathan had caused me, and I was free from the fear of being committed by the law for a crime.

And that dream I had. That dream that I had about two months before Nathan's call, where I was screaming at the top of my lungs as loud as I could at Nathan.

So much repressed anger and grief, feelings of betrayal coming out. I could forget that now. I would be leaving soon, like I often did after a breakup. Go start somewhere fresh, somewhere new again. And I did. I took off on my road trip, singing melodies, feeling light, free and easy. My car all packed up, camping gear ready, about two weeks later.

Jennifer Lin Phillips

Chapter 27: My Desert Oasis

The highway in Kansas leaving Oklahoma was a long straight two-lane backroad that crossed through the beautiful country. There was so much symbolism there, as I drifted in and out consciously with my mind, through what felt like the veil between illusory worlds.

I was driving straight and fast, then slowing my speed so as not to hit the yellow and orange butterflies crossing the two-lane road. They only flew from the right side of my car to cross rapidly, wings fluttering, across the dark pavement, courageously off to somewhere to the left of me.

I smiled inside at their flight.

The butterfly's effort to defeat the speed of the vehicles and the traffic. Where are they going? I thought. Why that way? And dang it, I hope I don't crush them. Watching them for miles upon miles trying to triumph over the two-lane road to safety, was very symbolic for me.

I was one of them.

I had travelled now nearly 3000 miles through the country and desert, and I was heading up from Oklahoma through Kansas to Colorado. I was one of them.

Sovereignty and the Goddess

Will they make it to where they are going? Shit. I just hit one!! And another one, damn it.

Oh, my goddess, it's hopeless. They're so small, wings so strong, but this highway, these cars, and the speed of travel. Ughh. Why me, why these butterflies? Why this long friggen' highway?

I just kept driving straight like that for miles upon miles. Holding the steering wheel with tense finger's, and casually slowing and speeding, to keep the numbers down of how many butterflies I would actually smash into.

In observation of my experience with them, on the backroad, after fleeing yet another disappointing encounter. Things were feeling so strange and dreamlike, like the butterflies were me. They were inside of me, and a part of me. Their journey was mine. I kept driving, they kept flying. I sent them waves of love and then I blessed them. I felt grateful for my own journey, and the fact that I had come so far all by myself. And we all kept fluttering along in the back country, in fierce determination to arrive to the other side of the highway, to wherever we were going.

I remember when I stopped to check my oil at the local gas station just off the two-lane HWY. Out in the middle of nowhere in Kansas.

Jennifer Lin Phillips

"You probably could go another 3000 miles with that car." the attendant told me as he pulled up the hood of my car to check the oil.

Below the hood, beside the heated engine was a butterfly. A yellow, black and golden butterfly. In perfect shape, lifeless and still. I picked it up under my finger and put it next to my radio inside my car. Such a beautiful, delicate creature, travelling so far, enchanting wing's in flight.

I got back in my car for the road again up North.

I nearly had a panic attack on the larger six lane highway I was now driving on. It was just as straight and just as bad.

Travelling 70 miles per hour for hours like that. Perfectly straight, no turns. I had been through a lot already. Now two weeks into my desert oasis journey.

Ojo Caliente Resort and Spa in between Santé Fe and Taos, New Mexico, had been the highlight of my journey thus far. Besides visiting my nieces and nephews in Idaho for three days of course. Oh, and camping near the town of Logan in Utah. Same name as my nephew.

I stopped to snap some photos of the church in town to send to my sis. I knew she would appreciate the name of the town I was travelling through. Named after my oldest nephew. Eight-year-old Logan, whom I had just spent three days with.

But gosh, this Hwy up through Kansas, my heart was pounding fast.

Two weeks into my journey and here I am feeling emotionally drained by my experience in Oklahoma. The six months of online dating came to an abrupt close after thousands of miles of travel. What a journey. What a trip. My head and heart were on a hamster wheel.

And it wasn't just that, but with the speed I was driving and the straightness of the highway, something happened. I was becoming short of breath, I was panicking and having trouble breathing. I was feeling faint, and with my thoughts and the letdown, and the sudden decision to leave. Everything was spinning.

I called David. He talked with me and I felt better as I slowed my car down to 50, 20 miles per hour under the speed limit. The dizziness was easing, and I was feeling a little bit grounded now. I had just been through so much in the past two weeks. My journey had been so exciting, but the time in Oklahoma didn't go as planned. David and I were not the match we thought we could be.

There was no room for me there anyways truthfully. A bunkbed he shared with his son on the weekends?

Jennifer Lin Phillips

What was I thinking?

I camped in the yard the few days I was there. The warm Oklahoma air was humid and nice. I awoke one morning after a storm, where thunder and lightning could be heard outside the pounding of heavy rain on my tent most the night.

It was exhilarating really, and I woke up to an electric pink rainbow in the pale morning sky. Well, maybe that was worth all those miles and the long courageous trip, I thought. Ha! Humm, yeah, maybe.

By day four, it was obvious things were going nowhere between David and me. He was a small town, Oklahoma guy, and extremely used to doing things his way. What was he going to do with me? From the bigger city, island girl and mystic?

I was obviously highly independent to be able to travel like I do. And after getting to know him, he really needed a down home girl. And what in the hell is he doing online dating for, with women halfway across the US?

A girl that says please and thank you, and yes sir, you got it. That's what he needs. A small-town girl. What in the world could he do with me? Ha. Out of all my girlfriend's, I tended to be the easiest going and, in many ways, the least high maintenance girl in the group. But standing here, in Tulsa, before this person.

Wow. Uuumm yes, clashing a bit.

I decided to take a hot yoga class at a small studio in town for an outlet and to clear my mind. I tried my best to relax and fit in there, in Tulsa. But there was no way I could live there. We both knew and could sense the awkwardness of our two world's colliding.

And as confused as I now was and very disappointed in the unfitting situation, my 6 month and only attempt at on line dating had to end.

Two hours from Colorado, I phoned my girlfriend Erin.

"Hi E! I'm just outside of Denver. Any room for me tonight? I've been in the car nearly ten hours now, and I am a bit tweaked out. Can I stay a night and visit with you?" I asked her.

She had been following my adventure on Facebook.

And had we planned it better, she would have met me in Utah, at the hot springs there.

The Mystical Hot Spring's in Monroe Utah. What a magical and rejuvenating spot.

Yellow, hot, sulfur water flowed up from the ground 24 hours a day there. You couldn't go barefoot, and you definitely could not take your eyes off the ground walking around the property. But omg. Bath tubs, hot sulfur water filling up white, vintage tubs on dirty cliffsides, with mountainous views beyond.

Jennifer Lin Phillips

Thankfully, the few hot springs I had googled and found were the right ones suiting my needs and desires. I spent two nights camping there and soaked up the heat of the desert and the sulfur springs quite carefully.

The perfect crystal to accompany me on my journey was from Arkansas. I had found it in the lounge there, where all guests sign in.

The lounge was eclectic and crammed with odd, dusty trinkets, heavy wool items and hippy clothes. I decided to purchase and include the white crystal in my collection and take it with me on my journey. It had these small pointed clusters that made the crystal appear to be like a white castle. I would use the crystal for guidance and protection for the miles to come. It was like a white snow castle, with snowflakes in beautiful shape and form filling the castle up with snow, from the inside.

With the yellow of the hot sulfuric water on light brown desert dirt. The elements had been absorbed into the white of the crystal, and my senses had also been imprinted.

The memory from my indulgent healing from the springs, was also in the crystal and once placed on the dashboard of my car, since leaving the Mystical Hot Springs of Utah, I intended for it to guide me safely.

It was so nice to be met by a good friend from Portland, Oregon, on that first night I stayed in Denver. She had made the venture to Colorado in pursuit of the mountain life. Her family had decided to begin a coffee company business in the area. IVibe coffee was a trendy name and she had been living in Denver about one year working hard on things, when I showed up at her apartment door.

Thank Goddess she had answered my call only a few hours earlier when I called her from that long, dirty highway.

When she greeted me at the door, she could see the weariness of my frazzled state. Helping me in with a girlfriend's warmth and I placed a small bag in her room.

"You can sleep with me tonight. Oh! And my friend from down the street is coming for some wine and hot tub here in a bit. I know you must be exhausted, but really, you should join us and talk about this crazy adventure you've been on. I know it would be good for you to connect and relax with us a little." Erin said sweetly and like a true friend.

Wine? Hot tub? Friends? Clear night sky? Stars are out......Share my travels?

Honestly, I was feeling quite emotional and wanted to hop in her bed and sleep awhile, but I knew she was right. I needed to vent. And breathe. Relax with good

Jennifer Lin Phillips

company and some vino.

I put on one of her swimsuits, which felt so good and reminded me of growing up with my two sisters'. We were always stealing each other's clothes and clean underwear.

Oh, the sweet joys of being a female.

Shortly after getting in the, brand new to me, hot pink bikini suit she let me borrow, Erin's friend arrived. We then took a few glasses of rose' in hands down to the tub and outdoor pool, which was lit up festively.

As we eased into the warm waters of the tub, I leaned into a few jets with my spine. It felt great to relax there and be uplifted by amazing company and surroundings that were now satisfying my sensuality.

The sizzle from the steam in the tub, rising from the hot water soothed me.

I was surprised at the depth of character her friend from down the street had, and he listened intently while I spoke. I almost thought he was gay, he was such a coherent and comforting man to be talking with. He quickly and happily offered his dearest insight and compassionate advice.

He was well travelled and well balanced in both his masculinity and his feminine nature's. I had been hugged, held and caught in their arms quite gracefully, after ten excruciating hours of breathing in highway air.

The following morning, I witnessed one of the most vibrant pink and horizontally elongated sunrise's I had seen in a while. As I looked out of my girlfriend's window, with an amazing fifth floor extended view, I exhaled with relief.

I glanced down at the mug of coffee in my hand.

I'm trying hard to remember now what the mug read, but it was just perfect for what I was feeling at that moment. Something about Gratitude. I'm so lucky, I thought to myself. Spirit is so good to me. Sure, I crash and burn. I do, but who doesn't? And well yes, it could be that I fall more than others, but that could be attributed to the quantity of attempts at flight.

Potentially many more than the average person.

Oh, who cares anyways! Whatever. I'm not going to overthink this. I'm here. I'm safe. I had been on the road only two weeks and there I was sipping coffee and witnessing the passionate paintbrush of Goddess' wand through tall elegant windows.

I chose to just be with it, the uncertainty, the fact that I was still floating there, perched high in the clouds, five stories up, being warmed by coffee and the golden sun

Jennifer Lin Phillips

rising.

I was starting to feel a little grounded finally. I took a few sips more from my cup and I took in deep breathes of gratitude. One, then another. I gave thanks to spirit for my safety, for harmony, and for dear friends.

The kind who pick you up and serve you coffee graciously with a view from high altitude places.

That morning, Erin guided me to Red Rocks National Park, which was very close by, for an afternoon hike.

"Just take your time here. I think you will love the energy in Colorado. Honestly, with as much as you enjoy the outdoors, this is a haven for activity. Why don't you get up to Red Rocks and hike around up there? The red of the rocks is incredible. You will love it. Let loose for a few days, and please don't feel rushed to get out of here."

Her words were exactly what I needed to hear.

I was already being energized by the expansive energy of the desert and I could sense the mountains nearby. On the contrary, Erin had been missing girlfriends from the Portland area most of the year. I think she was already really enjoying having me in town.

Picturing me hitting that freeway to drive back up to the Pacific NW only two weeks after I left the state, did not sound all that appealing to me. I was bored there. I couldn't go back yet. For what? The rain? With the fall and winter coming, I would go into a coma in no time. And here, in Colorado, it felt like summer still, as we approached the last few days in September.

I phoned my older sister from my afternoon hike up Red Rocks Park to let her know where I had landed.

"That's so funny Jen! I always pictured you in Colorado. With as much as you are into the outdoors, that place is perfect for you." My sister said to me over the phone.

Megan, my older sis, was no lover of the rain. Her and her family were happily settled in a home in the country, in sunny Idaho. I loved the rain. But I knew I wouldn't love it this year. I was desiring something alluring and perfectly new.

As I breathed in the smells outside where I was standing, I could feel myself opening. The air was different here.

Perhaps I could learn about the local plants and wildflowers. That was sounding pretty good for me right now, and I heard the wildflowers were spectacular here come summer.

My sister and I chatted as I walked around the park,

Jennifer Lin Phillips

observing huge red rocks towering high above me. The ground was dry.

I was really in the desert now.

This really is so cool, I thought. So very, very, very, very, cool. I was beginning to feel empowered again. Like four very's before the word cool empowered again.

Mmmhhhmmm, starting to feel something like an alternative cowgirl. Sorta dense, like heavy metal mixed with country. Not dense, like as in dumb. No, not that kind of dense. But dense like as in metallic, rainy.... but learning to be dry, dry like the country.

I was getting back in sync again with me and my surroundings.

And my sis, my older sis had always pictured me living here in Colorado?! I would have to plan a day, meandering through the small mountain towns in search of some leather cowgirl boots soon.

And then yes, after that, most likely find a beautiful and fast horse to ride!

Snow boots really was more what I needed with the season we were now heading into. I needed some snow shoes, bad. Thankfully, my landlord had given me an ice scraper for my car the day I moved into his condo.

"You will definitely be needing this." He grinned coyly as he handed it to me my first day there at the condo.

I just half grinned back at him, noticing the sarcasm in his mannerism, but happy to have my new winter instrument in hand. Well, this should be an interesting and icy winter, I thought to myself.

The falling of snow began in December sometime and continued all throughout the spring. It felt like a newborn baby, a tiny little miracle, every time the snowflakes fell. The sun still shined too, while strong winds whistled hard through the cracks of windowpanes. The winter dried my fair skin that had grown accustomed to the soothing moisture from NW rains. But it was mystifying really, watching the flakes fall for months and months on end.

I took photos of cherry blossom trees in bloom come spring. Big reddish pink buds hanging from branches with leaves, and covered in heavy, white snow. So pretty. I thought everything was just so beautiful frozen over with snow and ice.

And just maybe the shape of the buds would be preserved like that forever.

They have been at least, preserved like that, frozen, pink, cherry buds, in my mind's eye ever since.

Jennifer Lin Phillips

The irony of being in Colorado, with hot springs nearly all around the state to explore, just a few months later. I was admiring that white crystal that I had found at the hot springs in Utah that I had placed on the dashboard of my car as a compass. I was reflecting by my apartment window after a snow.

I was going to make a grid.

I was going to set some new intentions with all my new crystals, some which had just arrived, sent from a girlfriend in NY.

Her and I had just done a trade for services, and she and her daughter were now taking my Medicinal Chaga tincture for their health and vitality. Perfect timing for them to be on it really, now with the winter coming.

I decided that I would place most of my crystals elegantly on my shiny golden serving tray that I had brought with me on my journey. Great for serving tea with. But really, how perfect for an offering, a golden serving tray.

Well if that isn't a sincere message to the Divine.

I was getting excited now. All my experiences the past month were spiraling together somehow, and I was weaving them like a quilt.

I would set the tray just below the window I was

standing in. With the blinds half open, that way they could catch the rays from the sunlight beaming in.

I glanced at my ice crystal, turning it in my hand slowly.

A snowy tower and castle, I thought as I watched small snowflakes beginning to cover the fabric top of the outdoor covered pool. The pool which was now closed for the season.

It was only a few months into my desert journey and standing warm inside of the condo I was now renting. While some thing's had been closed for the season, the whiteness, the purity, and the sense of a new beginning was fresh somehow and gliding with intention on the altitude of the thin Colorado air.

I did manage to stay warm throughout most of the harsh Colorado winter. I took a part time job doing caregiving again. The client I cared for three times per week was in excellent shape at 91 years old.

Jack lived in the elegant suburbs known as Highlands Ranch. He lived in a nice home, with an electric fireplace. Most nights after our days had been completed, we would talk and hug by the warmth of the fire. I could tell the touch was good for him.

I think it was grounding the both of us really.

His home was a few minutes down the street from the

Jennifer Lin Phillips

YMCA, where we would walk laps around the basketball courts below, in linked arms, usually just one day per week together.

Jack was positive, charming, and had a rosy glow about him.

His life so far had been filled with love and a radiant vigor. His eight children did a beautiful job looking after him. And his son and daughter that lived nearby, were the two that had hired me on to care for him. Well, they had agreed to hire me through the company that I was working for.

I would cook in Jack's home for the both of us most days. And we would watch the weather change from the kitchen windows. On the colder days, we were happy to be inside, while the shocking Colorado wind whistled and screeched outside the glass windows.

I could sense Jack's helplessness somedays. Especially if the sun had been hidden away by thick, white, clouds. I was eager to cheer him with my smile and with my words whenever I was around him.

And on the days in between my shift with him, he would reheat the leftover's I had made. I tried to cook extra too on the days I was on shift, in hopes to deter him from running out for fast food on the day's I wasn't there. Homemade pie or a simple dessert, I even made homemade crust for him.

Well, he was my only sweetie that winter and spring. And I tried to keep him stocked with something to satisfy his aging sweet tooth. A chocolate candy bar with almonds for a quick snack. I would load those up for him in the fridge while I was away.

Often, after a workout, we would go for a snack out. Or grab a burger at the local burger joint. He seemed to have a fetish for those, and I know he enjoyed seeing the workers at a few fast food chains. I could tell he liked that they remembered him, and they would ask him about his week. I know he enjoyed the outlet and having the familiarity. It felt good for him to be recognized and I think it enhanced his liveliness. He had a sense of community there with them, over food, an outlet outside of his church and his family.

It had been a few cold months since I had seen Chico. The friendly and outgoing guy I had met at my friend's BBQ, my third day in Colorado. He was reasonably smooth that day, and had managed to get my phone number, just moments after I had asked him about the shoes he was wearing.

"Give me your number and I will send you the website where I got these. Awesome deal. Lots of great finds." He said casually standing outside in the last few days of the Colorado summer.

I was drinking a beer and celebrating the final leg of my

Jennifer Lin Phillips

journey. I was thrilled to have landed there in Colorado, now sitting in ease, in a chair outside, at a friend's BBQ. I was still debating in my mind, I wasn't sure whether to stay in the desert, or to travel on and go back home.

I was soaking in a sense of belonging that night though.

The group at the BBQ was so inviting, relaxing to be around, and the energy was fresh to me. Two bridesmaids were there that night, and I was the third out of a group of nine of us, all connected by a bestie back in Oregon.

The coincidence of being there with these new friends that had roots back to my bestie and hometown filled me with intrigue and delight. I relaxed in the new wave of people and then headed back to Erin's that night to rest.

Chico texted me while I was dressing for bed, later that night to talk. He had an urgency to connect with me. Almost a desperation, and it was somewhat alarming to me. Had he been having trouble with women lately, I thought? Is he struggling here in Colorado? He had arrived from Florida maybe a month, three weeks before me, and maybe things weren't going all that well for him?

He seemed like a cool guy, despite his urgency to hang out with me. Which was slightly annoying in pair with my unclarity as to where my life was going.

But he had such a friendly smile and demeanor and I felt like I was open to getting to know him better.

My focus now was to decide whether to stay in Colorado or head back up north to my hometown. So, I really was needing to put my energy there, on making that decision. I could sense that Chico and I were different from one another, sort of like that opposites attract kind of thing. But how much of an attraction that was there, was yet to be determined.

It was an exciting coincidence that we had both been orbiting the states, and had been brought together in a new town, right around the same time. Surrounded by similar friends and all these new possibilities.

I stayed out that weekend in Avon, where I met my girlfriend and her boyfriend that lived out there in the cute, small, ski town. Tall Aspen trees gleamed with golden yellow leaves. My first night out there was just incredible.

Long, silent, clear skies, and twinkling stars above the railroad tracks off my friend's back balcony. Aspen trees glowed all around, and you could see ski lifts trailing up and down snowy hills.

The following morning, I went to grab coconut milk from the market to accompany a few cups of fresh morning coffee.

Jennifer Lin Phillips

I pulled into the parking lot of the local market and turned off the engine to my car. I glanced down at the yellow butterfly I had still sitting in the console there, that I had found under the hood of my car a week before.

From the long narrow Kansas backroads, here it was, still sitting near the driver's seat of my car.

There was a half-moon out that morning, and I acknowledged its morning whisper, with squinting sleepy eyes. The yellow of the insect's leaves reminded me of something. I held the tiny butterfly in my hand again with admiration and with wonder.

As I exited my car door, the yellow of the Aspen trees all around the valley could be seen for miles and miles. One of the main varietals of trees in the area there. The branches of leaves were waving in the air, and they looked like fluttering yellow butterflies, wing's flapping, circling the valley. The thin, wispy Aspen leaves were flying preciously as they do, all around the quiet mountain town.

They had made it, the yellow butterflies, travelling so far to the other side of the highway like I did. The essence of the yellow butterflies had magnificently landed here too.

Chapter 28: Underlying Issues

I cannot really put into words the amount of turmoil and sadness I am feeling as I write this portion of the story of my life journey and my struggles. It could be that the pain from my experience is still so fresh to me.

Like watery dew drops on the leaves of Camelia flowers that nearly froze. I'm still waiting for the sunlight to suck dry the wet moisture from my aching limbs.

I sit at the cafe attempting to write. The coolness from the air coming off the vent and hardwood floors is chilling me. I've experienced trauma before, it feels like this. The body goes cold, as the feelings are really felt and acknowledged and then allowed to process. I pulled my long scarf around my shoulders closer to me, but the air from the vent is still creeping up the legging of my left leg.

I could sense a dark storm cloud above me just now. I was in the bathroom, considering writing this next chapter of my life, when I felt the dark cloud move over me. The stormy cloud above my head and shoulders resembled the ones we were chasing that afternoon, just outside of Denver, on the back of my

Jennifer Lin Phillips

new friend's fancy, vintage motorcycle.

I captured a lightning bolt on camera that day.

We had been riding and chasing the storm that was coming towards the city for miles, on the back-country roads of Colorado. We were approaching the storm, and dark grey was quickly taking over the clouds along the horizon.

We needed to turn back around and fast. The thunder was rolling in now too and flashes of lightening appearing closely after the roaring noise's coming from the sky.

With Jeff and I on his bike, and his friend on another bike, we were speeding quickly away. Leaving the storm still brewing closely behind us. Wheels now rolling away from the rain that was, in reverse, chasing us now.

I had decided to start dating. What choice did I have? Stupid question, I know. We all have choices, and I didn't have to start dating, but really, Chico had left me months ago. He left me in the cold Colorado winter to go and celebrate his 45th Birthday with old friends and family back in the state of Wisconsin, a week before Thanksgiving.

A Vintage motorcycle just like Jeff's was, red even,

single headlight flashed just now across my face. I'm still typing here at the cafe in Oregon. Observing the pretty Native girl in her black, thick, number 69 in print on her leather riding jacket.

She's about to order a latte, maybe tea or black coffee. She's in need of a warm drink, and she's standing in the line just in front of where I am sitting.

I sit here still, writing and remembering this past year, on an old vintage chair with floral print, in the corner of the popular and cute neighborhood cafe known as Insomnia Coffee.

The thunder from the engine of the motorcycle just outside, brought me to presence. Looks like a cute couple out for a rainy-day ride today.

Jeff and I weren't a couple. We had been on a few dates. But honestly, I talked about Chico nearly our entire lunch one day. Jeff even comforted me, as I apologized for the tears streaming down my cheeks. He must have been wondering what in the world I was doing dating, but I know he could tell that I was needing a friend.

I couldn't sit at home in my closet any longer. Dating was a good option to have for a girl like me. I needed to connect, to be admired and complimented, and I wanted to be taken out somewhere new. I was just

Jennifer Lin Phillips

sitting at home most nights restless, hoping to hear from Chico and I was starting to deteriorate mentally, emotionally, physically. I am a young woman of 38 years, and time is passing. I can't let some guy whom abandoned me bring me down so low. It was still important for me to enjoy the rest of my youth a little.

I was still so new to the area too. I couldn't hibernate the entire 7 months of my lease. And I had already spent the Holidays alone.

Both.

Thanksgiving and Christmas too. The Christmas I spent in Colorado was by far the saddest, most lonely ever. I mean if you were to be judgmental about it. I was laughing hysterically to myself, sipping up noodles of top ramen and nibbling sautéed potatoes on the couch of my small one-bedroom condo that snowy winter, 2016.

At least I was laughing about it. I had just left my girlfriend's apartment where I was dog sitting for her, in her cozy apartment by fireside. On the drive back to my own apartment across town, I realized that all the grocery stores were closed on Christmas Day accept the infamous fast food chain, McDonald's.

I honestly didn't feel sad. I wrote the Holiday off as couldn't get any more pathetic, unless I had tripped and slipped on the icy sidewalk and sprained my leg and had to be rushed to the Emergency room.

Whew! Thankful at least that wasn't my sad Holiday story. All right, success.

I just giggled and laughed to myself about the odd serenity of my aloneness. This was quite humorous, and I binged on Mooji videos on my only day off from work that week.

The Isness of Being as Mooji likes to call it. I was sitting in the Isness of my Being. Unravelling myself in the gooey spiral of never-ending peace and tranquility. I let in the softness from the blanket covering me.

Happy as a clam strip, I thought. I am warm and sipping noodles that were flavored like shrimp. Just catching up on some much needed rest, and yes, I heard it was some big Holiday out there, something like Christmas that day.

I had been waiting for Chico to get back to me, my loving arms. Our first month together was incredibly sweet, and it felt rapturous with his strong, caring arms around me each night.

I was seriously in love. And the endorphins rushing through my system held me in an ecstatic serenity.

Yes, I knew it had only been a few weeks. But I felt it.

I knew that I was really falling for him somehow, when I blurted it out one night on the couch. We had been cuddling that night, watching a little mindless television, when I decided to go off to sleep. He was staying up to unwind a bit more, over a few more tv shows.

"Okay babe, see you in bed. Love you." I said as I kissed him goodnight blushing. Oh, my my......what did I just say?! We both looked at one another in surprise.

"Okay, goodnight Boo," He said back to me.

The next day he texted me that he loved me too. It was sweet, and I felt like we really had found love. He was the guy I had been waiting for the past five years, and it felt so good just being with him.

We spent one month and one week together. He helped me get furniture from a local furniture company off credit, and rather easily, we had a one-bedroom apartment, just for the two of us.

I paid our rent.

Well, it was my apartment, and in my name. But I was so happy to have him with me. We spent every day together for that month and week, until he abruptly left. He had talked about it for maybe five days and then off he went, with the 70$ I gave him for gas money. Off he went to go celebrate his Birthday and the Holidays without me.

Abandoning me in a new town in the chill of the icy

and white Colorado winter. He left me there to fend for myself in the cozy home we had just created together.

He told me that he needed to sell his motorcycle and make some quick money. He had just had a great interview and had practically landed a job at Harley Davidson, which was seriously just a jaunt down the street from the condo I was renting.

What was he doing leaving right now?!

"I need money now. I can't wait another month to get paid." He said. "It will take me two weeks and I will be back here with a couple grand. I will be back soon babe, don't worry."

I think it was about a week after he left me, that I checked the drawers of the red dresser that I had just bought, to see if all his jeans and sweatshirts were gone. Yep. Every single one of them. On his side of the closet were a pair of summer slippers and a few t-shirts hanging.

My heart sunk to the floor.

What had just happened to me?

Barely a trace of him anywhere. The rooms were spinning on me. I felt nauseous. The room I was in was getting smaller, as the intense pain now squeezing my

Jennifer Lin Phillips

heart nearly collapsed me into myself. I curled up on the bed we had shared for weeks. And it felt like the walls of the condo would crumble on top of me at any moment.

Like a hurricane, leaving me lying in dusty, broken wood and rusty screws.

In the hall closet were some of his toiletries, and his sleeping medication. How could we spend every day together for a month? How could I feel like we had fallen in love like that? Why did he suggest to me our first night together in the condo, where we slept on top of one another on the small air mattress I had from camping that summer, "Let's be the couple everyone is jealous of. Let's be like that babe." And then he kissed me with heat just outside the front door.

Our first night together. We slept like we were one that night. And the night after too. And he said he hadn't slept that well in years. Probably close to ten of them. How could he just up and leave me?

"Two weeks babe. I will be back soon." He said.

He had a box full of medications. Mostly sleeping pills. Which confused me right away. I have never had issues with sleep. I can sleep anywhere from 7-12 hours, happily, easily and with deep pleasure. How could any doctor write prescriptions for this many pills? What kind of doctor does that? I thought as I looked at his stash of bottles.

Gotta have a clear conscience to get good sleep, I thought. Where is all his anxiety coming from?

That first month we had together, some nights I would come home from doing an outcall therapy session, open the front door and watch him as he opened his arms for me to come sit with him and cuddle up. On the chair I bought for him. I was so incredibly melted there. In his arms. Smelling his skin. His pheromones drove me crazy. I loved him. There was probably nothing I wouldn't do for him already. I just wanted to be there. Right there, smelling him. Kissing the skin on his neck and breathing in the love I felt with him near me.

How could he just up and leave me? Take nearly all his things he had just moved in only a month before? Well, he had abruptly moved out of the last place he was staying, rent free, with my help. I could sense he was trying to avoid his friends that day.

He didn't owe them anything. And apparently, he didn't owe them a goodbye either.

What kind of person does that?

And just what is he telling the universe if he really does want to be back here with me in two weeks. You aren't telling the Universe that, by moving almost every article of clothing you own out of the nice dresser I let

Jennifer Lin Phillips

you have both drawers of.

"I took my clothes to give some to my friend's, I've been meaning to declutter," He said over the phone when I asked him about it.

"Wow. That sure sounds like a lot of extra work for you." I told him back.

Now if I could only get the real story. The truth. Just what the hell is this person thinking and doing? Maybe it wasn't really any of my business anyways. If this person makes me feel weird and manipulated bad, what's it matters to me. Drop him. He's not consistent, and he doesn't know what the hell he is doing. Not to mention what he really wants from me, or life.

"Yes. I could stay in Wisconsin through Christmas." He said to a friend over the phone before he left, with me in the room.

When I asked him about it later, it was like I had made the whole thing up. I could've sworn he said that, I thought to myself, suddenly considering if I had heard him correctly or not.

"I never told you I love you." He said months later over the phone.

No, I guess he never did tell me that. He texted it to me.

It was baffling really. To feel like he could lie straight through his teeth. Does he even know what he is doing to himself when he does that? He's 45 years old. Doesn't he understand the repercussions from the universe. Has he not learned a thing?

I almost felt bad for him. I did. I saw him spin circles around himself. Like a dog chasing his tail. Like he thinks he's really going to catch it one of these times. God, isn't he exhausted with his own nonsense? He's about to wipe himself out. And I just wanted to help him. To love him. To bring him back around to integrity. He can do this, I thought. I have felt his heart. His love. He is a good man.

But really, did he mean anything he said? Or was he just so good at telling everyone something different that even he is confused. I'm thinking the latter. He's just so confused. He will figure it out. He will. He's going to get that shit together. He is. He's nearly there. I've got him. He's got this. It's good. We're good. Really, we're going to get it together, it's all good.

I convinced myself.

November of 2016, off he went to drive 12 hours on slick and icy roads back home to sleep on the couch of his old place. To make a few thousand dollars. He

Jennifer Lin Phillips

didn't even want to sell his motorcycle. It was his baby. Custom built. He said he put ten grand into it. Just get clear, I told him. The universe can't handle all your mixed messages. Can we please get clear here? I love you.

Two months, it took for him to get back to me. We texted every day. He told me how sorry he was, and that after the darkest point comes the light. I believed him. He wanted to be with me. He just made some shitty choices. Some quick choices that now had put him back even more.

He never sold his bike. He came back in mid-January. And his first weekend back was a mess.

He sent me out for hamburger buns at 10:30pm our first night together, after we finished the bottle of wine, I had brought home for us.

As I searched for the closest grocery store in the town, I was still getting familiar with half tipsy, I couldn't believe what I was doing. Out on the hunt for hamburger buns, how inconsiderate of him, I thought.

But I had agreed to it. Why couldn't I say no to him? I just wanted to please him, win his love.

I ended up getting lost that night, his first night home

with me after two months apart. I drove to a Thriftway halfway across town. I got the stupid, cheap buns and tried to smile as I gave the cashier my hard-working money. I was still trying to get my rent paid, just barely getting by in this new town. Not that hamburger buns are expensive, but seriously?

When I made it back to the condo, I found a parking spot a few blocks away. Now that his jeep was parked in my parking spot. Which I happily gave up for him and his nice new car. Bbbrrrr it's cold in January in Colorado, I thought as I walked quickly back to the condo that evening in the cool night air.

I walked in the door irritated and felt taken advantage of. Our first night together and I am already out on a scavenger hunt for hamburger buns. Isn't anything this person does or envisions easy? WTF and Why the F not?!

I gave him some attitude when I came home with the buns that night, "Maybe you should just go stay out at your cousin's in Westminster. I can't handle you. And the tv? It's been on all night long!"

I didn't watch tv. I turned it on once over the two months he was gone. For about thirty minutes and then off it went.

He scarfed the food down and crawled into bed. I could tell he was stressed, but already he was stressing me out too. I just wanted to be near him, close to him.

Jennifer Lin Phillips

Who the fuck needs hamburger buns when you have your love. Just enjoy it, just turn off the tv and love me. That obnoxious thing was on all night. All that noise, oh my god and the commercials, killing me! I can't imagine why this person has sleeping problems.
Sleep is a natural thing. You must be natural in your being to feel natural sleeping.

I went to sleep a little upset his first night back. God can't this person just figure out simplicity. Can't he just breathe and be with me? Talk with me? Love me and my feminine nature of Being? Oh, my Goddess, I am going to need some help with him. Please help me Goddess. I really do want us together and I want to be happy with him, and him with me.

We were such opposites really. Which was a huge part of the attraction there between us. I just wanted to win his love, have him get it together, and experience that deep love we had felt so strongly months before.

Where is all this pain coming from? I thought. As he hung the phone up on me again. Why can't he communicate to me? His father had died, unexpectedly, a stroke in his home, a few weeks before and he was grieving.

He had moved that early February to St. Paul for a job at Harley Davidson. Yep, in a completely different state. He moved for the same job he would have had in

Colorado, with me, living in our quaint cozy apartment sweetly, comfortably, in ease, together.

When his Dad died, he was grieving hard. It was near St. Patrick's Day, because I remember the picture, he sent me of him in a green hat and beads that day. The frown and sadness on his face was heartbreaking. At least he was communicating with me, I thought. He hadn't been very good at that from that first weekend he returned to Colorado.

I took a flight out in April to see him. He was working overtime, and still processing the pain from the death of his father. I had barely seen him since he left Colorado that past November. And like many people in pain, he drank and smoked weed the entire week I was there visiting.

My last morning with him and our only day together he had a hangover. He worked the day before, was gone fifteen hours and stumbled into his apartment door, nearly falling over right there.

"What did you do?" I asked him. "You drove like that? You could've killed yourself or someone else. Why did you drink so much?" I was shocked and paling over in disbelief at his condition.

Jennifer Lin Phillips

He just looked at me angrily. Took his clothes off and passed out on the mattress we had moved to the front room. Our little fort.

I knew the password to his phone. And I got into it that night. Loads of pictures of the models working the motorcycle event that day, even sending one to a buddy and bragging. And yet he hadn't taken one picture of me, or us together while I was there. The one time I tried, he pouted. He was grieving. Okay, fine, I'll back off.

And his friend Julia. They had been communicating nearly every day, and even five minutes before picking me up from the airport, an hour late, and five minutes before stumbling in drunk that night. And yet he barely called me. The woman he was trying to build a relationship with and said he wanted to commit to.

But the facts were, I was the woman there visiting with him, Julia was not.

"She's my friend of thirty years, a longtime family friend." He told me. Yes, okay, I get that. But I am here too, can you please let me in? I would think in disbelief at his inability to open and be present with me.

He was irate at me for getting into his phone that night and harassing him the following day with questions.

"Where are the pictures of us, we took?" I asked feeling like a crazy person.

There was one picture of us together in his phone. One.

Where is the sweet guy I fell in love with? Where is the guy you seemed to be only months ago? Can someone tell me, where is he? Yes, I get that you have a past. You have dear friends that you can count on. But don't you want a future? Don't you want to put in for that now? With the woman you've been playing hide and seek with for six months already? What am I doing to myself? I would think.

Why am I insisting on being with this man?

I left St. Paul to return to Colorado early Monday morning, our last night together didn't go well.

He sat on the couch, watching a movie, still a little hung over. I wanted his attention. I wanted it so bad. I was talking to him. I was asking him why he was so absent sitting there? He just looked at me, he didn't pull me in, he didn't comfort me.

Why did I fly out to visit this person? Why won't he comfort me, I was raising my voice now. He asked me to get out of the way of the tv that I had bought for him, that he still owed me money on. Stupid tv.

Jennifer Lin Phillips

Stupid weed, stupid drinking, stupid Chico. Fucking asshole, spending my money to come out and see him. Stupid asshole for ignoring me. And I swung at him and punched him in the arm.

He took me to the airport the next morning. I slept in his room that night and him on the couch by the tv. I got maybe an hour cuddling him that morning before I had to leave to make my flight. We got out of his truck, and he came around to help me with my bag.

I was about to cry, and he pulled me in. He hugged me and held me there. He kissed me and said to me;

"You want me to fall in love with you, you want love, then watch what you say to me."

It's true, I had lashed out a few times. It's fucking true. But the silence and pain he put me through was practically unbearable. I am no mute. I can't just keep standing by, my life on hold, while my partner goes around making poor decisions and neglecting me for six months.

I can't just be your mute, loyal girlfriend, while my needs go unnoticed again and again.

I looked at him with tears coming now.

"I don't think we will see each other for a while. I'm sad because this trip didn't go that well, and I probably

Sovereignty and the Goddess

won't see you again for a long while." I said to him.

We kissed goodbye both hesitantly. I could tell he didn't want me to go. And I can still feel his hand on my hip. His eyes looking into mine.

That was 10 months ago. And the last time I touched him or kissed his mouth, the two lips that I couldn't get enough of. The two lips that I was so happy just to kiss.

After I returned to Colorado, we didn't talk for nearly two months. He felt violated at me punching him, and I was on the verge of a nervous breakdown with how he had been treating me since our honeymoon month together.

I was so depressed some day's and felt completely taken advantage of. If it weren't for some dear friends, I might not have had the strength to get out of the tub some days.

Trying hard to stand and wash the suds from my naked frail body. I felt like I was 400 lbs., trying to pull myself up to rinse from my soothing bath. Trying to pull myself out from the dark depression that had oozed into my bloodstream. Affecting every muscle, every cell.

Jennifer Lin Phillips

As much as it felt like I was 400 lbs. In all honesty, I had lost 10 lbs. that winter after he left me. I was down to 117 lbs. And hadn't been that skinny since I had mold poisoning on Kauai.

In May, I contacted a moving company and storage facility. I had my things moved to a local storage garage. I would figure out what I was doing, and where I would go to next, later that summer.

I was heading up back to Oregon to complete my road trip, and see my nieces and friends, my family. I cleaned my condo in Denver to utter perfection, said goodbye to my friend Jeff, whom I never slept with, barely kissed and whom could barely get near me.
No matter how much of a gentleman he was.

I was still in so much pain over Chico. I could still feel his body next to mine every night, how we used to cuddle up together so tight. And that one time, how he made love to me. It was his heart he gave to me that time. And I could feel myself open, as he poured his heart into me, with every ecstatic thrust he gave me.

I think I locked his heart inside of mine that night. With a small, dainty, copper key. My pink heart locked in with his.

A few weeks later, I dreamt of us nose to nose one night, breathing one another in deeply. With our eyes closed, nose to nose, we were breathing in, together like that, in my dream. Heartbeats pulsing like one, breathing each other in. It felt kinda like bliss. It did.

How could I move on from that feeling, I was addicted to its memory? I wanted to, but really, how?

I slept at my friend Angie's house in Boulder my last night in Colorado. Then left early the next morning, heading back up to Idaho for my older sister's house.

This crazy road trip I was still on, ha and wow.

I had faced some inner and outer struggles, but still so much newness. The adventure had led me into some dark places inside of myself. And many bright experiences outside. Trying to unravel it would be my next important mission.

I did feel strong. I was proud of myself for making it on my own in a new town again. I had made some new amazing friends too. Visited a handful of luxurious spa's and hot springs. And I had also learned how to drive well in the dangerous and icy snow.

I had overcome some hurtles that wanted to take me down, and although I have mostly shared my grief with all of you, of my time in Colorado. There were many sunny days. And on those days, I would walk around the lake, and watch the geese fly. Or go hiking with Angie, in the mountains of Boulder. I did two sweats that winter in the snow with her too. In T-pee's out in the cold, expansive and white mountains.

Yes, native sweats. Two of them. The first one I nearly fainted from the heat and the amount of anxiety that was there in my heart over Chico.

The instructor of the group asked me to breathe low to the ground. Get low and lie close to the earth.

"The cold from the earth will hold you, as you process your current feelings in all of this steam." He said to me over the brutal, intense heat.

My second sweat was easier and subtler. She mixed herbs in with the wood that burned in the hole there in the ground, inside of the tent.

I spoke about my crystals in that sweat. I talked about the essence of my being, and what I felt was a part of my mission here on Earth. How the crystals hold the messages from the stars. The galaxies. I felt like my role on the planet, was to help share the intelligence of the crystals with others. And how they could heal and guide us.

We sweat that night in the snow, for our ancestors. We were clearing the karma of our ancestors, the leader of the sweat reminded all of us there inside of the tent that night. We had been doing that for lifetimes, I thought to myself, as I sweat hard for my Grandparents too that night.

I had many beautiful experiences there, in sunny Colorado. I did. And I relished the memory of all my experiences in different ways. Some of them loved me back. While others, nearly killed me.

I was reflecting now, driving back up north to Oregon. I spent a few night's in Idaho with my adorable niece and three nephews. I drove up the beautiful Columbia River Gorge the last few hundred miles of my journey.

I was shocked at the lusciousness of this land in Oregon, my home. I was now out of the desert and being embraced by the wet blue river.

The water was blue, elegant, wet, rippled.

I drove peacefully and watched closely, as the blue water would shift, and flow being shaped by land and rocks. The blue Oregon river weaving across the land.

My friend Jesse, from Kauai, texted me as I drove up the Columbia River.

"I'm coming up the river!!" I texted him back.

"That's Beautiful Kinipela!" Which was my name, Jennifer, translated in Hawaiian.

Jennifer Lin Phillips

Jesse and I had been talking about me coming out to visit him in Hawaii, on mama Kauai for nearly three years now. He was one of my dear friends whose words pulled me from the tub some of those painful mornings, while the ice in my heart melted a little.

Melted and streamed from my eyes. The ice that had been trying to freeze me like Colorado snow. It just dripped down from each eye, back to the tub, then down the long, metal drain. Mixing in with city water, then returning to ice, dirty ice shaped on concrete.

Perhaps this summer I would go back to Kauai and swim. I could really use the ocean right now. Perhaps Jesse and I would connect this summer again, over on the islands.

I gave thanks for my journey, my friends who helped me along the way, and landed safely in Portland that evening. I was going to stay at my dads for a few weeks. I finished up my long journey and ended up at my Dads. I was home.

Home in my heart a bit more and ready for some rest.

Chapter 29: What's up Kauai

Jesse was a Portland Native also. We had met years before on Kauai and did the little things, like send a text every few months. Make that hour-long call once a season or so, to stay connected and aware of the current trials and tribulations of each other's lives.

We also almost always made sure to visit and rekindle our kindred friendship every time he and I both were back home, in Oregon.

Our relationship was unique, but we had always solely just been friends.

For three or four years he had invited me out to come visit him back on Kauai where we had first met, when him and his girlfriend had rented the one-bedroom cottage from Nathan and me.

He's a surfer, free spirited, successful in his business, well-travelled, and stands in his heart, with integrity often. He is an amazing communicator, and he's attractive and healthy.

But so far, my attraction for him was on the friend level. I didn't get crazy butterflies around him, and he stood a few inches shorter than me, but our friendship, yes, it was deep, compassionate and solid.

Our conversations were always uplifting too.

Jennifer Lin Phillips

Could there be more than just a solid friendship between us? He had been pushing for us to get some more time together, a getaway over on the islands for some time. Like four years. And perhaps all we needed was time together to let our amazing friendship grow into something more.

I loved his soul, and our spirits had so much aligned. We understood the "Aloha," the ability to dream, to hold your vision. And watch as it blooms, petal by petal into fruition.

But was our chemistry right? I did one of those astrological tests and we stood at 56% compatible. Are those tests really that accurate?

Our chemistry wasn't electrifying, but it wasn't stale either. It was built on trust, honesty, not trying to control one another and on sharing openly.

I knew that I was safe with Jesse. His heart is pure gold. And with the year and turmoil I had just been through. An island escape sounded like an uplifting and healthy way to heal and recover for me. I hadn't been back to Kauai in so, so long. I hadn't returned since visiting Nathan nearly four years prior.

What a rollercoaster ride I was on. Still fantasizing about and processing all kinds of feelings including love and desire for Chico, the reckless man who couldn't quite get it together.

I had just landed in Oregon, and now planning an escape to Kauai. Jeff, the guy from Colorado, who was ready to take me riding on that gorgeous red cruiser motorcycle per my request. Well, he was hoping I make the trip back to Colorado to get to know one another better. There was a little crush there between us for sure, once I let my guard down.

But here I was, spinning, dreaming, and seeking the next appropriate step for my healing.

If only I could get my feet planted on solid ground somewhere please?!!

I had to decide soon since my funds were just enough for one of the above. Back to Colorado or an ocean retreat and adventure.

All my senses were reaching out towards the islands. I could feel the ocean calling me. So, that was it, I made the decision. I was heading towards a dear friend and the crystalline blue waters of the Pacific Ocean. I was heading back to Kauai.

Two months after landing in Portland, shortly after the incredible firework display down on the Willamette River. I packed up my favorite swimsuit and loaded the plane with my massage table. Island Bound. I was in serious need of an island retreat. An absolute fool proof way to refresh my beat up and wounded soul.

Heck, I deserved it.

Jennifer Lin Phillips

From the Columbia River to the big bad ocean surrounding the Pacific Island Chain.

My journey was coming full circle from when I left Oregon the previous year. And in returning to the islands. I realized my journey was making a figure eight. That's the infinity sign. Stands for Eternity. I'm tracing the land, and I'm making the choices I need to make. Step by step, mile by mile. I can continue, I must.

I was heading that way towards the Pacific Ocean anyways, and I need a good swim.

I also needed to make sure that I didn't belong living on the magical islands for good.

Considering that my furniture and things were in storage in both Colorado and Portland, I had some options. This wild haired, travelling gypsy girl with belonging's all over the states. And a little change in her purse.

So, I've jumped around a bit. Seen a few things. I'm courageous and I am meant for travel. I am, I'm, I'm tired. I am..... You can't hold me down.

Oh, my Goddess, I am almost forty, I need to grow the hell up. Wait a minute, growing up is for idiots, and I live like a child of the moon.

But who am I really?

I am a free spirit. And free spirits need to breathe.

Exhale.

Jesse had been one of my best guy friends. He was always there when I needed him. Just to talk, to vent. Talk story and hear about one another's travels. He was an amazing friend to me. He paid for my flight to Oahu and I spent one week there, reconnecting with old friends and visiting some of my favorite local places.

Then I paid for my inner island flight and headed to the oldest and greenest island, Kauai.

Somehow, while loading my massage table onto the scale at the airport, travelling between islands, I threw my back out. I couldn't believe it. Just turning slightly left and picking up 45 lbs. in a weird way. Ouch! Pinched nerve, I could barely walk.

I sat on the short plane ride in pain and nervous as to how long this awkward injury would take to heal.

I realized too that the timing of such an injury was odd. Ironic. Being that I had been sent to the emergency room with a broken back on the very island I was heading to.

I've been working on this book, seven months. And often, I feel a tightness, a swollen, tight pain, inflamed

Jennifer Lin Phillips

still, in that part of my back where I fractured my vertebrae. The pain deepens while sitting up and writing for hours, while editing. It always tinges pain right there, on that injured spot, the vertebrae L4, on my left side. The receptive side of my body, the feminine side. That had been neglected for so many months in that relationship, years even.

Some injuries do that. They don't heal all the way, ever. Some wounds don't just heal. But they can get better with time and with hope.

I could easily assume that me throwing my back out at the airport, was a relapse of trauma. An old injury that will never heal fully.

Jesse picked me up from the airport and I asked him to grab my table from inside off the luggage carousel. I was holding my body awkwardly and carefully and was in a ton of pain. Walking slowly and with caution.

He helped me up and into the side of his truck door. Both of us shocked at my sudden weak condition.

He had brought a beautiful red flowered lei for me and adorned me in it by placing it around my neck gently. On his neck was also a lei, made from the puka shells that he had collected from walking the long and sacred beach of Polihale.

It was so beautiful to be greeted like that by him. The Aloha way.

We drove to his place in Kapaa' to drop off most of my things. Emma jumped up off the floor and onto the counter to say hello. Tiny and black, with those sweet and curious green eyes. Kitten, Emma. I picked her up and she purred sweetly there in my open and dark freckled arms. It only takes a few days on island for those freckles to pop out, covering me like the skin of a cheetah or leopard. I giggled at my unique island tan.

Jesse's roommate was supposed to have moved out, with two of the three main cats. But instead, she stayed, and brought home another feline creature, a kitten.

I guess Jesse's roommate had made no effort to leave. Which was fine with me because I didn't really know their agreement. Jesse and I were just friends. On our way to seeing if there was more there between us. But he told me she was supposed to have been gone months ago.

I was happy to have the extra female energy around, as a buffer to mine and Jesse's relationship. But I was going to need to have space to work, which with her there, the only space would have to be outside somewhere.

The other thing, I was allergic to cats.

Jennifer Lin Phillips

He had made reservations for us that night up at the lodge in Kokee' State Park. The hikes and the views of the waterfalls were breathtaking up there. If only I was in good enough condition the following day to get out, walk a little and spot a few of them.

I couldn't believe the amount of pain I was in. I was moving like a turtle, moving rather slow. I hadn't been out like this since the actual injury.

There was so much red in the landscape heading up the Waimea Canyon. But the island was known for its red dirt. We passed by the small local shop that made t-shirts out of the red soil on our way up to the Kokee' Lodge. And red shirts dangled casually on hangers in the warm outside air.

I had done the drive up the valley canyon many times before, when I lived on island two different occasions. The air is much cooler up Kokee', and has more moisture in it from off of the valley clouds. Being up there always reminded me of home back in Oregon. I would make trips up there often to escape the heat from the south shore sun.

I could make the drive again and again just for the outstanding views of the valley.

We stepped out at a few spots along the road, and posed smiling together, snapping a few selfies with his selfie stick. Standing high up the elegant hillsides, one could nearly feel the density in the air at such an altitude, with breezes coming from towering waterfalls far off in the distance behind us.

Although I was in a lot of pain still. It was so good to be in the company of such a loyal and loving friend. I was so thrilled really, to be on another journey in the outback of Kauai, with my surfer friend Jesse.

I loaded up on aspirin, and that night we cooked, laughed and had wine up in the cottage he had rented.

At dusk, we drove to the end of the road that looks out over the Kalalau Valley Mountain Range. The Kalalau Valley trail is 11 miles in, and is entered through the opposite side of the canyon from Kokee' State Park. I did the entire 11 mile hike in once. Ironically with another friend of mine named Jesse. I was wearing a fifty-pound pack that long hike in and on my feet were flip flops.

We watched as the clouds above the valley shifted and moved. They were dark in color, and there was rain pouring down hard out over the ocean. The water in the clouds created some of the most beautiful colors.

Jennifer Lin Phillips

Pinks, oranges, purples, greys, white swirling around the vibrant glow. We took a handful of photos that night from the sun going down.

The peak of the hillside was extremely windy. And drops of rain began coming in. The dark rain clouds hovered over the dark blue ocean water out below and beyond our two shivering bodies standing out in it all, witnessing the magic.

We hopped back in the truck to head back to the cabin to warm up and get some rest.

The following morning, we grabbed a cup of the strong and bitter Kona coffee in the old lodge. I still wasn't in any condition for a hike, so we decided to head down the long, winding hill for the beach. We were headed to yet another sacred spot, Polihale Beach. Our plan was to walk the long beachside and scavenge for shells. I was needing a swim too, in that magnificent and soothing ocean salt water.

The road to Polihale was rough. Potholes every few feet. Big ones. Bump, thunk, bump, holding on to the side of the door for fifteen minutes, at least, until we landed in heaven. The destination we arrived at was stunning and well worth the long dirt road out.

Sovereignty and the Goddess

"I never want to leave this beach!" I yelled over to Jesse after getting out of his truck. "Unbelievable, oh my Goddess, thank you for bringing me here."

"Of course, Kinipela. Let's find a spot to chill, put out some chairs and then head down the beach for those puka shells I was telling you about. The ones that are strung on my necklace." Jesse said back to me.

I really had been admiring that necklace he wore since he picked me up from the airport. And now I was beaming from ear to ear at the adventure I was on. I was entering a state of total bliss. The fresh breeze was amazing. I felt so alive and so thankful to have my two feet standing right there in the warmth of the brown sand.

The pain in my back was slowly easing.

He pointed down the beach to where the shells were.

I was positive that I could make the long trek down to the reef and small ponds where the shells mostly collected. Maybe a 45-minute walk. The shells were also spread out in piles and pockets all along the hot sandy beach as well. Where the tide came out and swirled them around in enchanting spirals.

The sand burned on that beach. It was so incredibly hot it could burn each one of your toes right off. And

Jennifer Lin Phillips

toe nails too.

I was determined to brave the heat. Bare foot, I walked on the sand for at least thirty feet, then took off running for the water. Yikes. Stinking hot, that sand.

Ouch, I better be careful, my back was still on the mend.

I jumped in the water and Jesse followed me in. Splashing around in the warm waters felt so natural. I belong here, I thought to myself. Legs flapping like a well-earned mermaid tail.

We submerged ourselves in the water and the heat steaming off from our feet cooled. It felt so right to freshen up some in the bright and soft rays of the rising morning sun.

What a morning ritual the beach was.

I had performed that one often.

I loved that ritual nearly as much as I loved anything or anyone in my life. It made so much sense to me. The beach, in the morning, is truly my language. The language that spoke to every cell in my body. It had to be one of the most invigorating yet calming of activities, that my soul craved again and again.

And if I stayed on the mainland too long, I felt stuck in

both my body and mind. Stuck on pavement.

We hung around all day. I swam in and out of the water for hours. Like the real mermaid I am. Or as my niece calls me sometimes, just like Ariel.

After making the long trek to the small ponds for shells and back. I passed out under the umbrella we had set up and dozed off to sleep, exhausted. Surprisingly the pain in my back was nearly gone.

While sleeping I was taken to a vibrant green land and it felt like I was on a canoe floating. It felt like the land dropped off into somewhere beautiful, and I was taken in deep. There were voices around me speaking to me. I was listening to their words as I floated on in lush green jungle. The voices calmly explained to me that this body, the flesh on our bones, is only just that. And that one day we will merge with the Great Spirit.

I had the feeling like I was even standing over myself floating by, watching myself on the canoe, yet being guided. Then, I woke up. I woke up with this knowing that I had been taken to another land by the Hawaiian Spirits....maybe back in the valley somewhere.

Jesse came down the sand towards me, where I was lying on my towel, hiding out from the mid-day sun under the umbrella still.

Jennifer Lin Phillips

I explained to him my dream and how touched I felt to had been taken somewhere special. He then mentioned to me the belief's about Polihale, the beach we were on. Just out beyond the hillside and valley, the ocean is vast, beyond the beach I was lying on. He said that the Hawaiian people believed that when one dies, along those dark green hillsides by the water, you leave the Earth plane from there.

And suddenly my dream made sense to me. I had been guided by the spirits to where this special portal is. Where one leaves their flesh and bones behind, to merge with the infinite life beyond. Beyond the green of the island.

I was so thankful. So very thankful to have been shown the gleaming way there.

When we left the beach after packing up, two owls hovered together along the side of the dirt road out. They were about to make a catch together I think of some sort, and they were hovering over the brush, wings moving rapidly.

Jesse leaned over to me in the truck admiring the two owls out of the window on my side. And then he told me, that the owls were believed to be a sign of Good Fortune in Hawaiian culture.

Sovereignty and the Goddess

Had it really been four years since returning to this incredible island that felt like a second home to me?

Back in Oregon I had heard of some interesting news from a few of my friends from Oahu. We had made time to meet up for a talk at the hotel they were staying at. Which was just down the street from my apartment, while they were visiting the state that summer.

Chris asked me if I had talked with Nathan. I told him that I hadn't in almost a year, and that we had ended up losing the house.

Chris waited to tell me in person, but he had phoned Nathan a few months back to set up a time to visit with him. Nathan hung up the phone rather anxiously within minutes of his call, explaining that he was busy and needed to go. The King confirmed to Chris that Nathan was still in fact at the house on the beach, because the Queen had just gone down to gather some flowers. Most likely the Pu'akenekene flowers from the tree my client had brought over for us years before.

That tree was probably in full bloom now.

I had been lied to and cut out from the house that I had worked hand in hand on. Who knows whose idea it was to cut me out, and for how long they had been

Jennifer Lin Phillips

plotting the big lie. But it happened just a week before I was to take off on my desert road trip, just like that.

Yep, yeah, I know! Always the hard working and loyal female that gets the short end of the stick. Huh. Mmmhhhmmmphhh.

When I heard the news, I sent Nathan an email that contained two sentences in it. "I heard that you are still living at the house, is that true? If so, wow, you are quite the actor!"

And I never heard back from him. Nor did I waste my time in writing him again. I knew that spirit would take care of me. I would meet the right people, continue with my life, and keep moving forward.

And, I also knew I had a book coming.

I just didn't know it was going to include my business with him. I didn't know that I wanted to talk about and exploit my dealings with abusive and manipulative men.

But truth is. They are everywhere.

In politics especially. And the way the system is set up. The banking system. How nearly most of the wealthy are given tax breaks or even worse know how to use the law to completely avoid paying any taxes at all.

While the middle and lower class go around judging one another. Make sure you are a good citizen. Pay your taxes. Go ahead and fund violence, pay for war. Go ahead and take my money to destroy other countries. Sure, I will fund the destruction of the planet through the biggest assault on mother earth, oil drilling.

It's just that, greed and manipulation is nearly inevitable with the way the system runs.

And why would the King want to cut me out? I worked my buns off on that house, and nearly lost my life. Oh, these dictators, these politicians, they want to take all the credit and rule the entire planet. While everyone knows that there is a hard ass working woman, if not a group of them behind every ruler.

Just look at the world we currently live in. I'm not here to man hate, truly I adore men. I just don't trust a handful of them anymore, nor is it my duty to please them. Like our culture ingrains into us at a young age. Hand over your power, be a nice girl. Standing up for yourself sure ain't ladylike.

Thankfully, as more and more women gain power on the planet, those messages are changing and have changed dramatically over the past few years.

I soon realized that my book wasn't just about me and my story. But about all women who don't have the same rights as men. The women who are abused and

Jennifer Lin Phillips

neglected. Shamed, overqualified and cut out. I want to include the innocent and qualified men who are simply trying to compete, to find success and take care of their families. In a system that is pretty much designed to destroy one's health and freedom.

I know the answer is Peace. Taking responsibility for one's own healing. Self-love, self-care, proper diet, healthy thinking. Making loved ones and the light of the Self a major priority.

But what is it, the top 1% of the Population owns 99% of the world's wealth? That does make things a bit more challenging for the rest of us. Most of the time, my fridge is practically empty. But I never feel like I don't have enough. I work hard on taking care of me, being there for the people I love, and I work hard on providing a healthy service for the public.

I am the rarest being on the planet. There is only 1% of people on the planet with red hair and blue eyes. I have a unique perspective, this is all I know, and I have a warrior's soul.

I am not just a girl in the world, although most of the time, that's all I want to be. Have my rent affordable, quality food affordable. Be in a system that really flourishes and where people really honor and respect one another.

Goddess knows yes, I am privileged. I can shower whenever I want to. I can pay my own bills. I have clean water. Deodorant, floss, lotion. Omg I love lotion. But man, the system is rigged. And people are power hungry. While woman after woman holds the grounds for healing on this planet. Unnoticed, unappreciated and under paid.

I am a woman, a phenomenal woman. A woman of the universe. A star light. A mother child. A wild woman. And I want my sovereignty too.

I knew I had some karma to work out on that island. After one week of being on island, Jesse and I drove past the house. Made me sick inside thinking about how I was treated and how greedy some people are.

After two weeks of being on island again, I broke out in a rash on my legs mostly. I had gotten ring worm from the cats at Jesse's place. Most likely from the oldest cat whom would bring home live chickens and gnaw at their throat until they died right there by the back-screen door. Not exactly a sanitary environment, but once you live on one of the more remote islands for a while, you soon realize you aren't on the mainland anymore. You in the jungle baby.

After running into Sharon at the art fest one evening in downtown Kapaa'. The woman and healer that I first came to the island with fifteen years prior, I knew that I was on my way to healing up and making some new discoveries.

Jennifer Lin Phillips

She too had gone through the awful ringworm the summer before. And it was one of those things that island cats can carry and pass on to sensitive people.

I was beginning to get fever from the outbreak all over my legs in little red circles, maybe twelve of them, and didn't want things to get worse. I decided that I should leave the island soon.

My last day on the beach, Jesse and I went to a gorgeous spot up North Shore. I had my pink rose quartz triangle on me. The one that the Brazilian teacher of the crystal course had given me.

As we took photos and walked along the shoreline out past black rocks that curved around the corner in shallow water, I knew I was walking to find resolve. I prayed for my healing. For my karma on this island to be healed, and for my health and wellbeing to be renewed. I wasn't even sure if I wanted to come back to Kauai.

The energy there was getting weird.

I looked up towards the rocks that were scattered up the shoreline and saw three big rocks piled up on one another. The rocks were a peace offering, standing alone holding sacred intention. Surrendering its solid material form to the big of the mighty sky.

But while looking at the rocks on top of one another, the offering looked weak. It wasn't complete, and I knew what needed to be done. I had a tiny shell in one hand, and my rose quartz triangle in the other hand. I placed the pink crystal balancing it on top of the rocks below. And on top of that, the tiny shell. I bowed my head in prayer and reverence. I said my prayers for healing and peace, and for the renewing of my karma on the islands. And the karma of the island for the people living there.

I took a picture of my offering, recited a few more prayers on my walk back. My feet now stepping in the light blue of the shallow water.

I left the island later that day.

Jennifer Lin Phillips

Chapter 30: My Dreamwork

When I flew into Oregon. I stayed at my friend Dominique's before settling into my own apartment again in my favorite neighborhood, Hillsboro. I was gathering myself. I had furniture in storage, and I needed to heal from the nasty ringworm which had invaded my system.

I was exhausted from all the travel that summer also. And truth be told, broke. A dear friend helped me move my things from my storage unit into my new cute apartment. The storage unit containing my things, was on the same property that I had lived on for a few years before my Colorado trip. It was an easy move and only took a few hours.

I was practically settled in by the days end. Just a few days after the big Solar Eclipse that streamed through and could be seen clearly through parts of Oregon.

It sure felt good to be home. I had spent the day after the eclipse up at Mt. Hood at my friend's cabin for a few days. I was grounding myself up on the trails and taking in the mana from the beautiful mountain that towered high above the city.

My senses were telling me that this would be a season in my life for deep reflection. For deepening bonds with the people I love and care for. And for really exploring my life's history. The story of my life thus far.

I placed my crystals around my cute one-bedroom apartment with fireplace. My blue Andara ended up on the windowsill in the bedroom and was taking in power from the tall Pine trees that were gathered out past the swimming pool.

I walked past the Andara maybe two weeks after settling back into my hometown and could feel the breath of the ocean. Waves splashing upon waves, and I took a few deep breaths. The waves were still with me. The energy I had just gathered from my one-month trip to the Hawaiian Islands was still with me.

I breathed in deeper to feel the ocean only an hour away from me just westward. Just past the beautiful and fresh Tillamook Forest.

I was settling back in from my travels. The ocean was still breathing with me and that is when it dawned on me that I needed to share the story of my journey. Of my plight over the waters. My deep love for my own path and for my own truth. I was still trying to understand it all. Why I have chosen the ways that I have chosen.

I exhaled the saltwater that naturally breathes through me. And a few days later, I started this book.

Jennifer Lin Phillips

Since writing consistently, my dreams have become more vivid, and have shown me the secrets of my life. My dreams have taken me to places inside of myself that only I would know the reasons for.

After returning to Oregon, I met someone who came to me with an incredible amount of love. Every time I would see him, gifts for me and adoration. I was being romanced and the attraction between us was also stimulating and good. Although this new man in my life was twelve years younger than me, he was showing up as a man. A man whom wanted to adore me.

Things moved quickly, and they ended just as fast. After three months of solid dating. We weren't sexually compatible and because of the age difference there was such an absence of experience on his end, that I found myself bored at our conversations. Yes, he had a lot of love for me. But the relationship wasn't going to make it.

I knew that it wasn't, when I had a dream about me examining my own yoni. Pulling my lips out a little to make a pink heart with their folds. In the dream I felt unhappy with the feeling's I was getting from him. I was examining my yoni like the love vessel that it is. My love vessel, my choice to how I use it.

And my current love was expecting me to have sex multiple times per day with him. I didn't enjoy that. It felt like an addiction, but it was also the sexual chemistry between us.

I could tell that I felt violated by his needs and his disappointment in me for pulling away from him. It felt like my body was not even my own and there was no way that I wanted to meet his demands. I was now being completely turned off from having sex at all.

We were on different rhythms, and that was all that I needed to know to go ahead and move on. He was incredibly giving and loving, just not the right soul match for me. And I couldn't invest more energy and time into something that wasn't going where I needed it to.

A week after our breakup. I began to process a lot again. I began to investigate myself, what I wanted, and how to heal the loneliness I was feeling again at his absence.

I had dreams of my bath tub overflowing, while I waited for my long-lost love to appear. My true love.

I realized from that dream that I use my tub as an escape from the sadness I feel at not having found him. I am in that tub four times a week. And as much as it soothes me, I was shocked at my discovery that it is a

Jennifer Lin Phillips

tool I use to mask my lonely heart.

One night shortly after the break up. I dreamt I was wearing a long Hawaiian skirt. Just like the one I found soaked in saltwater, in the public bathroom at the beach on Oahu. That was my very first trip over at the age of just twenty-three.

The hand sewn, and beautifully textured Hawaiian print skirt had been left there on the bench, sandy and soaking wet in a ball. I knew that it was a very special gift for me. From spirit. The prints on it were gorgeous, old vintage Hawaiian style. Black, brown and yellow print. The skirt was a few sizes too big for me, but after I took it home to wash it, I wore it often anyways and let it dangle around my fair white skin.

In the dream, I was wearing it. It flowed down my long legs and swayed around me. I had an amber aura in my dream, and I was in my healing space. The energy around me felt medicinal, sacred, connected. I was being swept up in my own amber glow when the woman's voices came in. The voices were singing, sacred Hawaiian chants around me and over me. The female voices were surrounding me, protecting me, guiding me. I felt so safe, and so welcome. Like they were my mother, my grandmother, my sisters. They continued to chant, and I awoke mystified.

As Spring approaches in 2018, I now have a few more months to save some money and find my direction again. My lease will be coming to an end very, very soon. As I examine my life, the people in it that I love, and what matters to me, I am coming closer to making my next choice.

It isn't easy being a travelling gypsy girl, wandering and courageous warrior woman, whose got a little sense for style. I will continue to take my steps with confidence and with sincere attention.

I have furniture here in Oregon, a storage unit full in Colorado, and my heart that yearns for the ocean to swim.

This journey, this wanderlust is real to me, and what I have known my entire adult life so far. Knowledge seeker, this is what I have become. My roots are thick and deep, but these wings, they expand over mountains. They expand over sea.

I know that the beauty of creativity and my longing for freedom and adventure will continue to guide me safely. If I continue to dance in harmony with her, and her with me.

I was cooking eggs in my kitchen that morning. My hands reached for the box of bagged tea that I had on the counter. I opened one tea bag of Yerba Matte tea. The water on my stove began to boil, containing the fresh water that I had collected from the spring out

Jennifer Lin Phillips

towards the coast.

As I placed the tea bag into my mug, I noticed she was watching me closely. Fully present in her gaze, with beauty emitting from her being.

I was so busied. Somewhat flushed and frazzled. I was working on creating a healthy breakfast for myself.

She noticed the state that I was in. And she looked over to me. I stopped what I was doing to take her all the way in and acknowledge that she was there with me.

I wasn't surprised to see that same expression on her face. The one I saw often as a girl. I could sense someone else there in the room with us, and I realized quickly that it was my little sister. We were all together there in the kitchen now.

The look on my Mom's face was one of incredible beauty, slight annoyance, and bright and full presence.

As I walked over to her, her radiance was engulfing me now.

My hand reached out to her. And the inside of my delicate palm caressed the cheek of her glowing ivory skin.

"You are so beautiful Momma." I said to her sitting there.

Sovereignty and the Goddess

Her eyes peered into mine and she said, "I am?"

It was then that I turned into a puddle there before her. I was not a young girl in the dream, but I turned into what felt like a three-year-old before her now. Chin tucked in and down, blushing, sadness mixed with shyness.

I responded to her crying now, "Mmmmmhhhmmmmm....."

She giggled and laughed aloud. Her motherly nature showing play and delight. She said coyly back to me, "Mmmhhhhmmmmm...." As if she were tickling me all over sweetly with her tone.

It was then that her spirit touched me through her eyes. And I knew that she was really there with me in that dream. She was, and she wanted me to know that. She was there with me and had been all along.

The tears exploded from my being. I woke up weeping for my mother. The woman whom had left me nearly twenty-five years prior. I was only a girl then, just barely a teenager.

I have missed her nearly every day since then.

I woke up wet faced in my bed, now fully understanding one solid truth. She had never left me.

Jennifer Lin Phillips

Then a few nights ago, I had another vivid dream.

In my dream I was moving and twirling, and dancing with the land. My arms moved around me in ease. There was a friend nearby in my dream. He possessed the same fire energy and spark that I feel streaming through me often.

As I danced in my dream, out in the distance, the lava was flowing, and moving hot along the land.

I pointed out towards where it was burning crimson red and glowing. I pointed to my friend so that he could also see the lava moving nearby.

While observing the lava move, in my heart and my mind, I could feel the lava grow and expand with every twirl I took. It was speaking to me. The lava told me that every breath and gesture I give, I am honoring her.

And she burns further along the land, through me, because she is the heat of creation.

I kept dancing. And watching. The lava was red and hot and moving still. From where I was standing, the lava even resembled the lights that turn out in the galaxy, sparkling, swirling, popping, burning.

I took a few more breaths, inhaling the experience, and my new revelation of this great mystery.

Lava began to stream down both sides of my cheeks, pouring from the red of my hair. It was just like in the painting of Pele that I had seen at the King's house years before. It poured from the strands of my auburn hair elegantly and around my fair face.

It steamed, it burned, it sizzled and then I awoke.

Alive.

Jennifer Lin Phillips

Sovereignty and the Goddess

CPSIA information can be obtained
at www.ICGtesting.com
Printed in the USA
FSHW021021240719
60351FS